Radio Plays

CU00693380

Caryl Phillips is the award-winning author of eleven
five volumes of non-fiction, in addition to numerous radio plays, scripts and essays.
His latest fiction, *A View of the Empire at Sunset* (2018), focuses on the life of
Dominican-born writer Jean Rhys. Identity, migration and history are among the main
themes of his writing, which also stands out for its formal daring.

Bénédicte Ledent is honorary professor at the University of Liège. She has published
extensively on Caryl Phillips and has worked on numerous editorial projects, the
latest of which is a special issue of *The Journal of Commonwealth Literature*, edited
in collaboration with Daria Tunca and devoted to postcolonial biographical fiction.
She is co-editor of the book series Cross/Cultures.

Radio Plays

The Wasted Years
Crossing the River
The Prince of Africa
Writing Fiction
A Kind of Home: James Baldwin in Paris
Hotel Cristobel
A Long Way from Home
Dinner in the Village
Somewhere in England

CARYL PHILLIPS
Edited and introduced by
BÉNÉDICTE LEDENT

methuen | drama
LONDON · NEW YORK · OXFORD · NEW DELHI · SYDNEY

METHUEN DRAMA
Bloomsbury Publishing Plc
50 Bedford Square, London, WC1B 3DP, UK
1385 Broadway, New York, NY 10018, USA
29 Earlsfort Terrace, Dublin 2, Ireland

BLOOMSBURY, METHUEN DRAMA and the Methuen Drama logo are trademarks of
Bloomsbury Publishing Plc

First published in Great Britain 2023

A catalogue record for this book is available from the British Library.

A catalog record for this book is available from the Library of Congress.

ISBN: HB: 978-1-3503-0006-4
        PB: 978-1-3503-0005-7
        ePDF: 978-1-3503-0007-1
        eBook: 978-1-3503-0009-5

Typeset by RefineCatch Limited, Bungay, Suffolk
Printed and bound in Great Britain

To find out more about our authors and books visit www.bloomsbury.com
and sign up for our newsletters.

Contents

Preface

I spent a great deal of time during my teenage years with my head in a book, or else sitting up in bed with my small transistor listening to radio drama. Both pursuits served the same end; to transport me beyond my present circumstances and in the direction of a world (or worlds) that might stimulate my imagination. I was a dreamer who was fascinated by the lives of other people, and reading books and listening to radio plays formed the bedrock upon which I dreamed.

I eventually attended university and studied English Literature, which meant that I continued to read. Did I continue to listen to radio plays? Occasionally, but I was more concerned now with the theatre. It is probably no coincidence that the first stage play I directed, Harold Pinter's *Silence*, had originally been written for radio. It is a short poetic piece, with three voices speaking out of the 'darkness' across time, each character trying to connect with the other. I had, of course, spent many years listening to work like *Silence*, so the stage play's intense interiority didn't feel strange to me.

Upon graduation, I decided that I wanted to write, and the novel was the form I felt most drawn to. I think I implicitly understood that the solitude and single-minded dedication that are necessary to complete a book were better suited my character, for I had already decided that I didn't possess the kind of collective sensibility that one needs in order to successfully work in theatre. However, at this juncture, my biggest problem was that I had very little idea as to how one might go about constructing a novel. I also had the additional problem of having to earn a living.

Within a year or so of leaving university, I was lucky enough to be the recipient of two strokes of good fortune. First, a stage play that I had written was accepted for production at the Crucible Theatre in Sheffield. It was a beginning – an affirmation that I was a writer of some kind – *and* I would be paid. Second, I was approached by a BBC Schools Radio producer, who was making a series of short dramas which were to be broadcast in school assembly halls around the country. The producer asked if I would like to contribute, and assured me that I would be remunerated.

This would be my first experience of working in radio drama. Having completed my assignment, I would get on the tube and take my ten- or fifteen-minute script into a small studio in central London where the actors and producer were gathered, and together they would read the short piece before recording it. The process was swift, and the atmosphere was devoid of the collaborative clutter of the stage. I enjoyed the process, for my imagination was unfettered, and geographically I could range anywhere, and also move freely in time.

I understood that these early offerings were little more than extended sketches, but I soon settled down to write my first radio play, *The Wasted Years*. Reading this play again – for the first time in nearly forty years – and the eight plays that followed, I'm taken aback by how closely related in theme these plays are to my fiction, non-fiction and theatre work. Without wishing to deconstruct myself, it's clear that issues to do with home, migration, celebrity and sexuality are present in a great number of the radio plays, as they are in my other work. I can also see how, in these plays, I am preoccupied with form, in a manner not too dissimilar from the formal concerns that are threaded through my fiction.

The process of commissioning *The Wasted Years* was reasonably straightforward. I had an idea, I spoke with my agent, who then spoke with the BBC, and eventually a contract was drawn up. After this first play, which was produced at the BBC's Pebble Mill Studios in Birmingham, the subsequent eight plays were produced by the BBC in either London or New York. During this period, I was fortunate to work with two extraordinary producers, Richard Wortley and Ned Chaillet, who were at the helm for all except the final two plays. Armed with a notion of what I might want to write, I would meet with one or other of them for lunch or dinner. Generally, by the end of our meal, we had an agreement. I would go away and write the play and, depending on whose production it was, either Richard Wortley or Ned Chaillet would contact my agent and then make the arrangements whereby we would have a studio available and a date by which I was supposed to deliver a script.

Sadly, this informal planning appears now to be a thing of the past. As I read through the plays, I couldn't help feeling that this body of work might never have passed the scrutiny of today's commissioning committees, or survived the inspection of those bureaucrats whose job it is to measure 'potential impact'. Either the content or the form of the plays, or both, would probably have raised eyebrows. It troubles me that, these days, publishers, theatres, media production companies and others try so hard to *measure* the value of unwritten work, as opposed to just taking a chance on the writer's imagination.

I am grateful to Richard Wortley and Ned Chaillet for their loyalty and support, and to the editor of this collection, Bénédicte Ledent, for her efforts in tracking down the original scripts and collating and presenting them in a single volume. Rereading the plays transported me back to my youth when the BBC Radio Drama department was almost as important to me as the books on my shelf. That I had a chance to work in the department, and with such outstanding producers and studio managers and actors, has been one of the great blessings of my life as a writer.

Caryl Phillips
13 January, 2022

Introduction

DISTANT NOISES OF OTHER VOICES: A COLLECTION OF CARYL PHILLIPS'S RADIO PLAYS

Bénédicte Ledent

Caryl Phillips is one of the most respected Anglophone writers of his generation. Born in the Caribbean (St Kitts), raised in England and now Professor of English at Yale University, he is internationally known as a prolific essayist, a published playwright for the stage and an award-winning novelist with eleven novels to his name. What is less commonly acknowledged is that he is also an accomplished radio dramatist. Nine of his radio plays were broadcast by BBC Radio 3 and Radio 4 between 1984 and 2016. His very first play, *The Wasted Years*, is the only one among them that is in the public domain. Aired when its author was only twenty-six, it was one of the winners of the Giles Cooper Awards, a prize sponsored by Methuen and the BBC, and as such it was included in an anthology entitled *Best Radio Plays of 1984*, a volume containing six scripts selected for their strength and inventiveness.[1] The typescripts of Phillips's other eight plays have remained unpublished to this date, in spite of their undeniable quality and originality. They have only been accessible via their author's papers, which are housed by the Beinecke Library at Yale University – with the exception of his latest radio play, *Somewhere in England* (2016), which is not yet part of these archival holdings.[2]

It seems important to make all these radio plays available to a large readership, for, even if they might be regarded as 'minor' pieces for generic reasons, they are creative works in their own right and constitute an integral part of Phillips's literary universe. As these radiophonic texts contain in a nutshell the author's hallmark mix of formal audacity and sharp social criticism, they are most likely to be of interest for newcomers to his work. Yet, these plays also represent invaluable resources for the growing body of Phillipsian scholars, because they offer compelling points of comparison with the rest of Phillips's writing, both thematically and formally, and can therefore help to grasp the full scope of this writer's literary achievements.

The nine radio plays in this collection are presented chronologically, according to the dates when they were first broadcast, which provides an idea of the development of Phillips's radiophonic art over more than thirty years. What is striking is the impressive consistency of his output for radio: except for *Writing Fiction*, a radio play broadcast in 1991 and focusing mostly on the mid-life crisis of an English writer with a waning reputation, all the texts relate to the existential predicament of displaced individuals and are linked in one way or another to the African diaspora. Among the nine plays, it is also possible to distinguish three more specific, yet interconnected, thematic clusters.

The first group, which includes *Crossing the River* (1985), *The Prince of Africa* (1987) and *Somewhere in England*, testifies to Phillips's long-lasting interest in the aftermath of the slave trade and slavery and how this historical episode has radically and irrevocably shaped the world in which we live. Very much like his 1993 novel *Crossing the River*, these three plays powerfully remind us that 'There is no return'[3] or, to borrow the words uttered by a character from *The Prince of Africa*, that 'Our past and present and future are inextricably interwoven' (91). These historical plays also confirm that the fates of Black and white people are intimately linked in the wake of the Middle Passage, and it is therefore not surprising that even if they concentrate on the African diasporic experience they should also include well-developed white characters, for example the crew in *The Prince of Africa* or Joyce, the English lover of Black GI Travis, in *Somewhere in England*.

A second thematic strand emerges in *A Kind of Home: James Baldwin in Paris* (2004), *A Long Way from Home* (2008) and *Dinner in the Village* (2011), three fictionalized biographical narratives focusing on artistic figures from the African diaspora – respectively James Baldwin, Marvin Gaye, and Richard Wright and C. L. R. James. As the titles of the first two plays indicate, their protagonists are plagued by a sense of unbelonging, in constant search for a place that they can call home. This interest in the life stories of tortured artists with irreducibly complex identities also pervades Phillips's non-fiction and fiction, most notably his latest novel, *A View of the Empire at Sunset* (2018), which dramatizes episodes in the life of famous writer Jean Rhys, a white Creole from Dominica.

The other three plays, *The Wasted Years* (1984), *Writing Fiction* (1991) and *Hotel Cristobel* (2005), can be brought together as well, in spite of their different settings and contexts. Sensitively evoking the quandaries of individuals in crisis at the end of the twentieth century, these texts focus respectively on a teenager from a migrant family settled in England, a writer faced with declining fame and the absurdities of the English literary scene, and three emotionally scarred individuals interacting in an island of the post-independence Caribbean. These radio dramas display an extraordinary capacity on their author's part for acute social observation, combined in the latter two plays with touches of humour that are rather unusual in Phillips's fictional world, with the possible exception of his film script *Playing Away* (1987). In 1984, a critic described *The Wasted Years* as 'socially conscious drama at its best'[4] and this most fitting depiction of Phillips's first radio play can undoubtedly extend to *Writing Fiction* and *Hotel Cristobel* as well, as they also address issues linked with race, class and gender.

It is clear from this brief thematic overview that this body of work is bound to prove a treasure trove for anyone who wants to further explore Phillips's deeply humane and politically radical fictional imaginary. However, it is perhaps on the formal level that his radiophonic production is likely to help scholars and students working on his fiction to get an even better insight into the specificities of his writing. What follows will specifically focus on Phillips's approach to characterization and his use of experimental narrative techniques, which seem to display genuine kinship with some features of radio drama as a genre.

When asked by interviewers about how the characters in his novels take shape in his mind, Phillips has consistently answered over the years that he first needs to hear their voices to be able engage with them. It is 'the one thing that's *absolutely* necessary', he recently declared.[5] And indeed his novels are replete with the (often inner) voices of marginalized or damaged individuals who have been left out of traditional historiography. The connection between novel writing and audio drama is easy to make if one recalls that it too basically relies 'on the human voice rather than visual identification'.[6] This has several implications that can be illustrated through the radio plays collected in this volume and which by extension can apply to Phillips's fiction as a whole. To start with, this vocal dimension creates a unique closeness between the characters and the readers because the latter are, as it were, spoken to directly. This produces a form of intimacy that in turn generates a non-judgemental understanding on the part of the reader and promotes a form of affective communication with the protagonist that is absent in the narrative universe of the play or the novel. The disembodied voices of the children sold into slavery in the radio play *Crossing the River* are a good example of how such intimacy can be achieved. A similar sense of intense closeness is equally perceptible in *Writing Fiction* when one is given access to Lawrence Wilson's writer's notebooks, or in the voice-over passages in *Somewhere in England* in which Joyce confides her emotions.

The centrality of the vocal at the expense of the visual also makes for elliptical and economical narratives where many elements remain implicit. The numerous short scenes that make up *A Kind of Home*, but also the other biographical plays by Phillips, are an example of this concision, which obliges readers to use their imagination and transforms them 'into active makers of meaning', to use the words of William Stanton in relation to the listeners of radio drama.[7] What matters in such a context is not so much the plot, the storyline, but what the characters have to say about their suffering and their painful groping towards an understanding of who they are. This is confirmed by a note dated May 1985, found in Phillips's archives, in which he outlines the rationale behind a project of a radio play set in the hold of slave ship (untitled at that stage, but presumably materialized in *The Prince of Africa*):

> I see the play as an essentially more 'reflective' than 'dynamic' piece of drama. The impact of such a huge crime seems to me better dealt with through voices that search for meaning and definition, rather than voices that are bound by the parameters of a rigid adherence to exposition and denouement.[8]

Clearly, such a statement captures the essence of the radicality of Phillips's characterization, which is to a large extent inherited from the practice of the radio dramatic genre.

The same can be said of his approach to form and structure. Radio drama is known to be a fluid medium that makes it possible for narratives to move smoothly and quickly across time and space. Such flexibility is particularly noticeable in Phillips's most experimental texts for radio, *Crossing the River* and *The Prince of Africa*. In the former, the triangulation between Africa, the Americas and England creates what Suzanne Scafe has called a 'dreamscape of topographies and histories that are at once discontinuous and overlapping',[9] resulting in an economical but nuanced coverage of some two hundred years of history. Likewise, *The Prince of Africa* opens with a character generically called 'African', who is successively on board an eighteenth-century slave ship, enslaved on a nineteenth-century New World plantation and migrating from the Caribbean to England in the twentieth century. But Phillips's more conventionally structured radio plays, too, abound in flashbacks and flashforwards as well as in sudden changes of scenes, which are the narrative reflections of a world literally shaped by dislocation and instability. One can find in *The Wasted Years* constant temporal shifts that make it possible to alternate between the experiences of the first and second generation of Britons from the Caribbean while in Phillips's formally more conservative biographical radio plays chronological disruptions help to shed light on the nature of the protagonists' malaise. Unsurprisingly, the majority of Phillips's texts for radio also contains various references to crossings of the Atlantic, a symbolic space that is crucial in any evocation of the lives affected by the original transportation of slaves across the ocean.[10]

'I learned a lot about what was possible in the form of the novel from "experimenting" in radio drama',[11] Phillips said in an unpublished online interview conducted in 2013. One of the things that his fiction owes to the subversive temporal and spatial shifts that are possible in radio drama is undoubtedly the fragmented form of his many-layered novels and the comparative logic that underlies them. His fiction often puts past and present side by side, with a view to showing, as he also does in his book-length essay *The Atlantic Sound* (2000), that 'the past surges like a mighty river . . . It empties into the present'.[12] Likewise, Phillips's travelling texts create resonances and invite comparison between characters with very different backgrounds who do their best to survive in the face of traumas brought about by mankind's eternal tendency to reject the Other.

*   *   *

This collection of radio plays is a long-standing project which would not have been possible without the unfailing help and support of Caryl Phillips. I am very grateful to him. My thanks also go to the Beinecke Rare Book and Manuscript Library for facilitating my visits to New Haven and to the Beinecke librarians for their kind assistance during my research in Caryl Phillips's archives.

Notes

1 Caryl Phillips, *The Wasted Years*, *Best Radio Plays of 1984* (London: Methuen, 1985), 85–141.
2 Caryl Phillips Papers. General Collection, Beinecke Rare Book and Manuscript Library, Yale University.
3 Caryl Phillips, *Crossing the River* (London: Bloomsbury, 1993), 2.
4 John Wain, 'Towny Smartiboots', *The Listener*, 22 March 1984.
5 Maria Festa, 'On Writing, Reading, Interpreting (and Pan Africanism): An Interview with Caryl Phillips', *From the European South*, 3 (2018), 125–32 (128).
6 Leslie Grace McMurtry, *Revolution in the Echo Chamber: Audio Drama's Past, Present and Future* (Bristol: Intellect, 2019), 5.
7 William Stanton, 'The Invisible Theatre of Radio Drama', *Critical Quarterly*, 46(4), 2004, 94–107 (95).
8 Caryl Phillips Papers. General Collection, Beinecke Rare Book and Manuscript Library, Yale University.
9 Suzanne Scafe, 'Home/lessness, Exile and Triangular Identities in the Drama of Caryl Phillips', in Mary F. Brewer, Lynette Goddard and Deirdre Osborne (eds), *Modern and Contemporary Black British Drama* (London: Palgrave Macmillan, 2015), 62–76 (70).
10 There are no real allusions to journeys across the Atlantic in *Writing Fiction*, with the exception of one of the minor characters, called Rudy, who suggests that his mother came to England from the Caribbean.
11 Email to Bénédicte Ledent, 20 July 2013.
12 Caryl Phillips, *The Atlantic Sound* (London: Faber & Faber, 2000), 220.

The Wasted Years

Broadcast Details

BBC Radio 4, 12 March 1984. Directed by Vanessa Whitburn.

Characters (in order of appearance)

Mr Teale
Solly Daniels
Tagger
Interviewer
Cynthia Daniels
Chris Daniels
Roy Daniels
Tracey
Headmaster
Jenny
Gym Teacher
Bates
Children

Notes on the Play

This play focuses on the Daniels, a family of West Indian descent living in England in the 1980s. It explores the identitarian difficulties met by second-generation youths from a migrant background, as well as the disappointed hopes of their parents, who came from the Caribbean in the 1960s. Raised with his brother Chris by their now single mother, Cynthia, Solly Daniels attends a mostly white comprehensive school. His experience of racism in this context feeds his anger and complicates his relationship with his mother and his supportive teacher, Mr Teale.

The story contains several points of comparison with Caryl Phillips's first stage play *Strange Fruit* (1981) – which was revived to much acclaim in 2019 and was republished by Oberon in the Modern Playwrights series – and it also echoes some sections of the novel *The Lost Child* (2015), notably the school days of Ben and his brother Tommy.

The Wasted Years was selected for the Giles Cooper Awards as one of the best radio plays of 1984, when it was first broadcast. It was aired again by the BBC in 2017, which bespeaks its ongoing relevance.

Noise coming from a classroom as the bell has just gone for the end of the day.

Teale I said quietly, 5C. This isn't Saturday afternoon down at the match, it's a school, and, Deakin, put that chair back where it belongs.

Sound of the kids jeering.

Shut up, all of you. I said put it back, Deakin, and put it back now.

Solly He don't have to do it, for it's the end of school.

Tagger Well, I wouldn't do it, I can tell you that much.

Teale What was that, Daniels?

Solly Nothing.

Teale Don't 'nothing' me, lad, I'm a bit longer in the tooth than you.

Tagger (*giggles and whispers*) A bit what?

Teale Tagley, shut your stupid mouth, boy.

Tagger Sir.

Teale Daniels, I'm still waiting.

Solly I said he don't have to move it if he don't want to for it's the end of school now.

Teale I see. You're not by any chance trying to tell me my job are you, lad?

Sound of some of the kids starting to giggle.

The rest of you move, and move quickly and quietly or I'll have you all back here in detention tomorrow night. (*Groans.*) Go on. Daniels, you wait here.

We hear them disperse until only **Teale** *and* **Solly** *are left.*

Teale I think we better have a talk, don't you?

Solly I don't see what for.

Teale I don't see what for, Mr Teale.

Solly Mr Teale.

Teale Look, Daniels, haven't you got rid of that chip on your shoulder yet? It'll not do you any good once you get out there.

Solly I haven't got a chip on my shoulder.

Teale Hasn't it ever occurred to you, Daniels, that people notice when you misbehave. When Tagley and the other lads do it they . . . well, they see them all as one, find it more difficult to single them out, but with you, it's as if you're a natural target and you will insist on placing yourself in the firing line won't you?

Solly I'm no worse than anyone else.

Teale   Well, I'm not sure if I'd go that far but what I will say is if you're going to leave school at the end of the week and go out into society with a kind of 'come and get me' attitude, then they'll come and get you; and they'll swallow you whole.

Solly   Who will?

Teale (*laughs*)   Who will? Daniels, there isn't a lad in the country of your age who's not going to have to run the gauntlet of interviews, careers people, dole people, social security, police; it's not like it was when I first started teaching anymore. And don't look at me like that – it was only nine or ten years ago. These days we don't send you out to your apprenticeships and your office-boy jobs. Everybody's head is on the block and I can promise you there are people out there happily doing the chopping. (*Pause.*) You've never liked school have you?

Solly   I did to start with but people started to get at me.

Teale   And so you began to throw away all your talent and energy into causing trouble: don't you see that's playing the wrong game, Daniels, and if you try and play that out there you'll be eaten alive. Doesn't your mother want you to get on?

Solly   Course she does and I don't cause trouble, it's you lot. You pick on me.

Teale   Why not try for her? Or for yourself even.

Solly (*gets upset*)   I have been but there doesn't seem to be any point, does there? If Tagger or any of the others do something then you let them off. If it's me I get sent to the head or put in detention. If there's a load of us running down a corridor then I'm the one who'll get stopped and given lines. Always me like it's a big joke to you, then you always have a talk to try and make me feel bad, like I'm a crook or something.

Teale   Nobody thinks you're a crook.

Solly   Well, I'm not! (*He gets up and runs out obviously upset.*)

Teale   Daniels, wait. Daniels . . .

Newsreel: voice-over of West Indians arriving off the boats in the fifties and 'BBC' **Interviewer** *talking.*

Interviewer   . . . these dashing chaps in their colourful hats and big smiles all seem to be finding the cold a bit much as they file gingerly down the gang plank. Let's go and talk to one or two of them. How are you finding it here?

Answer   Well, it's cold but I think I'm going to like it.

Interviewer   And how long are you planning to stay with us?

Answer   A few years, three or four.

Interviewer   I see, then back to the sunny Caribbean, eh?

Answer   I hope so.

Interviewer   And your wife here, is it?

Answer   I think we'll both like it here. Everyone seems so friendly already.

Interviewer   Ah good. And you, sir. First impressions favourable?

Answer   Well, it's the motherland isn't it, and I'm just pleased to be here.

Interviewer   Quite. You look well prepared, sir.

Answer   Well, I was over here in the war, RAF pilot, and I'm used to it.

Interviewer   And how long are you planning on staying with us this time?

Answer   About five years should be sufficient, but who knows. I might stay longer.

Interviewer   And I think I speak for the British public when I say as long as there is work to be done we'll always be pleased to have you here.

Answer   Thank you very much.

Solly *is running across a wide playground.*

Solly   Tagger! Tagger!

He nears **Tagger** *and slows down out of breath.*

Tagger   I thought you weren't coming.

Solly   I had to listen to Teale first.

Tagger   What's he say?

Solly   Nothing much.

Tagger   Oh come on, what's he say? He must have said something.

Solly   Normal stuff. Going on like he might expel me.

Tagger   How come? We've only got three more days in this dump.

Solly   I dunno. Always bleeding picking on me. You wanna go behind the bogs for a quick fag?

Tagger   What for? It's after school and we can have one in the street or on the bus if we want.

Solly   I know but if my brother sees me he might tell my mum and she'll kill me.

Tagger   Then you'll kill him, won't you?

Solly   Well, someone else might see us and tell her. A friend of hers or something.

Tagger   All right then, but Batesy and Johnson are behind there. (*Pause.*) Well, still coming?

Solly   I don't know. Forget it then.

Tagger   It's up to you.

They walk on a little and we hear the noise of traffic as they leave the school playground.

You coming down the club tonight, Solly?

Solly   Suppose so. Don't care really.

Tagger   What's the matter with you? You've gone all funny.

Solly   How?

Tagger   Sort of quiet.

Solly   It's just the club, it gets on my nerves sometimes.

Tagger   I reckon that's cos you haven't got a bird. Still, you could get one if you wanted one though.

Solly   Yeah, I know I could but I don't want one.

Tagger   Well, there ain't much else to do down there except hope someone'll buy us a drink.

Solly   Haven't you got any money either?

Tagger   Course not but someone might have.

Solly   I don't know if I want to go now.

Tagger   Look, have a fag and shut up. It's getting dark and nobody will see us. Well, they won't see you at least.

Solly   That ain't funny.

Tagger   Just a joke that's all, just a joke. (*Pause.*) I forgot to ask you. Will you do that maths quiz for us? I'll give you another fag if you do.

Solly   Yeah, course I will.

Tagger   Great. It's even worse than homework and it's supposed to be a game. Hang on a minute. (*Lighting a fag.*)

Solly   Look, you coming or not?

Tagger   Funny that; that's what my bird always asks me.

Solly   Very funny. Come on, will you?

Tagger   No need to bite my head off you know.

Solly   I ain't feeling too bright.

Tagger   You ain't the only one. My old man says if I don't have a job in six weeks he's kicking me out. I told him that if all dads acted like him then the streets would be teeming with millions of homeless teenagers. So he clouted me for cheek. (*Laughs.*) I know what I was going to ask you. What did your dad used to do, I mean for a job like?

Solly   I don't know.

Tagger   Well, he might have been a millionaire, or a footballer or something. You can never tell. Ain't you interested?

Solly   No. What you don't know you don't miss. There's loads of people like me, you know. It's nothing special.

Tagger   Yeah I know, I never said there was anything special.

Solly   Well, why do you keep going on about it?

Tagger   I don't. I just mentioned it, that's all. There's nothing wrong with that is there?

Solly   Suppose not. (*Pause.*) Look, come on, let's run, no point in hanging around here.

Tagger   All right then. (*He begins to run.*) Last one into Fairfax Road is a wanker.

Solly   Hang on a minute.

The front door slams and **Cynthia** *shouts through from the kitchen where she is listening to the radio news.*

Cynthia   Christopher? Solomon?

Chris (*shouting back*)   It's me, Chris.

Cynthia   And where's your brother?

Chris   I don't know. I haven't seem him.

He moves to go upstairs.

Cynthia   Where are you going. Christopher?

Chris   Homework.

Cynthia   You mean you can't come through and kiss me or say hello or something like that. Is it a house of ghosts I'm living in now or what?

Chris (*beginning to run up the stairs*)   I'm in a rush, Mum.

Cynthia (*tired*)   Everybody's in a rush, everybody's busy, nobody's got time. I don't know what kind of a world you all think you're living in. Jet age this, and space age that, and all I'm beginning to feel is my old age. Jesus, if only I'd have realized what I was taking on.

On a train.

Roy   You still cold, darling?

Cynthia   I thought England in July would be warmer than this, Roy.

Roy   Well, it's a different world over here, me dear.

Cynthia   Seems like it.

Pause.

Roy   Look at the cows over there in the field. Jesus Christ, most of them look better fed than the people back home.

Cynthia   That's not fair. We have ample food back there.

Roy   So why the people them look like stick insects?

Cynthia   Here it's a land of plenty, it's exciting, like your first day at school. A brave new world is what they call it on the radio.

Roy   In a way it is. You don't think so?

Cynthia   I'll wait and see but I'm glad we've come this far, we can't turn back now.

Roy   Turn back? We soon going reach London then pow! Things really start to take shape.

Cynthia   I hope so. I really hope so for I can see that unless you come prime minister by next year all you going do is moan.

Pause.

Roy   You feeling all right, Cynthia?

Cynthia   I guess I'm just a little frightened, Roy.

Roy   Well, you don't think I'm frightened too?

Cynthia   Are you?

Roy   Course but . . . but there's hope here, space to grow and develop, and England is not a normal island, it's special.

Cynthia   I suppose it is.

Roy   And the way I see it we must work and save up some money, and put down a deposit on our own property. Then, when the time is ready and we are settled and secure – then, and only then, we can start to bring children into the world so they can take over where we started.

Cynthia   I want two children, Roy. To keep each other company. Solomon and Samantha.

Roy   And I want the boy to be a doctor and the girl to be a nurse.

Cynthia   I thought you wanted the boy to be a lawyer.

Roy   Or a lawyer. It's a fine profession for a young man, especially if what I hear of England is correct. For you can't go wrong if you have an education, and that he must have, they must both have it, and no matter what happens we must try and give them that at least. If nothing else some learning for a future.

Cynthia   In that case we make the right decision in coming here.

Roy   Of course we did. All they really going to learn back home was how to starve and suffer and live without a job.

Cynthia   The train's slowing down, Roy. This must be London.

Roy   Look! Look! A red double-decker bus. Well, Lord, I never thought I'd live to see a red double-decker bus – and a policeman. A bobby with a helmet. And look, my arse, a bowler hat! (*Pause.*) Cynthia, I want one of them.

Cynthia   If you do, well, I don't see why not.

Announcement: voice-over – 'This is London Waterloo! London Waterloo!'

Roy   Well, we've arrived and the second part of our life is just beginning.

Cynthia   But I'm still frightened, Roy. I don't know what's going to happen, you know.

Roy   But that's all part of the excitement, girl; that's what's meant by being on the move.

Cynthia   Lord, I can feel my blood pumping like it's ready to just burst out of my body.

Cynthia *is in the kitchen sitting alone in the dark. It is so quiet that perhaps one can hear a clock ticking away on the wall.*

Cynthia (*in a very hushed whisper*)   Well, Roy, I'm still trying, you know, I really am, and the blood still pumping. (*Pause.*) They've become a bit like what you were, Roy. Headstrong boys. They always played rough, even as babies. Always covered in bruises but never crying. Neither of them. Well, Solomon did to start with: You remember that, but he soon learned to hush up when his brother came along. Yes, a brother: I know we wanted a girl but I'm happy with Chris; he's a good boy. I'm more than happy with him. (*Pause.*) And I can't be too hard on them. I just can't, not after what happened.

Chris   Mum?

Cynthia   Who is it?

Chris   It's me, Chris. Why is the light off?

Cynthia   Christopher? Where are you? (*Light goes on.*) Oh good, I can see you now.

Chris   Who were you talking to, Mum?

Cynthia   Nobody. Just myself. I must have fallen asleep. (*Standing up to fill the kettle.*) Even a simple little secretary job seems to be starting to tell on me. At my age. (*She laughs.*)

Chris   Are you all right, Mum?

Cynthia   Yes, dear. Just tired. You go on and finish your homework and I'll bring you up a cup of tea.

Chris   I've finished.

Cynthia   Oh, I see, Well, you can talk to me then.

She goes to put on the kettle.

Chris   What about?

Cynthia   Nothing. Just anything. Talk. Or maybe we have to draw up an agenda before you can talk with your mother.

Chris   But I can't think of anything to say.

Cynthia   Don't worry. I'm sure we'll manage to find something to say, something to talk about. (*Pause.*) Well, sit down then.

Chris   Why don't you give up work, Mum?

Cynthia   And then what will you eat, you tell me that?

Chris   Don't you get a pension?

Cynthia   I hope that's a joke.

Chris   Well, some people get them before they're sixty.

Cynthia   Well, not me.

Chris   Solly might get a job.

Cynthia   And I'll win the pools, eh?

Chris   I'm only trying to help.

Cynthia   I know you are. (*She kisses him.*) Tea or coffee?

Chris   Tea.

Cynthia   Tea what?

Chris   Please. (*Pause.*) Mum, what's a period?

Cynthia   Nothing that you'll have to worry about. Why?

Chris   It's just that I heard some girls talking about it and I thought it meant how long a lesson takes but they laughed at me.

Cynthia   What were they saying?

Chris   Just stuff about being late which is why I thought they were talking about lessons.

Cynthia   I see. And what do you think they were really talking about?

Chris   I'm not sure.

Pause.

Cynthia   Samantha. If we had a girl we were going to call her Samantha.

Chris   That's awful, sounds like a princess.

Cynthia (*laughs*)   She would have been a princess and she'd have been able to tell you all about periods.

Chris   You tell me then.

Cynthia   I've got two princes instead and I'll tell you both when I'm ready and not before. Now take this and go to bed, you look tired.

Chris   But football's on tonight.

Cynthia   I said you look tired so you're going to bed.

Chris   No point cos Solly always wakes me up when he comes in.

Cynthia   Well, you should tell him to come in more quietly.

Chris   I do but he never listens anymore. He just shouts. And at school he just ignores me. I think he's trying to pretend I'm not his brother.

Cynthia   All boys are like that but I'll talk to him if you like.

Chris   Do you think he'll listen?

Cynthia   Of course he'll listen, I'm his mother, aren't I?

Chris   Teachers keep saying things to me about him.

Cynthia   Like what?

Chris   Like why can't he be like me and stuff like that.

Pause.

Cynthia   Is it upsetting you, Christopher?

Chris   It gets to me a bit. Annoys me. It's like they think he's a freak or something, Mum. They talk about him like he's not real.

Cynthia   And what else do they say to you?

Chris   Nothing.

Cynthia   Are you sure?

Chris   Yes.

Pause.

Cynthia   Go to bed, son. I'll speak to your brother when he comes in.

Chris   All right, goodnight.

Cynthia   Goodnight, son.

We are at a discotheque where the music is loud and punkish. They are not really playing any Black music.

Solly   But it's no good coming somewhere if you haven't got any money.

Tagger   Well, we've only just got here, Solly. What's the matter with you?

Solly   And what about the school disco on Friday night? I haven't got any money for that either.

Tagger   Well, nick some from your mum's handbag. That's where my dad gets his.

Solly   I ain't nicking it from home.

Tagger   Well, that's up to you, ain't it?

Solly   Yeah, and I ain't nicking none.

Tagger   Well, we can't have a drink till my bird gets here. But she might have a quid or something.

Solly   Tracey?

Tagger   I've only got one bird, you know.

Solly   Yeah I know.

Tagger   You should get one. At least you'd have someone to buy you a drink then. (*Laughs.*) What about Jenny Bates. You ain't trying to tell me you don't fancy her cos I know you do.

Solly   Who says?

Tagger   I say. You never shut up about her but it'll only come to nothing cos you're too chicken to say anything in case she tells you to get lost.

Solly   I'm not scared.

Tagger   I didn't even have to ask Tracey. Her mate Sandra, or whatever her name is, she told me. And what's the first thing Tracey starts talking to me about when I took her out: kids and getting married. I said yeah I want all that Trace but there's a few more years to wait as yet. I'm only sixteen for God's sake.

Solly   I know what you mean.

Tagger   Do you, hell. If I didn't know you better I'd think you were . . .

Solly   Who, me?

Tagger   It's like you're scared of them. Is it cos you're coloured, you think they might tell you to get lost?

Solly   You don't know what you're on about. You sound pissed already.

Tagger   Oh yeah? And what would you know about it.

Solly   As much as you.

Tagger   Sure you do. Anyway shut up, here comes Tracey.

Solly   I'm off to the bog. I'll see you later.

Tagger   Why, are you thinking of moving in there or something?

Solly   Get stuffed, Tagger.

We mix back to the discotheque later where the music is still playing and the scene seems to be in full swing. **Solly** *is standing on his own and* **Tagger** *comes across with* **Tracey**.

Tracey   Hello, Solly. Where have you been?

Tagger (*a bit pissed*)   Watcher, Sol, me old mate. What you doing over here all by your tod then?

Solly   Same as usual. I couldn't find you. And how come you've been drinking?

Tracey   Yeah that's what I want to know. Me dad got laid off this morning and he gave me and me mum a fiver each to go and commiserate for him as he was going out with his mates. I've got about forty pence left cos he's gone and drunk it all in record time.

Solly   I might have guessed.

Tagger   Not all of it. She had an orange juice. (*He laughs to himself.*)

Tracey   How come you ain't dancing, Solly?

Tagger   Cos it ain't 'roots, man', not vital music, that's right ain't it, Sol?

Tracey   Shut up will you, Tagger.

Solly   I just don't feel like dancing. I'm going now anyway.

Tagger   Well, you're going to have to run quickly if you wanna catch her up for she left ten minutes ago.

Tracey   Catch who up?

Tagger   Jenny Bates of course. You mean you don't know about Solly fancying her?

Solly   On your bike will you, Tagger. I'm off.

Tagger   If you wanna go out with her ask her.

Solly   It ain't none of your business if I do.

Tagger   You ain't ever had a bird have you?

Tracey   Oh shut up, Tagger.

Tagger   You shut up! You're scared of asking her, aren't you?

Solly   Shut your face or I'll fill it for you.

Tagger   Yeah, you and whose army? You think I'm scared of you just cos you're black.

Tracey   Tagger! Shut up! He's just drunk, Solly. He don't even know what he's saying.

Solly   He better not say any more or I'll hit him, mate or no mate.

Tracey   Tagger, shut up. I'm going for my coat then we're off. See you later, Solly.

Tagger   I wonder what it's like never to have been able to pull a bird.

Tracey   Shut up, Tagger! See you, Solly. You better go now.

Solly   Yeah, see you, Tracey.

He goes.

Tracey (*in a lower voice*)   You behaved like a pig.

Tagger   It's him and all his pretending about not wanting a bird. Makes me sick.

Tracey (*in a lower voice*)   He don't really fancy her, does he?

Tagger   Course he does but he never says nothing about it. You can see in the way he just looks at her.

Tracey   Oh God, speaking of Jenny Bates here comes her brother with that stupid git, Johnson.

Tagger   They better not try anything cos I've got my flick-knife with me.

Tracey   Don't be stupid. Put that away, Tagger.

Tagger   I can handle myself.

Tracey   And so can they but nobody has done anything so don't start any trouble, eh?

Tagger   I don't want to start any trouble. Have we got enough money for another drink?

Tracey   I suppose so if you have half.

Tagger (*glumly*)   All right then.

Tracey   I'll get it. Wait here, and for God's sake behave.

Cynthia's *bedroom. She is lying awake and we hear the bedroom clock ticking. We hear the sound of* **Solly** *creeping up the stairs but the steps are creaking despite his attempts to keep it quiet.*

Cynthia (*shouting through*)   Solomon, is that you trying to creep up the stairs without me hearing you?

Solly   I was just trying to keep quiet so I wouldn't wake you up.

Cynthia   Yes I'll bet you were. You'll have to grow wings, boy, before you can get past me like that. Come, I want to talk with you.

Solly (*he has come into the bedroom now*)   What about?

Cynthia   What about? Haven't you got any manners?

Solly   I just asked you what you wanted to talk to me about.

Cynthia   I know what you asked me, Solomon.

Solly   Well, what's the matter?

Cynthia   You, you're what's the matter.

Solly   I haven't done anything so I don't see why you're getting at me.

Cynthia   Who's getting at you?

Solly   You, you are. Always bickering and telling me what's wrong with me, telling me what to believe and how to dress, and what to wear, and what to say, and none of it makes any sense does it?

Cynthia   You mean nothing I say makes any sense to you?

Solly   No, none of it. It's all just words, words, words, and it don't add up to anything real. Like when you keep saying don't I feel I owe you something.

Cynthia   Well, don't you?

Solly   Like what?

Cynthia   Like the fact that you've got clothes on your back for instance.

Solly   And I'm supposed to feel grateful for that? I thought that's what you were supposed to do anyhow if you had kids.

Cynthia   Well, open your eyes, Solomon. Some parents don't.

Solly   Well, they're stupid then, aren't they?

Cynthia   And do you think I'm stupid? Well? Do you think there's something the matter with me?

Solly   No! I told you it's them. Not you.

Cynthia   You should feel proud, Solomon, you should hold your head up high and realize you're just as good as the other boys, you're just as English as them.

Solly   That's it! That's just it! You don't know what you're talking about, do you? I'm not just as English as they are and I don't know why you keep going on about it.

Cynthia   What do you mean you're not just as English as they are? Of course you are.

Solly   Well, you go tell them that and see what they say to you.

Cynthia   'Us', 'them', 'we', 'they': what's got into you, Solly ? Why all the dividing all of a sudden? It's not the way I brought you up.

Solly   I know, Mum. But it's different from just straightening your tie, and grinning nicely! I am different! They can see that.

Cynthia   Don't shout or you'll wake up your brother.

Solly   I might as well wake him up cos he's gonna have to hear this sooner or later anyhow.

Cynthia   Hear what?

Solly   Hear that it's not the truth what you say.

Cynthia   Then what is the truth, Solly ? What is it that I'm either too stupid or too ignorant to know?

Solly   I don't mean it like that.

Cynthia   Like what?

Solly   Like to tell you that you're stupid or anything.

Cynthia   Well, don't stop now, you might as well go on. And what is it that you say your brother will have to learn?

Solly   He'll have to learn that they don't like him even if he does come top of the class every time. It don't make any difference in their eyes.

Cynthia I see and you think it's all about wanting to be liked.

Solly I never said that, what I meant was that it'll change for him too.

Cynthia What'll change?

Solly I don't know, Mum. (*Pause; he is getting upset.*) Why don't you ever explain things to us?

Cynthia What do you want to know?

Solly About you and Dad, for instance.

Cynthia I don't see what that's got to do with your lack of interest in your schoolwork, do you?

Solly No, but it's real talk isn't it? Isn't it?

Cynthia Don't shout at me, Solomon. Just remember who you are and where you are.

Solly I know that.

Cynthia Well, if you don't like it you're perfectly free to go, understand? I won't have you here any longer unless you have some respect, understand?

Solly Why can't I ask questions?

Cynthia Go to bed, Solomon, it's late.

Solly I said, why can't I ask questions?

Cynthia You can but when I say bed I mean bed so please go. And I expect an apology from you.

Solly What for?

Cynthia You'd better think about that yourself. Well? (*Pause.*) Well?

Solly I'm sorry.

Cynthia Go to bed, Solomon. I sometimes wonder just who it is you really think you are.

In the brothers' bedroom.

Chris Is that you, Solly ?

Solly No it's the Ghost of Christmas Past.

Chris What time is it?

Solly I don't know, do I? I'm turning the light on.

Chris What for?

Solly So I can see, dummy. (*He turns it on.*)

Chris God it's bright, Solly.

Solly Light bulbs usually are.

Chris   Aren't you coming to bed?

Solly   No I've got to write a letter first.

Chris   Who to?

Solly   Prime Minister. Asking her for a job in Parliament.

Chris   Doing what?

Solly   Oh shut up will you.

Pause.

Chris   You been arguing with her again?

Solly   Brilliant, so you've got two ears.

Chris   What about?

Solly   About why you're such a dick.

Chris   No, really.

Solly   About how she keeps on about how the sun shines out of Britain's backside.

Chris   No she don't.

Solly   Just listen and you'll hear her. She's got her job with Dr Chandra but she must leave his place and travel in a sealed capsule to get to work and back home. She never sees or feels anything.

Chris   Yes she does.

Solly   Like what, creep? Like the number of gold stars in your report book?

Chris   No, I don't know. (*Pause.*) Will you be long?

Solly   Why?

Chris   Cos I can't sleep with the light on.

Solly   Well, put your head under the blankets.

Chris   Then I can't sleep cos I'll suffocate.

Solly   Well, you'll have to suffocate then.

Chris   Is it a love letter?

Solly   Shut your face, is it hell.

Chris   We get our exam results tomorrow.

Solly   I said shut your face, I'm writing.

Chris (*whispers*)   You shut yours.

Solly   You what?

Chris   Nothing. I had a talk with Mum today.

Solly   So, you're not the first and you won't be the last.

Chris   Did she tell you about it?

Solly   About what?

Chris   The talk.

Solly   No, why should she?

Chris   No reason.

Solly   Well, shut up then.

Pause.

Chris   Solly?

Solly   For God's sake.

Chris   What's a period?

Solly   A what?

Chris   A period. I heard some girls talking about it today.

Solly   It's what they get when they're not going to have a kid.

Chris   Is that all?

Solly   Well, what did you think it was?

Chris   I didn't know.

Solly   Just shut up now, will you? I want to finish this.

Chris   Then will you turn the light out?

Solly   No I'm going to sit here all night until the bulb blows up, goodnight.

Chris   I'm not thick you know, Solly. You don't have to talk to me like that.

Solly   Who told you that or did you learn it in General Studies?

Chris   That's not funny.

Solly   And neither are you so shut up or go back to sleep.

Pause.

Chris   You always wake me up.

Solly   Well, if you don't shut up I'll put you to sleep for good, right?

Newsreel-type interview: in the street.

Interviewer   And, sir, can I ask you what you think of our coloured brethren?

Answer   I think there's far too many coloureds over here and they ought to be sent back to the jungle or wherever it is they come from.

Interviewer   The West Indies.

Answer   I don't give a damn where it is. All I know is I didn't fight a war for this country just to see the likes of your sort handing over our spoils to niggers and watching them take our women from us.

Interviewer   Thank you, sir. And you, madam, what do you think?

Answer   Well, they're dirty for a start-off. Never see any washing on the lines outside of their houses. And they let their children run around with hardly any clothes on.

Interviewer   And you, sir. Do you think there's a colour bar problem?

Answer   Don't know, do I?

Interviewer   Well, then, do you work or socialize with any coloureds?

Answer   A few and they're all right. Keep themselves to themselves.

Interviewer   So you don't have any complaints against them?

Answer   A spade's a spade. A white man's a white man, that's all there is to it.

Interviewer   Thank you, sir. Madam, can I ask you about the coloured folk over here. Do you have any contact with them at all?

Answer   What?

Interviewer   I mean at work, or in the local pub.

Answer   I don't mix with darkies. I was against letting 'em in and I still am.

1966: **Roy** *and* **Cynthia** *are lying in bed.*

Cynthia   Roy? (*Pause.*) Are you awake?

Roy   I can't sleep, Cynthia.

Cynthia   What's worrying you?

Roy   I don't know. Seven years in this country and we still don't get no place as yet. I guess that could be worrying me.

Cynthia   But at least you're working. We have a nice bedsit and soon we can maybe put down a deposit on a house.

Roy (*laughs*)   When? I could have built a house by now with my own two hands.

Cynthia   When things pick up a bit.

Roy   I sometimes wonder if things ever going to pick up, you know, England just win the World Cup, hippies in the street, everything peace and love, and we still ain't going no place. How come everybody else is happy and we still in the shit?

Cynthia   We have to give it time, Roy. I think we maybe expected too much too soon from England. Maybe we place too much burden upon her.

Roy   Well, if that's the case she's certainly getting her own back now. Today, at work, the foreman asked me if I fancy doing some overtime but not to tell any of the others. When I ask him why he just wink at me he say that it's a secret between the two of us for they don't like spades. Well, I let that one slip by, but when he bowl me the one about he's only paying me half rate for the overtime for he is doing me a favour, I have to drive the ball back down the wicket and into his damn mouth because he must think I'm a fool or something.

Cynthia   Why didn't you tell me this before, Roy?

Roy   Why? (*He laughs.*) Do you tell me every time someone push you in the back, or drop your change on the counter, or call you nigger, or push you off the bus, do you tell me every time? No you don't and you know why not? It's because if you did we'd be talking all day and we'd never get any peace of any kind in the evening. There would be too much misery between us.

Cynthia   So nobody talks to you at work?

Roy   Yes, man, people say things like 'Bring the hammer, Roy', and 'Take the hammer, Roy', and 'Bring the spanner, Roy', and 'Take the spanner, Roy', they talk to me all right.

Cynthia   Well, you can always change the job, can't you?

Roy   And do what? We have enough problems saving up as it is at the moment and I can't risk a less secure post than this otherwise we never going be able to afford to have some children and bring them up nice and properly. All I've got to look forward to at the moment is more, 'Bring the goddamn hammer, Roy', 'Take the goddamn hammer, Roy'.

Cynthia   I could go out to work, Roy.

Roy   How many times I must tell you that I prefer it if you stay at home for the man should support the woman like back home.

Cynthia   But we can save faster if I work too, don't you see that?

Roy   Yes I see it but I don't know if it's right, you know. I just can't tell, Cynthia.

Classroom just before the start of the day and all the commotion of the kids arriving.

Tagger   Give it us here. I'll do it.

Voices of the classroom: 'No, let Steve . . . It's only a knife . . .', etc.

Only the 'y' to do now. Anyone coming?

Voice   Not yet, Tagger. He's bound to notice when he opens his desk.

Tagger   Well, that's the whole idea isn't it, birdbrain?

Voice   Hang on a minute, here he comes.

We hear the sound of a terrible commotion and chairs scraping, etc. as they try to get into place.

Tagger   All right, Solly.

Solly   Yeah. Why, what's up?

We hear the sound of sniggering.

Tagger   Nothing. What makes you think there is?

Solly   Because I know you and I can tell when something's up.

Voice   There's nothing up, Sol. It's just Tagger still smashed from last night.

Solly   Yeah, noticed you didn't come across and offer me a drink.

Tagger   I told you it wasn't my money that I was spending otherwise I'd have been the first across. You know me.

Solly   Yeah I know, Tagger. Better than you think.

Voice   Hold up a minute, Teale's coming.

Sound of **Teale** *coming in and closing the door.*

Teale   Morning. (*Murmured reply, hardly audible.*) It's happened at last. You've all lost your tongues. Well? I said, 'Morning'.

Class   'Morning'. (*In various shades of protest.*)

Teale   'Morning, Mr Teale', or 'Morning, sir' would have been better but I suppose I'll have to be thankful for what little I get from you lot.

Voice   Don't be like that, sir.

Teale (*mimics*)   Don't be like that, sir. There's no spark in you lot is there? No spirit? A wasted generation.

Voice   We're not wasted, sir.

Teale   Well, prove it then, behave, work, dress smartly, take some pride in yourselves and all the rest.

Voice   You sound like the man from the Army Recruiting Office, sir.

Teale   Well, that's not exactly what I had in mind, thank you very much. Right. Register. Andrews . . .

Voice   Sir.

Teale   Askew . . .

Voice   Sir.

Teale   Bates . . . Where's Bates, anybody?

Voice   Late, sir. I saw him coming to school but . . .

Teale   I know. I know. Had to stop for a quick fag. (*They all laugh.*) Collins . . . Daniels . . . Deakin . . . Evans . . . Fairbairn . . . Francis . . . Grahams . . . Harris . . . Hawley . . .

The register fades, then we go back to the classroom where **Teale** *is still taking the register.*

Teale   Tagley . . .

Tagger   Sir.

Teale   Tattersall . . .

Voice   Sir.

Teale   Thompson . . .

Voice   Sir.

Teale   Watson . . .

Voice   Sir.

Teale   And last and by all means least. (*The class laughs.*) Williams.

Voice   Sir?

The class laughs even more.

Teale   Quiet, quieten down now. The joke's over with. (*They shut up.*) Now then, as you may or may not be aware there is a school disco on Friday night to celebrate the releasing of your horrible selves onto the unsuspecting world out there. (*A cheer.*) I don't know what you're all so happy about. I'll give it a week and you'll all be begging at the school gates to be let back in.

Voices   'No chance, sir' – 'You've got to be kidding' – 'What, into this dump?', *etc.*

Voice (*in a quiet voice*)   Here, Tagger, look.

Tagger   Oh God, he's opening it. (*Suppressed laughter.*)

Teale   Well, anyway, when you have a discotheque you need people to do exciting things like serve soft drinks, serve food, prepare the school hall, hang up decorations, do some disc-jockeying, and lots of other thrilling things, and seeing as it's for your benefit we, the staff that is, don't see why we should have to be bothered with such details. I'm sure you all agree. (*Boos.*) So we need some volunteers. (*Silence.*) Well, come on then. Don't crush me to death in the rush. Solomon Daniels, how about you?

Solly   Eh?

Teale   Eh? What kind of an answer is that? And what are you doing, lad?

The class bursts out laughing.

Solly   Nothing.

Teale   It doesn't look like nothing to me. (*Moves towards him.*)

Solly   I'm not doing anything.

Teale   Well, I'd like to see what's in your desk too. (*He lifts up the desk lid.*) I see. You do know how to write with a pen and a piece of paper don't you, Daniels?

Solly   Course I do.

Teale   Course you do. Why, then, carve 'Jenny' into your desk lid like some imbecillic, love-sick ten-year-old?

Solly   I didn't carve it into my desk.

Teale   Well, somebody did and it's you who was poring over it when I was asking for volunteers.

Solly   I wasn't poring over it.

The school bell goes.

Teale   All right, you lot hoppit to your lesson. Daniels, you stay here. I'd like a word with you yet again.

Tagger   See you later, Solly.

Teale   I said hoppit and that means all of you. And fast.

They all leave and then it goes quiet and we are left with the sound of the two of them alone in the room.

Teale   So, you didn't carve the name into your desk then?

Solly   No, I just said I didn't.

Teale   Then who did?

Solly   I don't know.

Teale   Let's try it from another angle then. How long has it been there?

Solly   I've never seen it before,

Teale   So it must have been done either last night or this morning, right?

Solly   I suppose so.

Teale   And who is this Jenny girl anyway? Your girlfriend I presume.

Solly   I don't know.

Teale   You mean you don't know who the 'Jenny' might be referring to?

Solly   I said I didn't do it, all right, so I didn't do it.

Teale   And I'm saying that somebody did it and it's wilful damage to school property and whether you like it or not, or whether I like it or not, it's part of my job to find out who it was.

Solly   Well, I don't know what you're asking me for cos I didn't bleeding do it.

Teale   I don't think there's any reason to adopt that tone of voice.

Solly   What tone of voice?

Teale   You know what I'm referring to.

Solly   No I don't. All I know is that you're calling me a liar and if you call me a liar I'm gonna tell you to piss off, cos I'm not a liar.

Teale   I'm sorry, Daniels, but your behaviour's becoming a bit too arrogant even for me. I'll meet you outside the head's study in five minutes. If you can't or won't talk to me then you'll have to talk to him otherwise you'll be in very serious trouble, understand? Understand?

Solly   No, I don't understand.

Teale   Well, to be quite frank with you I'm a little baffled myself, Daniels. Tell me, is it that you don't trust me, you think I can't relate to whatever it is that's getting to you?

Solly   Nothing's getting to me.

Teale   Oh come on, I was your age once myself. Girls, getting a job, convincing your parents of the most basic and obvious things, younger brothers and sisters, it's all common, but it seems to have hit you harder than most, doesn't it?

Solly   I don't think so.

Teale   Look, I'll be frank with you. I know I'm not coloured but I think I do understand some of what you're talking about.

Solly   Like what?

Teale   Like, well, like . . . Well, you're not really talking, are you?

Solly   No.

Teale   Just plain insolence and stubbornness.

Solly   I don't want to talk to you, don't you understand?

Teale   I think I'm beginning to. Outside the headmaster's study in five minutes.

Inside the **Headmaster**'s *study.*

Head   But you actually have no proof that the boy did it.

Teale   It's not so much the desk itself that worries me, Headmaster, it's his attitude in general.

Voice   Well, from what I've been hearing you're not the only one worried by the boy's behaviour.

Teale   Fair enough but I think it would be good for him if you tried to talk with him, not so much as a judicial figure of authority, but more as a friend, a counsellor. He's standing outside waiting.

Head (*laughs slightly*)   Mr Teale, I appreciate your concern for the boy's welfare. Indeed I think it's admirable, but if I were to waste my time as counsellor to all the boys, and indeed some of the staff too, then I'd have no time left to run the school. I think it's perhaps time you took the bull by the horns and dealt with an issue yourself, Mr Teale, instead of delegating like some lily-livered community worker.

Teale   Instead of what?

Head   Instead of delegating, Mr Teale. Instead of passing the buck.

Teale   But there comes a time, Headmaster, when a boy needs to be pushed slightly more rigorously, especially when things are going wrong for him.

Head   And you have my full permission to do so, and to discipline the boy as you see fit.

Teale   But I'm not asking for your permission to punish, I'm asking for your co-operation in guiding the boy as safely as possible out of this school and into the world out there. I'm asking you to back me up.

Head   To do your job for you?

Teale   No, dammit, to help me do my job!

Head   I think you had better calm down, Mr Teale, or else resume your duties – that is, after all, what the local authority pay you to do.

Teale   I see.

Head   And when they promote you through the various scales, head of department, then deputy head, then finally, possibly, to headmaster, then I think you'll begin to understand what it is that I am talking about.

Teale   Maybe.

Head   Yes, indeed, maybe, but one can but hope. Good morning, Mr Teale.

Teale   I haven't finished yet.

Head   Well, I have. Good morning, Mr Teale. (*Pause.*) Oh and you can send the boy on his way. There seems little point in his propping up the wall outside all day, wouldn't you say.

Teale   Yes, Headmaster.

Girls' toilet.

Tracey   Here, Jenny, I've been looking everywhere for you. (*Pause.*) What you doing in the bogs?

Jenny   Nothing.

Tracey   Yes you are. What are you doing?

Jenny   I'm just reading, Tracey. Just leave us alone.

Tracey   Let's see.

Jenny   No, leave off.

Tracey   Let's see. (*She snatches.*) Oh God, it's not a letter from Solly Daniels, is it? I don't believe it.

Jenny   Give us it back. It might be.

Tracey   You don't like him, do you?

Jenny   I don't know him.

Tracey   But you don't fancy him?

Jenny   He's all right.

Tracey   But what'll your mum and dad say?

Jenny   I haven't done anything yet.

Tracey   I know, but what would they say? And what about your brother?

Jenny   I said I haven't done anything yet.

Tracey   I know, but I was just wondering, that's all.

Jenny   I heard you and I don't want to hear anymore.

Tracey   Well, it's up to you.

Pause.

Jenny   Give us it back, Tracey.

Tracey   'Dear Jenny, I know that I don't know you very well so please forgive me for just writing to you like this.' Where did he learn to write like that?

Jenny   I don't know, do I?

Tracey   'You see, I'm a bit shy of saying anything right out to you in case you tell me to get lost or something. I suppose I'm being a bit cowardly about it, aren't I?' Too right he is.

Jenny   Give us it back, Tracey.

Tracey   'But I'd really like to go out with you after school tonight, to the pictures, or just a walk if you like. Please let me know what you think and I'm sorry for not just asking you straight out. Yours sincerely, Solomon Daniels.' Solomon Daniels!

Jenny   Well, that's his name, isn't it?

Tracey   No it's not, his name is Solly.

Jenny   Which is short for Solomon, stupid. You know like Tagger's last name is Tagley but everyone calls him Tagger.

Tracey   All right I know, I know. You don't have to go on.

Jenny   Well, if you know how come you're pretending you don't? And anyhow it's up to me, isn't it, if I want to see him or not?

Tracey   Course it is, but I've already said I think you're mad. Here, you can have your letter but for God's sake hurry up or we're gonna be late for the next lesson.

Jenny   All right I'm coming, don't bite my head off.

Tracey   You're day-dreaming like you're in love already.

Jenny   Oh shut up, Tracey. You must have an electric mouth the amount you talk.

Behind the toilets in the playground.

Tagger   Hi, Sol, all right?

Solly   No, I'm not.

Tagger   Do you want a fag?

Solly   No, I wanna know why you got me into all that with Teale and don't say it wasn't you cos I know you.

Tagger   It was only a joke, Solly.

Solly   I might have known.

Tagger   No need to be like that, how was I supposed to know that Teale would come and have a look.

Solly   That ain't the point, is it?

Tagger   Yeah, I know, but anyhow what happened?

Solly   Give us a fag and I'll tell you.

Tagger   Here, have one.

Solly   Cheers.

Tagger   Well, what happened then?

Solly   Hang on a minute. Let me get it lit will you.

Tagger   Okay. (*He lights the cigarette.*)

Solly   Well, he just kept asking me who done it and I just kept telling him to mind his own business cos it wasn't me. Eventually I must have told him to piss off once too many times cos he sent me to see the Head. I stood outside while he went in then he just came out and told me to get lost.

Tagger   What, you reckon the Head must have told him to get lost?

Solly   I don't know what happened but that's the end of that as far as I'm concerned.

Tagger   You didn't split on me then?

Solly   Course I didn't split. I'm no grass, you should know that by now.

Tagger   I knew you wouldn't split. Not you. Come on I'm off to the shop. Coming?

Solly   Yeah, I want some chewing gum.

Tagger   Chewing gum? What do you want that for?

Solly   It's games this afternoon. Helps you concentrate when you're playing.

Tagger   You've been watching too much *Match of the Day* mate. You'll be wanting vaseline to rub on your legs next.

Solly   At least I can kick a ball which is more than you can do, you slob.

Tagger   You must think you're Luther Blissett.

Solly   Who says?

Tagger   I says.

Solly   On your bike, Tagger. Let's go.

Tagger   Hey, Solly?

Solly   What?

Tagger   I was a bit pissed last night. Tracey says I should say sorry.

Solly   Don't worry about it, it's okay.

Tagger   And will you still do that maths quiz for me?

Solly   Yeah, don't worry, loads of time.

Tagger   Great. I haven't got a clue,

Solly   Okay.

Tagger   You don't mind do you?

Solly   I wouldn't be doing it if I minded, would I?

Tagger   No, suppose not.

Solly   Well, there you are then. Come on, man. Let's go.

1969: We are in a room somewhere. We can hear noise from another room. A bedsitter of some sort. The noise is a football match with a radio commentary. Then a baby starts to cry in the room.

Roy   But I can't take this place anymore, it's killing me, it's driving me mad. After ten years I'm about to become a madman in England. They can put a man on the moon but I'm still living in a bedsitter with a wife and child.

Cynthia (*comforting the crying baby – about eighteen months old*)   Quiet, Solomon, your father's tired too.

Roy   Still trapped in the same damn stupid nothing dead-end job and every place you turn these damn evil people calling you name this and name that. And you can't go out and find a next job to double the money because of that child, and we can't find the money to put down a deposit on our own property – you know I don't know what the hell we still doing here, you know I just can't figure it out.

Cynthia   Roy, you're just tired.

Roy   Course I'm just tired, woman, but you have to ask yourself what it is I'm tired of. I'm not a young man anymore, you know, I can feel the years slipping away from me, the best years of my life going down the drain and passing out of sight. In this place. In England!

Cynthia   But we can't go back home. What about Solomon, he has to have his education here. There's nothing back there for him, we both know that, Roy, that's why we're here in the first place.

Roy   But we're not going anywhere in this country, we're going backwards.

Cynthia   But we've got to keep trying. We've got to make sure that we don't fail, for our sakes, but more so for Solomon; we owe him success of some kind.

Roy   And we owe ourselves something too. Sanity in England. Solomon shouldn't have been born so soon then we could just dig up and try a next place for work, a next city, or America even.

Cynthia   Solomon is the best accident that ever happened to me. I don't regret anything so please don't talk that way about our child,

Roy   Don't 'Please' me anymore, woman, I've had it. I turn up early for work, I have the union on my back. I turn up late, I have the boss on my back. My child is ill so I stay at home and I have everybody on my back, and this country don't have as many spare jobs as they like to make out so I can't just tell them to go to hell or otherwise what we going to eat? (*Pause.*) I can't take my child in the park for the loose dogs come and chase us and one of us end up stepping in filth, and if we go out together is only a matter of time before somebody shouting at us 'Nigger, go home' or 'Jungle Jim, do us a dance', and the Beatles singing 'Get Back' and people singing it to us, and you want us to stay here? We can't even go out together cos nobody will babysit for us so I mean what the hell am I supposed to do, eh? I mean you want to go mad in England? You want our child to go mad here, to get used to being called 'nigger' in England? Eh? Eh?

Cynthia   Roy, I'm having another baby.

Roy   You doing what?

Cynthia   I'm pregnant.

Roy   Why?

Cynthia   What you mean why?

Roy   When you find this out?

Cynthia   This morning.

Roy   Well, that's it, then you must get rid of it.

Cynthia   I can't kill it, Roy.

Roy   You must get rid of it! We can't afford to feed a next mouth and I don't want another child in this country. One going be enough of a problem as it is.

Cynthia   Roy, I can't just get rid of it. It belongs to us, for better or for worse; it's our baby.

Roy   You crazy or what? I kill you before I see you bring a next child into this world.

Cynthia   Roy, I want to have the child.

Roy   And how you going feed it? It's only one pair of hands I have.

Cynthia   We'll find a way.

Roy   What you mean 'we': you didn't hear what I say? I gone now for sure, woman. I'm going home if you have a next child.

Cynthia   But you talk to me as if it had nothing to do with you.

Roy   And I could say the same about you and your decision to have the thing.

Cynthia   But it's wrong to . . .

Roy   And it's just as wrong to bring a coloured child into this damn world as it is at the moment. You don't see that? Well?

Cynthia   But I've waited ten years for our two children. Roy, I'm getting too old to wait for a next chance.

Roy   Well, it's you who must make your decision. I've said what I've got to say, understand? Well?

Cynthia   Roy, please . . . (*The door slams.*) Roy . . .

The baby starts to cry.

We are in a noisy school changing-room and the kids are getting changed for an afternoon game of soccer.

Solly   Whose side are you on, Tag?

Tagger   I don't care. I don't feel like playing anyway.

Solly   That's cos you can't.

Tagger   Here we go again.

Solly   Boring you am I?

Tagger   Yeah, but I nearly forgot, I've got something for you.

Solly   What?

Tagger   You'll have to cross my palm with silver first.

Solly   Sod off. What is it?

Tagger   A letter from Tracey.

Solly   Tracey?

Tagger   Given to her by none other than Miss Jenny Bates. As opposed to Master Bates.

Solly   Give us it here.

Tagger   Well, aren't you going to open it up then?

Solly   Yeah, when you've gone.

Teacher   Right, you lot. Out there now! And that means now.

Tagger   See you in a minute then, Solly, and try and control yourself as you read it.

We hear them all trooping off out leaving **Solly** *alone.*

Jenny (*voice-over, reading the letter*)   Dear Solly, thank you for your letter. I would like to go to the pictures with you tonight and I'll be at the Odeon at seven if you still want to go. Maybe it's best not to tell anybody at the moment cos my dad's a bit funny about me going out with boys. Sorry it's so short but I've got to rush. Yours sincerely, Jennifer Bates.

Teacher   Well, Daniels? Waiting for Christmas are we? Get out, lad! Get out there, show us some of that old black magic.

On the football pitch. We hear the whistle, shouting, etc. The sound of the ball being kicked.

Voice   Here! Pass it over here!

Voice   Through ball! Through ball!

Solly   Here! Here!

Voice   Solly!

Solly   Aghh!

Voice   That's a foul, sir. Penalty!

The whistle goes and voices are raised in anger.

Teacher   What kind of a tackle was that, Bates?

Bates   It was an accident, sir.

Tagger   Send him off, sir. That was disgusting.

Bates   Shut your gob, Tagger.

Teacher   Bates! If I hear any more from you, or see another tackle like that, you'll be off, okay?

Bates   It was a professional foul, sir.

Teacher   There was nothing professional about thuggery even before the Jimmy Hills of this world gave it a nice label, understand?

Bates   Sir.

Teacher   Are you all right, Daniels?

Solly   I think I might have twisted my ankle.

Teacher   It's just a bit bruised but you better go off. Can you walk?

Solly   I think so.

Teacher   Give him a hand, Tagger.

Solly   No, I'll manage, honest.

Teacher   Okay. (*He blows the whistle.*) Penalty.

There is argument.

Solly *goes into the house and slams the door.*

Chris   You limping, Solly?

Solly   No, I fell in a puddle and one of my legs shrunk.

Chris (*hushing him up*)   Quiet, Solly, Mum's ill.

Solly   What do you mean ill?

Chris   She's in bed not feeling too good. I had to ring up Dr Chandra and he came round and said we had to stay with her.

Solly   What's up with her?

Chris   Nothing serious, just exhaustion, he said, and worry.

Solly   Exhaustion? She works for him doesn't she? Trying to work her to death is he?

Chris   He said it was worry really. She's got too much on her mind.

Solly   So where is she now?

Chris   Upstairs asleep. He gave her some sleeping pills and said we had to check on her from time to time.

Solly   What, all night?

Chris   Yeah, why, were you off out?

Solly   Pictures.

Chris   Where you get the money from?

Solly   None of your business.

Chris   I bet some bird's paying for you.

Solly   Well, that's how much you know.

Chris   Well, you're not still gonna go are you, Sol?

Solly   Why not? You're here to look after her.

Chris   It ain't fair, Solly. She's your mum too. (*Pause.*) Don't go, Sol. Phone up whoever it is and say you can't.

Solly   Don't tell me what to do.

Chris   I'm not.

Pause.

Solly   Is there anything to eat?

Chris   Beans on toast. You're not going then?

Solly   Let's have some of that. I'll go and sit with her first.

Chris   Okay.

Solly   Hey.

Chris   What?

Solly   Did he say there was anything else the matter with her?

Chris   No, he said she'd be all right as long as she got some rest, that's all. Just some rest.

Solly   What you looking at me like that for then?

Chris   Like what?

Solly   Like it was my fault she's ill.

Chris   I'm not.

Solly   Yes you are.

Chris   You keep shouting at her. (*Pause.*) I heard you last night.

Solly   I wasn't shouting, it was her.

Chris   I only heard you.

Solly   So you think it's my fault.

Chris   I didn't say that.

Solly   You think I've made her ill just cos I ain't a creep.

Chris   It's more you than me.

Pause.

Solly   You say that again and I'm gonna kick your head in.

Chris   So what?

Solly   You know what. And you're beginning to get on my tits as well so shut it.

Chris   I won't.

Solly   I said shut up!

*We hear **Chris** coming downstairs and going into the kitchen.*

Chris   I said it's your turn to go and sit with her now, Solly. Were you asleep?

Solly   Let me finish my cup of coffee first. It's like being on guard duty outside Buckingham Palace. What time is it?

Chris   Nearly eleven. You could take your coffee with you if you wanted.

Solly   I wanna drink it here.

Chris   I don't reckon she should go to work tomorrow.

Solly   It's up to her.

Chris   Don't you care?

Solly   Course I care, or how come I'm here?

Pause.

Chris   Was it that Jenny bird that you were supposed to be going out with?

Solly   Why?

Chris   Someone told me you fancied her.

Solly   Who?

Chris   I can't remember. (*Pause.*) She's okay though, isn't she?

Solly   Suppose so.

Pause.

Chris   Are you glad to be leaving school?

Solly   Can't wait. Hate the bloody place.

Chris   But you didn't always used to though, did you?

Solly   So what? They treat you like you're a kid.

Chris   Not all of them though. Tealy's okay, isn't he?

Solly   Used to be but he's getting just like the rest of them. Even asked me about Mum and how things were at home.

Chris   What did you say?

Solly   Nothing. None of his business, is it?

Chris   No. Suppose not. (*Pause.*) I came top of our class in the exams.

Solly   I could have been top of our class if I'd have wanted.

Chris   Yeah, I know.

Cynthia (*voice very faint from upstairs*)   Chris? Christopher?

Solly   She's woken up. I'll go.

Chris   Tell me when it's my turn.

Solly   I will, don't worry.

Chris   No need to be like that, is there? It's not my fault you couldn't go out.

Solly   It don't matter. She's more important than any bird, isn't she?

Chris   Yeah I know she is. You don't have to tell me.

Solly   And what do you mean by that?

Chris   I don't mean anything, why?

Solly   Well, you better not.

Chris   I don't.

In **Cynthia** *'s bedroom.*

Solly   Mum?

Cynthia   Solomon. Pass me some water from over the side there. (*He does so.*) Thank you.

Solly   You want anything else?

Cynthia   No. I just wanted to make sure you were all right.

Solly   We're fine.

Cynthia   You had something to eat?

Solly   Yeah.

Cynthia   Good. You can go back downstairs now if you want.

Solly   No, it's all right I'll wait here. You go back to sleep.

Cynthia   You can be a good boy. Both of you can be. (*Pause.*) It's late so don't stay up too late, and make sure Christopher goes to bed before you.

Solly   I will. Go to sleep now.

Cynthia   I'm just tired that's all, Solomon. Nothing to worry about. Nothing at all.

Solly (*concerned*)   You'll be all right, won't you?

Cynthia (*laughs painfully*)   I've done all right so far. I think.

In the bedsitter.

Roy   I don't care what you say, woman, I'm going.

Cynthia   But you can't leave me and Solomon and a next child on its way, Roy. How the hell we going to eat? How are we going to live with no money coming into the home?

Roy   Well, you'll just have to start working. This damn country just about grind me down to nothing and unless I'm leaving now there don't going be nothing left of me to grind down any further. I've already told the man at work that Friday is my last day.

Cynthia   How you going explain to our family back home, Roy? How you going tell them that you just walk out on me like that, you just leave me?

Roy   You think I'm afraid of what people think? You think you can blackmail me into staying here with you? You must be crazy . . .

Cynthia   Well, maybe I am crazy, but I can't just rip a child out of me body and throw it in the trash can just because you say to me that I must do so for you don't like England. All I'm interested in, Roy, is the education of my children. I never stood a chance and neither did you on an island where your opportunities stopped when you were fifteen or sixteen, unless you had money or you could win one of the big scholarships, and although we both had brains in our heads just look at the jobs that we end up doing, well? And in England why is it that we can't find the money after over ten years of struggle, we can't even find the money to own even the smallest of houses, we can't go out and enjoy ourselves, we can't do anything, Roy, except shout and curse each other, and lately I notice that we don't even do that because you too drunk by the time you come back in from the pub. All you care about is yourself and how things are bad for you. What you're forgetting is Solomon and the next child, Samantha, maybe. You forgetting what will happen to them. At least here they have a chance to get some qualifications, even if it means we must send them to school out of this one room, at least here they have a chance to be somebody, to be something and they don't have to go through all the pain and the humiliation of having to leave the island and their family to do so. You, Roy, you just trying to force me to kill so you can stay but you can go now, I don't care, you can go but I can't take them back to that.

Roy   And you know why? It's because deep down you're just ashamed of what you are, that's all. You're ashamed of the people you came from, the place you came from, you're ashamed of real life, aren't you?

Cynthia   No, Roy, I'm ashamed of you. You've tried but only for yourself. It's not good enough for me and my children.

Roy   Well, in that case I gone then! I can't stay here with you for you'll only be happy on the day when you wake up in the morning and look in the mirror and find you've turned white. Until that day comes you always going be unhappy, aren't you, always thinking you're something you aren't. You can keep the children for I going reclaim the sunshine and a real life.

Solly *is in the kitchen pouring out his cornflakes into a bowl. It is morning.*

Solly (*shouting*)   Chris, hurry up will you? It's half past eight. Chris!

Chris *comes in.*

Chris   What?

Solly   How come you aren't dressed then?

Chris   Cos I ain't going to school today.

Solly   How come?

Chris   I'm staying at home with Mum.

Solly   Does she want you to?

Chris   No, I want to. Just in case she faints again.

Solly   Do you want me to ring Chandra and tell him she ain't coming in?

Chris   No, I'll do it when she wakes up.

Solly   Okay.

Chris   Have you got any money I can lend, Sol?

Solly   What for?

Chris   Milk and stuff like that. I don't want to wake Mum up.

Solly   I've got a quid. Here.

Chris   Who give you it?

Solly   Do you want it or not?

Chris   Thanks. (*Pause.*) I'll see you tonight then.

Solly   I'll be back to take over. Make sure you look after her properly.

Chris   Course I will! What do you think I'm gonna do to her?

Solly   I don't know do I?

Pause.

Chris   Solly?

Solly   What do you want now?

Chris   Remember when she told us that we weren't called Daniels any more.

Solly   Yeah, so what?

Chris   Why did she change her mind back again?

Solly   I don't know. (*Pause.*) I think it was cos of Dad. Why, are you thinking of changing it?

Chris   Well, it's silly to have his name isn't it: if he's dead we might as well be called after Mum.

Solly   You don't half talk some rubbish, you know. Her name is Mrs Daniels cos she's called after him. We're Daniels cos she is, all right?

Chris   I just wondered that's all.

Solly   Well, you can keep wondering because that's all there is to it. Keep an eye on her and I'll see you later, okay.

Chris   Okay.

In the classroom.

Teale   Now 5C I've called you all back here after assembly for I've got a very serious and sad announcement to make.

Voice   Is Thatcher dead, sir?

They all laugh.

Teale   Quiet! When I say serious I mean serious. Yesterday afternoon, during the games period, two boys in this room, I won't say who they are for it's not important, what is important is that these two boys had money taken from their pockets by somebody, or some people in this room.

A murmur goes around the boys.

Now, unless any of you are unaware, this is known as stealing and I don't care much for thieves so will the culprits, or culprit, please make themselves known. (*Long pause.*) All right, seeing as nobody has the courage to speak out I'll be having the whole lot of you back here tonight until somebody does own up, is that understood?

Tagger   Oh God.

Solly   I ain't staying back.

Teale   Did you say something, Daniels?

Solly   I said I can't stay back tonight cos me mum's ill.

Teale   I see. Well, I'm sorry to hear that but when I say the whole class I mean the whole class, and that includes you. Now all of you get to your lesson quickly and quietly.

They all begin to move off noisily.

I said quietly.

The playground behind the toilets.

Jenny   Did you go to the bingo with your mum last night, Tracey?

Tracey   Yeah, but it was dead boring seeing as you decided that you didn't want to go.

Jenny   I never said I was going in the first place.

Tracey   But you never said you wasn't going either so I thought you were, didn't I?

Jenny   Well, you thought wrong.

Tracey   And I suppose you went out with Solomon Romeo Daniels instead.

Jenny   No, as a matter of fact I didn't.

Tracey   What happened? Your dad wouldn't let you out as usual?

Jenny   No. He didn't turn up.

Tracey   He stood you up?

Jenny   He might not have been able to make it.

Tracey   Well, he could have phoned you.

Jenny   He didn't know the number.

Tracey   It's in the phone book. He can read, can't he?

Jenny   Course. I don't care anyhow.

Tracey   I'll bet you do, anyone would. I'd kill Tagger if he tried that on with me.

Jenny   I don't know why. He gets away with everything else he tries on.

Tracey   Get lost. (*Pause.*) So what happens if he asks again?

Jenny   What do you mean what happens?

Tracey   I mean are you gonna tell him to get lost or what, cos he can't just not turn up.

Jenny   I don't know what'll happen, do I. It's not easy to tell.

Tracey   Yeah, well, I know what I'd do. Wasting a night like that.

Jenny   You can't just . . .

Tracey   Hey, hang on a minute. I don't believe it. Look who's coming over. He's got some front, hasn't he?

Jenny   Don't be like that.

Solly   Hello, I've come to explain about last night.

Tracey   Yeah, I should think so as well.

Jenny   Shut up, Tracey, will you?

Tracey   Well, he can't go round doing that to people.

Jenny   Shut up will you.

Solly   You see . . .

Jenny   Hang on a minute. Why don't you leave us alone for a minute, Trace?

Tracey   Oh, hark at her lovebird.

Jenny   It's not that, it's . . .

Tracey   Yeah, I know. I know when I'm not wanted.

She leaves.

Jenny   I'm sorry about that.

Solly   I'm sorry about last night. You see it's my mum. When I got home she was collapsed and I had to stay with her.

Jenny   Oh God, is she all right now?

Solly   Yeah, well a bit weak but I reckon she'll be all right soon.

Jenny   I thought it must be something like that.

Solly   You see I haven't got a dad.

Jenny   Why not?

Solly   I just haven't. He's dead. Chris and me have to look after her.

Jenny   I didn't know.

Solly   It's not your fault, I don't really talk about it much.

Jenny   I see. I'm sorry.

Solly   What for?

Jenny   That you haven't got a dad.

Pause.

Solly   Did you wait for long?

Jenny   About an hour.

Solly   Oh God.

Jenny   But it wasn't that bad though. This old man gave me a paper to read. Really boring. (*She laughs.*)

Solly   Well, how about tonight then?

Jenny   I can't. I've got netball practice.

Solly   Well, Friday then?

Jenny   That's the disco isn't it?

Solly   Yeah, how about meeting up at eight for the disco?

Jenny   Okay, great.

Pause.

Solly   Do you still mind about everyone knowing?

Jenny   Not now. Should I?

Solly   No. (*Pause.*) Sure?

Jenny   Course I'm sure. I'd better go now otherwise I'm gonna be late.

Solly   What's your mum and dad do?

Jenny   That's a weird thing to ask, isn't it?

Solly   Is it?

Jenny   No one's ever asked me that before.

Solly   You been out with someone else?

Jenny   Well, sort of, but not properly. I meant nobody, not even a girl, has ever asked me that.

Solly   Sorry.

Jenny   I don't mind. My mum's a housewife and my dad's a carpenter. Boring isn't it?

Solly   Sounds all right to me. At least he's working.

Jenny   Just, or so he says. Have you thought about what you're going to do yet?

Solly   Thought about it but not really done too much about it, if you see what I mean. Not a lot I can do except hope and wait and all the rest of those things.

Jenny   Suppose not. (*Pause.*) I've really got to go now, Solly.

Solly   Okay then. See you tomorrow. About eight.

Jenny   Okay then, see you.

In the classroom.

Voice   How long's this detention going on for, sir?

Teale   Till I tell you it's over.

Voice   And how come Daniels is allowed to get away with it?

Voice   Yeah, we all know who was in the showers first.

Tagger   Shut your face, Marsh, or I'll push it in for you.

Voice   You and whose army, Tagger?

Teale   Quiet! All of you. That's enough. You've been here nearly an hour now so you can go.

The noise of them all about to leave.

I said quiet – I'm going to have to think whether or not you lot deserve an end-of-term discotheque.

The noise of jeering.

And even if you do, I want you all on your best behaviour, otherwise it'll be one dance then hoppit for the lot of you.

The noise of them jeering, etc.

Now go quietly.

In the front room.

Teale   Seems like you've a very nice front room here, Daniels. I can see why you prefer coming here and putting up your feet rather than being in detention.

Solly   It's not my front room, it's me mum's.

Teale   Well, then, how's your mother?

Solly   Better I suppose. She's gone off to work. Why, did you want to talk to her?

Teale   No, no. It's you I came to talk with.

Solly   Well?

Teale   Why did you take the money?

Solly   I didn't take it.

Teale   Well, who do you think did then?

Solly   I don't know.

Teale   Well, some people think it was you.

Solly   What people?

Teale   It doesn't really matter what people, just some people. And I think it could have been you but I don't know why you would want to take money.

Solly   I didn't take any money.

Teale   Look, Solly, when I was younger I used to take things too you know. Sweets from the corner shop and things like that. Why? Sometimes just because I wanted them, which is a stupid reason. Now you're not stupid like I was. You must have had a reason. And the rest of your behaviour of late, it's like you're angry but you don't know what you're angry about. Is it the prospect of leaving school?

Solly   No.

Teale   Has something happened at home? With your mother?

Solly   I told you she's poorly.

Teale   Is that what's been worrying you?

Solly   No.

Teale   Has anybody said anything to you? Is somebody calling you names for instance?

Solly   No.

Teale   Well, what about this girl, Jenny? Presumably the Jenny is Jenny Bates?

Solly   Might be.

Teale   How long have you two been seeing each other?

Solly   We don't.

Teale   But you'd like to.

Solly   I don't want to talk to you anymore.

Teale   But you'd like to go out with this Jenny Bates, is that it?

Solly   I want you to go now. I don't want to talk with you.

Teale   Did you take the money for her? So you could impress her perhaps.

Solly   I want you to go I said.

Teale   I don't think there's any need to get quite so upset about it, Daniels.

Solly   I said I want you to go.

Teale   I'll see you tomorrow then I expect.

Solly   You might.

Teale   Oh come on, Daniels. Last day at school. You'll want to be there for that won't you.

Solly   I've told you I don't want to talk to you.

Teale   There's no need to shout. I'm going. (*Pause.*) Maybe I ought to have a talk with your mother. What do you think?

Solly   You can't talk to her cos she's out and I don't want you to talk with her, all right.

Teale   I'll see you tomorrow then.

Solly *slams the door behind him.*

Solly   Yeah, but that'll be the last time, then you can get stuffed.

In the boys' bedroom.

Chris   Can I have one of your blankets, I'm cold.

Solly   Yeah, take it.

Chris   Did you think Mum looked tired tonight when she came in?

Solly   Course. You would if you'd gone and fainted the day before and just spent all day at work.

Chris   What are you doing? I want to go to sleep now.

Solly   Well, I'm not stopping you.

Chris   Are you writing poetry?

Solly   No I'm not and stop trying to look.

Chris   You are, aren't you? (*Pause.*) Why won't you tell me what Teale wanted to know?

Solly   Cos it's none of your business.

Chris   Are you in trouble with him or something?

Solly   Course not.

Chris   Well, how come he comes to our house then?

Solly   None of your business.

Chris   Can you turn out the lights, please, I want to go to sleep.

Solly   I'll be finished in a minute.

Chris   Good, I'm tired.

Solly   I said I'll be finished in a minute, didn't I?

Chris   Okay.

Pause.

Solly   You ask too many questions.

Chris   That's cos you don't give any answers.

Solly   You reckon?

Chris   Yeah. Finished?

Solly   No. Shut up.

Chris   I heard you crying, Solly. After Teale had gone.

Solly   Who, me?

Chris   Yeah.

Solly   No you didn't.

Chris   I did.

Solly   You didn't, all right.

Pause.

Chris   What's up?

Solly   Nothing.

Chris   Why don't you talk to me anymore, Solly?

Solly   Cos I'm tired.

Chris   No, I mean all the time. Not just now. All the time, you never do, never. (*He begins to cry.*)

Solly   Who's crying now?

Chris   Stop getting at me.

Solly   I'm sorry, Chris.

Chris   No you're not.

Solly   I am. I didn't mean to make you cry.

Chris   You always do this to me, you're just not my friend anymore, are you?

Solly   Course I am. Chris?

Chris   I don't want to talk, I want to go to sleep now.

Solly   Chris?

Chris   I want to go to sleep, I'm tired now. Just let me go to sleep. Solly.

The **Headmaster***'s office.*

Head   But are you saying the boy took the money, Mr Teale? Or are you saying something else? I have to be frank with you, it sounds like another of your 'scratching on the desk' games.

Teale   I'm saying that I'm not sure if Daniels took the money but it's symptomatic of the hysteria his presence causes that almost all of his peer group seem to feel he did.

Head   And what do you propose to do about this?

Teale   I was hoping that a stiff letter to his mother might help. I tried to talk with her when I visited the boy's home yesterday afternoon.

Head   And presumably she would not talk with you either.

Teale   She was not in when I called round.

Head   Then write the letter, Mr Teale.

Teale   I was hoping that you might write it, Headmaster.

Head (*sighs*)   There seems little point, Mr Teale. I hardly know the boy and neither his mother nor the circumstances of his home life are even vaguely familiar to me.

Teale   So you refuse?

Head   You come in here with some half-baked story about a shower-room theft and a boy who has been causing you and the rest of my school trouble and you seem either incapable or unwilling to put the two pieces together.

Teale   So that's the end of that then, is it?

Head   Not quite, Mr Teale. Take a seat again, please. I've been watching your own conduct over the last term with some interest and I'm not sure if you're the right sort of teacher for a school of this sort.

Teale   What do you mean?

Head   I mean, Mr Teale, that this is a tough comprehensive school with, I have to admit it, a rather second-rate academic track record. It would seem to me that you'd be happier in a school with less demanding disciplinary problems where your liberal studies skills might flourish a little more easily. Have you thought about a transfer?

Teale   Well, when you put it like that, no.

Head   Well, might I suggest you do. It shouldn't be at all difficult to arrange, and there might even be a promotion involved if we were to choose the right school for you.

A train station.

Roy   You didn't have to come and see me off, you know.

Cynthia   I wanted to.

Train announcement.

Roy   I feel stupid, Cynthia.

Cynthia   If it's what you want then do it, just go.

Roy   It's not what I want.

Cynthia   Then why do it?

Roy   Ssh. Don't shout.

Cynthia   I'll shout if I want to.

Train announcement.

What am I supposed to tell the children?

Roy   Tell them their father was going mad in England and he left before he killed somebody.

Cynthia   And what kind of sense is that supposed to make to them, Roy? What kind of sense is it supposed to make to me?

Roy   I don't know.

Cynthia   Solomon, you understand your father?

Roy   Please . . .

Cynthia   Look good at him for it's the last time you'll ever see him.

Roy   Don't threaten me, woman.

Cynthia   I'll do what I like, Roy, you've no right to tell me anything anymore. Never! Never!

Train announcement.

Roy   I've got to go now.

Cynthia   Then go. But look good at your child and remember. And the one in my belly that you can't see is the same one you said you never wanted to see, and I going to make sure the child never going see you, so go! It's never going know nothing about you so just go – go!

In the kitchen – the clock – silence.

Solly   Who were you talking to, Mum?

Cynthia   Solomon?

Solly   Who were you talking to, Mum?

Cynthia   Your father. I sometimes hear his voice and . . . and it comforts me.

Solly   But you were shouting.

Cynthia   Was I?

Solly   Why don't you ever take us to his grave, Mum?

Cynthia   Please, Solomon.

Solly   Why don't you ever talk about him, Mum?

Cynthia   I don't know, dear. Don't you have to be at school?

Solly   I leave school today, Mum, to start up on my own. I've finished with all that. I'm big now.

Cynthia   I suppose you are.

Pause.

Solly   Just tell me one thing about him.

Cynthia   What?

Solly   Just one thing. Anything.

Cynthia   Your father was going mad in England and he left before he killed somebody. (*She begins to cry.*)

Solly   I don't understand. Why are you crying, Mum?

Cynthia   He was going mad in this country, Solomon. Working himself stupid for nothing but you two, both of you, you've got a real chance to make good here. Please, for my sake, make use of it.

Solly   What do you mean he was going mad?

Cynthia   I'll tell you, Solomon, but not now. I'm too tired. Too tired to think anymore.

Solly   Do you want anything?

Cynthia   Come here and hold me, son. Just hold me.

Solly   All right, Mum. All right.

She continues to cry.

Cynthia   Solomon, why do you shout at me, son?

Solly   I don't mean to, Mum, it just happens.

Cynthia   It's been happening for a while now, hasn't it?

Solly   I know, I'm sorry, Mum.

Cynthia   Sometimes what I think is best for you isn't always best.

Solly   What do you mean?

Cynthia (*laughs*)   I don't know. (*Pause.*) Do you think I've brought you up badly, Solomon? Do you think I've neglected you?

Solly   No, who says you have?

Cynthia   Nobody, it's just that I sometimes wonder. I sometimes wonder if I've failed.

Solly   You haven't failed, Mum. Nobody could have done what you've done. I know that and so does Chris. It don't really matter if nobody else does, does it?

Cynthia   No I suppose not.

Solly   It doesn't. I don't care what they say.

Cynthia   I love you both. (*Pause.*) I'm very proud of you.

In the school playground.

Tracey   What you reading, Jenny?

Jenny   Nothing.

Tracey   Yeah you are, I can see you, can't I? I'm not blind. (*She snatches.*) Let's have a look.

Jenny   Give us it back.

Tracey   Oh my God, I don't believe this. Poetry. Is it from him?

Jenny   Who else?

Tracey   He's a nutter.

> My heart cries out for you,
> And I feel blue,
> But the sun in the sky,
> And the warmth in your eye,
> Turns the world a brighter hue.

(*She laughs.*) What a load of crap. If Tagger wrote anything like that I'd tell him where to get off straight away.

Jenny   Give us it back.

Tracey   I haven't upset you, have I?

Jenny   No you haven't.

Tracey   I thought you were going out with him.

Jenny   No I'm not. I'm thinking of changing my mind.

Tracey   Why? Just cos we've been taking the mickey a bit?

Jenny   Maybe.

Tracey   Well, I think you're better off without him. I keep telling you it will just cause trouble.

Jenny   Maybe . . . but . . .

Tracey   But nothing. You'd get in a right mess. Come on, we're off to the shop. Coming?

Jenny   All right, I suppose so.

Tracey   He must think he's a poet or something, sending you poetry. Off his rocker.

Jenny   He's not off his rocker.

Tracey   Can I have the poem?

Jenny   What for?

Tracey   To show Tagger.

Jenny   No, it's mine.

Tracey   But I thought you said you might not go out with him no more or anything.

Jenny   I might not but it's mine, he gave it to me.

Tracey   But I only want to show Tagger.

Jenny   I still like him. I don't want you making fun of him.

Tracey   I'm not making fun.

Jenny   It's my mum and dad, Trace. They'd kill me, they really would. It's pathetic but I suddenly realized that it's serious. It'll never work, will it?

Tracey   You already know what I think.

Jenny   I suppose I'm just a coward. I feel terrible about it, Tracey. Honest. Really bad.

Tracey   There's nothing to worry about. It didn't even start really, did it?

Jenny   I suppose not . . . but . . .

Tracey   But nothing, come on.

Jenny   I don't like giving up. I don't really want to.

Tracey   You don't know what you want, do you?

Jenny   I don't know. Maybe I'll think about it a bit more.

Tracey   Come on, I'm in a rush.

Jenny   I'll not come tonight, will you tell him?

Tracey   Yeah.

Jenny   But I think I will keep going out with him. I've got to stand up to my parents some time, haven't I?

Tracey   Well, I'm glad I'm not you.

Jenny   I am or else I wouldn't have Solly.

Tracey   Oh God. When are you gonna start the family?

At home in the **Daniels***' house.*

Chris   Have you been at home all afternoon?

Solly   Yeah. Just reading and stuff.

Chris   Where's Mum?

Solly   Gone out to work.

Chris   She leave us anything to eat?

Solly   Normal.

Chris   I've got a letter for you.

Solly   Who's it from?

Chris   Mr Teale gave it to me.

Solly   Teale? (*He opens it.*)

Chris   What's it say?

Solly (*tearing it up*)   Nothing.

Chris   It must say something.

Solly   Yeah, it says the school is full of rubbish, which I know already.

Chris   Is that all?

Solly   Yeah. Make us some tea will you? I've got to go get ready.

Chris   You going to the disco tonight?

Solly   Yeah.

Chris   You're going with Jenny Bates, aren't you?

Solly   Might be.

Chris   She's all right, she is.

Solly   What do you know about it?

Chris   Same as you.

Solly   Oh yeah. Make the tea, shrimp. (*Pause.*) Chris?

Chris   What?

Solly   What's a period?

Chris   Get stuffed.

Pause.

Solly   Chris?

Chris   What?

Solly   Don't tell Mum.

Chris   Don't tell Mum what?

Solly   That I'm going out with her.

Chris   You mean you really are?

Solly   Don't sound so surprised.

Chris   That's great. I like her.

Solly   So what if you like her. And you don't even know her.

Chris   But it's good, though.

Solly   I suppose so. It's all right.

Chris   All right?

Solly   Don't shout. And don't tell Mum just yet.

Chris   Don't worry, I won't tell her. (*Pause.*) I won't split on you.

At the school disco. Music is playing loudly and it is in full swing.

Tagger   All right, Sol?

Solly   All right, I suppose.

Tagger   You don't sound it. (*Pause.*) I'm off to the bar. You want anything?

Solly   Yeah, Coke please. You want the cash?

Tagger   No, it's okay. If they sold pints here I might say 'yeah'.

Solly   I know you would.

Tagger   Anyhow, I came into a bit of money, if you know what I mean?

Solly   I know what you mean. I thought it was you.

Tagger *laughs. Then he goes off and leaves* **Solly**. *The music continues then* **Teale** *comes across.*

Teale   Didn't see you with the other helpers at six o'clock, Daniels.

Solly   Don't remember ever saying I'd come.

Teale   And I don't remember giving you permission to leave school early either. (*Pause.*) Well? Did your brother give you the letter?

Solly   Yeah.

Teale   And I suppose you gave it to your mother.

Solly   I'll give it to her later.

Teale   I bet. (*Pause.*) Well, what's to become of you now? A first brush with the police? Or have you already had a brush with them?

Solly   I've never been in any sort of trouble.

Teale   Well, one way and another you've certainly been trying hard enough this term.

Solly   I haven't got anything to say to you.

Teale   I did notice, but I could have helped you, you know. I can still help if you'll let me.

Solly   I don't need your help.

Teale   Maybe not but if you ever do then take this card. It has got my home phone number on it. You see, the headmaster is trying to get rid of me as well. Thinks I take too much interest in boys like you. And my wife, she thinks I'm a coward and I can't make up my mind whether you're coloured or Black or West Indian *or* an ethnic minority *or* Black British, and she reckons that's where I go wrong, but I've always said to her that you're just a lad to me, Daniels, and maybe that's where I've been going wrong with you.

Solly   Maybe.

Teale   But you see it's when I start to think of you as something different from just an ordinary lad that I'll pack it in. Does that make sense to you?

Solly   Maybe.

Teale   Yeah, I know. My problem. (*Pause.*) Go on take it. Put it in your pocket before your mates come back.

Solly   Okay.

Pause.

Teale   See you around then.

Solly   All right.

Teale   Good, I hope so. And stay out of trouble.

He goes off and **Tagger** *comes back.*

Tagger   Did he give you a going over?

Solly   Wanted to know where I was all day.

Tagger   Don't matter now, does it, you've left.

Solly   That's what I told him.

Tagger   Yeah, I'd have told him that too. (*Pause.*) Hang on, here's my bird.

Tracey   All right, Solly.

Solly   Yeah, how you doing, Tracey?

Tracey   Yeah, I'm all right but Jenny's not coming. She asked me to tell you.

Solly   What's the matter with her?

Tracey   Parents. She'll ring you tomorrow. You're onto a winner there.

Bates   Nothing's the matter with her, Daniels but there will be if I catch her with you. I don't like coons round my sister, right?

Tracey   Oh God. Push off, Bates.

Bates   Shut your face, slag.

Solly   You can't tell Jenny what to do.

Bates   I can tell who I like what to do, right, Daniels?

Tagger   Leave it out, Batesy.

Bates   You shut your mouth, Tagger. It's nothing to do with you.

Tracey   Yes it is, he's Solly's mate and my mate too.

Bates   I don't care if he's Solly's grandad. It's between Jungle Boy and me.

Solly   I've got nothing to say to you, it's between me and Jenny.

Bates   You what?

Solly   I said it's between me and her and you keep your nose out.

Bates   You're off your head, Daniels, you wog.

He hits **Solly** *who immediately hits him back and there is a fracas.*

Tagger   Leave off him, Batesy . . . Hit him, Sol, hit him.

Tracey   You bully, bully. Stop him, Tagger, stop him.

We hear a hell of a commotion but get the idea that **Solly** *is losing.* **Teale** *comes tearing across.*

Teale   Break it up right away. You want to try it on with me too do you, Bates?

Bates   No I don't, so get off me.

Teale   You telling me what to do, Bates?

Bates   No.

Teale   No what?

Bates   No, sir.

Teale   Right, stand there. You all right, Daniels?

Solly   Yes, sir.

Teale   Now who started this?

Tracey   It was Bates, sir. He's just a bully. A big stupid bully.

Tagger   Yeah it was. Solly didn't do nothing.

Teale   I think you better leave, Bates, and I don't want to see your stupid face around here again, understand?

Bates   You won't have to cos I won't be round here again. Come on, Johnson, let's go.

Tracey   Bloody animals.

Teale   Are you sure you're all right, Daniels, that's a nasty bruise you've got there.

Solly   I'm all right.

Teale   Maybe you should go home and get it dressed.

Tagger   I'll go home with him, sir.

Tracey   And me.

Solly   No, it's okay. I'll go by myself.

Teale   Are you sure?

Solly   I'll be okay.

Tagger   I'll call by tomorrow see how you are, Sol.

Solly   Okay then.

Tracey   See you, Sol.

Solly   Yeah, bye.

He goes.

Teale   All right, let's get back to the disco.

Tracey   I hate that Bates, you know. I wish someone would kill him.

Tagger   Yeah me too, but I don't know who. Clint Eastwood maybe.

In the kitchen.

Cynthia (*bathing his wound*)   So which boy hit you in the face?

Solly   It doesn't matter, Mum. It's finished with.

Chris   I bet I know who it was.

Cynthia   Who?

Chris   I'm not sure.

Solly   Good.

Cynthia   There, does that hurt?

Solly   No.

Cynthia   Well, sleep with your head the other way on the pillow tonight and you'll be fine.

Chris   Have you told him yet, Mum?

Cynthia   No.

Solly   Told me what?

Cynthia   We're going away together for a week as from tomorrow.

Solly Going away? Where?

Cynthia I don't know. The country, the seaside. Wherever you want to go.

Chris Great, eh?

Cynthia We all need a rest, and we need to talk, don't we, Solomon?

Solly Yeah, we need to talk.

Chris About what?

Solly About everything.

Cynthia Everything, Chris. You're big lads now. You've grown up practically before I've had time to blink. We need to spend some time together.

Chris Well, what we gonna do? What we gonna talk about?

Solly Dad.

Chris Really? And what else?

Solly There ain't anything else is there?

Chris Yeah there is.

Solly Like what?

Chris I don't know, do I?

Cynthia Right, that's enough of that. I think you ought to go to bed now.

Chris But, Mum . . .

Cynthia No argument. We've got to be up early in the morning, all right?

Chris All right.

Cynthia I'll wake you both up.

Solly Goodnight.

Cynthia Goodnight. Both of you, sleep well.

In the boys' bedroom.

Chris Are you still gonna go out with Jenny Bates now that you've left, Solly?

Solly Yeah. Why?

Chris I just wondered that's all. (*Pause.*) You're not saying much.

Solly I'm tired.

Cut to **Cynthia** *sitting alone.*

Cynthia You see, Roy, you were right. It's not for us. It was never for us. But that's what you never fought for. Nobody left for just themselves. Nobody stayed for just themselves. We came to fight for them.

In the boys' bedroom.

Chris   Do you wanna play soccer tomorrow?

Solly   I'll think about it. (*Pause.*) We can't.

Chris   Why not?

Solly   Because we're going away, aren't we?

Chris   We can play when we get there.

Solly   I suppose so. (*Pause.*) Yeah, I suppose we can.

In the kitchen.

Cynthia   And eventually the boys will find you in themselves, and in each other, and if they want to find you they can and I won't stop them, but I don't regret anything, Roy. I regret nothing. They'll never cut cane, or spend their lives herding scrawny goat, do you understand?

In the boys' bedroom.

Solly   I want to sleep.

Chris   Is your face still hurting?

Solly   No.

Chris   Good.

Solly   Yeah, I'll see you in the morning, Chris. In the morning, man.

He is falling asleep.

In the kitchen.

Cynthia   And as you always used to say, Roy, you get nothing for nothing. But when I look at our two boys, I know the price I paid was cheap. They've got a life now, Roy. We don't matter anymore. At least coming to England has given them a chance.

Crossing the River

Broadcast Details

BBC Radio 3, 7 September 1985. Directed by Richard Wortley.

Characters (in order of appearance)

Sarah
Ben
Will

Notes on the Play

Like the eponymous novel by Caryl Phillips published in 1993, this short radio play gives a voice to three children of the African diaspora, a girl and two boys, who remember when they were sold into slavery by their father in the eighteenth century. The three siblings are dispersed in time and space: Sarah is a slave on a West Indian plantation, Ben is a New Orleans minstrel around 1900 and Will is an angry young man who lives in twentieth-century Peckham and has problems with the law. In spite of their resemblance to the characters from the novel, the three protagonists in the radio play have their own individual personality and background and provide an enlightening complement to the chorus of voices that frames the later narrative. In addition, the fragmented structure of this radio play is one of Caryl Phillips's earliest formal experiments with a style that has become characteristic of his fiction.

Sarah Two men in my life. Both then and now. I cannot include my father. A daughter is nothing to a father. I just watched my father.

Pause.

No rain.

Pause.

I listened to my two men. Brothers.

Ben Today father will make another sacrifice. A cock. To the God of all land. And pray for rain. His crop is dry, burning.

Pause.

He is a lonely man. A tall, distinguished lonely man. We are all he has.

Will I stood on top of a great boulder and looked down. I could see them coming. With them were some of our people.

Ben Eight market weeks without rain. Father says we must live in hope.

Will Before them marched a man with a piece of crooked wood held high. As though to shield his face from the sun. I could not understand. He was one of our people. A warrior by his markings. Brave.

Sarah Two men in my life. Brothers. I am older now than I was then. We crossed the river. Together. Two men and a woman. With others. In a ship that stank of the vomit of a million sick.

Silence.

Ben God damn! I'm forever smudging the gloves. That's the last part, just peeling on the gloves and straightening up my smile. (*Laughs.*) Lord Jesus, a nigger playing a coon for the white man. That's minstrelling.

Will I thought he was gonna bite my balls off . . . the dog that is, not the copper.

Pause.

They've even got bars on the windows of my council flat. In Peckham it is. Suppose that's why I feel at home here. Don't care much for the neighbours, though.

Sarah After the man had finished I stood up. I knew it would be easier a next time. I knew a next time would soon come.

Pause.

Can you feel the movement?

Silence.

Ben My sister? It is dark.

Will From the top of the boulder I could see for miles.

Sarah   The ship made a loving movement. Like a woman rocking a child. And the sea spoke to us. Telling us to have no fear.

Ben   Please. Some light. I cannot live in this darkness.

Will   From the boulder I saw them coming. They did not hurry.

Sarah   We danced for a gentle storm. A small cloud to burst. Then heavy rain. But it would never rain. And father's crop would fail again.

Pause.

Father?

Ben   Father?

Will   Father. You let them take us. I can never forgive you. Never.

Sarah   But the motion was a loving one.

Silence.

Ben   New Orleans is the home of minstrelling. Though some might say Mississippi, but all they got back there is a few rickety shacks and a pile of bricks masquerading as a theatre. And the women? Jesus, I ain't never seen so many painted hussies outside of a whorehouse. Fact is it seems to me like Mississippi is one big whorehouse. But New Orleans is real grand. Style just how I like it. Women if you need them. But style all the while. Take my dressing room for instance. I got – now lemme see – three, four, five, nine, ten, no less than twelve genuine electricity bulbs. Three mirror glasses positioned so as I can see all sides of my face, and best of all a tub . . . not a regular size bath tub, but somewhere between that and a hand basin. (*Laughs.*) Who said Orleans ain't got style. Sonny Johnson, now he's my regular partner – he plays Mr Tambo to my Mr Bones. Excuse me, Mr Tambo. Yes, Mr Bones. Was your pappy ever a soldier, Mr Tambo? Yes, sir. He was in the battle of Bull Run, Mr Bones. He was one of the ones who run. (*Laughs.*) He just loves working with me and I guess I must like something about working with him. He's been on the circuit longer than me. Figure that's why he's got a Ford Model T standing outside looking bolder than a skunk in the wind.

Pause.

I begin with the white paint.

Sarah   My child was born perfect. She was born in a cutting in a canefield.

Slight pause.

Will   The social worker asked me if I needed help. I smiled at her and asked her if she wanted to have it off. After she'd gone I went out. I wore my black jeans and some shoes I'd had for ages. Blue. Black laces, though.

Ben   I guess I always begin with the white paint. Sonny, I don't know what he begins with. Mr Tambo on the banjo.

Silence.

Sarah   When the white men grouped before me I turned. I looked up at them.

Will   I felt no fear. I had seen them coming from the boulder. I took the crooked wood from the man and broke it in half.

Ben   But their skin is . . . is dead, the colour of death.

Sarah   Father's crop would fail again.

Pause.

There was no rain in the sky.

Silence.

Will you play?

Ben   I do not play with girls.

Will   We must hunt.

Sarah   But the plains are empty.

Will   We will hunt the ghosts of the dead animals.

Sarah   You are stupid.

Ben   We two?

Sarah   Both of you.

Will   You are a child. You cannot understand how men's ways are.

Sarah   You are boys playing at men. I heard father say so.

Will   And I heard you cried when they carried you for your cut.

Sarah   Boys do not understand such things.

Pause.

We all cried.

Will   Men never cry.

Sarah   Never?

Will   Never!

Ben   I *have* seen father cry.

Will   You lie.

Sarah   We must speak to each other. Always. Never argue. Why do you two always argue? Why do we never speak to each other?

Will   You are a girl.

Ben   I have seen father cry. Behind the village by the small lake. When his last wife died.

Will   He cried out of duty.

Sarah   He cried from love.

Will   Did you see him cry?

Sarah   I know . . .

Will   Women can never know the ways of men. Never. Never.

Silence.

Sarah   When the white men grouped before me I turned. I looked up at them.

Will   I felt no fear. I had seen them coming from the boulder.

Ben   But their skin is . . . is dead, the colour of death.

Silence.

Sarah   Then I saw father.

Silence.

Will   Though I felt no fear my legs were wet. The warm fluid burned. But I showed no pain.

Sarah   He ran blindly towards father.

Will   Father . . . father . . .

Sarah   He stopped and looked.

Pause.

The man with the cross struck him. He was one of our people.

Pause.

I am older now than I was then.

Pause.

They took me from the canefields. A doctor bound my breasts. The skin under my arms cracked and splashed blood onto the white bandage. Starve the . . .

Pause.

Starve the child to see how long a picaninny can live without food.

Pause.

They put my child – Mary. They put Mary into an empty room. Her skin began to turn grey.

Silence.

Will   Me, I wasn't doing nothing in my black Levi's and blue shoes with black laces. I began to walk through the puddles, splish frigging splash, then some bastard in a car deliberately drove into the gutter and sprayed water all over me. Alright, mate? Flash git in his Capri. I walked on a bit then stopped outside a shop window. Thought about the social worker. I'd love to give her one. Then I looked in the window. H. Samuel. The jewellers. Then this bloke came up to me. Looked like an ex-boxer. Face all smashed in and everything. He asked me why I nicked it. Nicked what, I said. It, he said. I saw you take it and run off. Run off where? Down the side-streets, he said. I'm on a main road. I've just come out of my council flat. Don't get lippy, sonny. What? Where is it? I ain't a mind-reader. I don't know what you're talking about. And who are you anyway? I'll have your guts for garters. My what? When I turned to go he grabbed me so I hit him. In the mouth. Hard. Hurt my bleeding hand. But he hit me back. Then called his mates in a van.

Ben   I guess I always begin with the white paint. After the white paint, the burnt cork.

Pause.

Sonny, Mr Tambo. Coon.

Will   I thought he was gonna bite my balls off . . . the dog that is, not the copper.

Sarah   I begged for Mary. He began to unbutton his breeches. The other man. Not Mary's father. Mary's father was still in the field cutting cane.

Ben   Singing, 'Coon, coon, coon, I wish my colour would fade. Coon, coon, coon, I'd like a different shade.'

Sarah   It fell out. Then stood up.

Will   I've got bars on the windows of my council flat. I'm used to the frigging things.

Sarah   And after the man had finished I knew it would be easier a next time. I knew a next time would soon come. But if Mary could only live. Suck somebody else's breasts.

Ben   God damn! I'm forever smudging the gloves.

Pause.

Can I name the four seasons for you, Mr Tambo? Sure I can. Pepper, salt, vinegar and mustard. (*Laughs.*)

Pause.

Then I straighten up my smile and wait. For Mr Tambo on the banjo.

Silence.

Sarah   I looked up at the white men then past them. I looked up at the sky. It would never rain.

Ben   I am proud of father. He is too old. They will not take him. They will take us. I know he wants me never to forget the family name. Never to forget our people.

Will   I ran from the boulder towards him. I stopped. I looked at her looking at the sky. Then back at the white men with the iron chains. Then father.

Silence.

Sarah   Can you feel the movement?

Ben   Please. Some light. I cannot live in this darkness.

Sarah   But the motion is a loving one.

Will   The man struck me. With the crooked wood.

Sarah   But father shall have sufficient now. The rains will not matter.

Will   He let them take us. I can never forgive him. Never.

Silence.

Sarah   Two men in my life. Both then and now. I cannot include my father. A daughter is nothing to a father. I just watched my father and listened to my two men.

Silence.

Ben   Today father will make another sacrifice. A cock. To the God of all land. And pray for rain. His crop is dry, burning.

Pause.

Eight market weeks without rain. Father says we must live in hope.

Pause.

And then I put on the white paint.

Will   I'm used to bars on windows.

Sarah   Mary's father was still in the field cutting cane.

Pause.

I listened to my two men. Brothers. My breasts hurt. I heard grey Mary cry.

Pause.

Father? Father? Today it will rain. Soon.

Pause.

Nobody listens.

Pause.

Then we all crossed the river.

The Prince of Africa

Broadcast Details

BBC Radio 3, 3 March 1987. Directed by Richard Wortley.

Characters (in order of appearance)

African
Brother
John Winston
Hotel Keeper
Boatswain
Cabin Boy
First Mate
Father
Auctioneer
Voices in the hold

Notes on the Play

This radio play is mostly set on an eighteenth-century slave ship bound for America with a full human cargo. Economically evoking the horrors of the crossing and its aftermath, it confirms Caryl Phillips's long-standing interest in the slave trade and slavery, which most visibly surfaces in fictions such as *Higher Ground* (1989) and *Cambridge* (1991). *The Prince of Africa* is based on an early stage play by Caryl Phillips, meaningfully entitled *Point of Departure*, which was never published nor produced. Both dramatic texts provide a nuanced rendering of the tense interactions between the captive Africans and the white crew during the voyage and beyond. With the author's usual ambiguity, these plays show, on the one hand, that neither faction can be regarded as monolithic and, on the other, that the two antagonistic groups have features in common, such as existential insecurity and difficulties communicating.

We hear the dull regular beat of a drum.

African   Marooned in the west. Washed up on the shores of England by the ever-insistent tide of colonialism. Jettisoned by an empire. Flotsam to be discarded. Proud of my history. Because I understand it. Understand it in order to survive. I look at you and ask: How is that you who were once free are now bound by the same chains that you sought to enslave others with? Chains of ignorance. Which is why you do not understand Brixton, or Liverpool, or Bristol. Inner-city riots. (*Laughs.*) I understand, because it was out of these three ports that you bought and sold me 200 years ago. (*Again he laughs.*) Why your surprise?

We mix through to the sound of water lapping up against the side of a slave ship. The beating of the water is abruptly broken by a loud and piercing scream.

Brother, you must try to dominate your dreams. Turn even your sleeping mind away from our family and home, turn it towards the future.

Brother   What future?

African   Tomorrow.

Pause. We hear the creaking of the ship's hull, and a medley of whimpers and painful cries.

Think no further than tomorrow.

We slowly mix through from the ship to a distant choir singing evensong. It is about 7.00 p.m. on an English spring evening. The year is 1780. We are in a small upstairs room in a cheap hotel near St Paul's Cathedral, London. **John Winston** *is sitting at a desk writing a letter.*

Winston   Dear Father, I write to you knowing full well that you will disapprove of my projected course of action. There is little I can do to disguise the nature of my intent, therefore I feel it important that I come directly to the matter. I have, due in part to my social standing, in part to my knowledge of the world and wide travel in my youth, been appointed Captain of a vessel. But, true enough, it is no ordinary vessel. As a Christian . . .

There is a knock at the door. We hear him struggling to cover up the letter.

Come in.

Enter the **Hotel Keeper**.

Hotel Keeper   Ah, Mr Winston, sir. I don't want to be disturbing you, but I thought you might be needing this. A nice pot of ale.

Sets down the beer.

Winston   Thank you.

Hotel Keeper   Help you sleep and forget the 'morrow.

Winston   Yes. Quite.

Hotel Keeper   Though you be luckier than most captains that pass through here, what with no wife to weep for you and create all that fuss. And a rich northern family you can come back to and find solace in when it's all done.

Winston (*takes a drink*)   I don't think there will be too many tears shed for me, Mr Squires.

Hotel Keeper   Oh?

Pause.

I don't mean to be prying like, but they do know you'll be setting sail with the Royal African Company then?

Winston *does not answer.*

Hotel Keeper   I see, sir. Well, sometimes it's the way things be.

Winston   Things have happened so quickly.

Hotel Keeper   Oh, I know, Mr Winston. I understand. Still, they must know there's no finer money to be made than 'passage' money. I mean it's quite possible for a man of your means to improve his family lot ten times over. You could mechanize the farming land you were telling me about. The money's a godsend.

Winston   But are the Blacks? Did God send them too, did . . .

Hotel Keeper   I'm sorry, Mr Winston, but I can't be arguing the church with you or any man. England's an island and every second man's a poor sailor, whether he likes it or not – you, you're just a man going off to do his duty. I can't be worrying about the niggers.

Winston   I see.

Hotel Keeper   I mean, have you not seen the blackie on his travels in the city, who dresses in silk and keeps a coach and footmen and other frippery. And there be plenty more like him. Well?

Winston   I have seen him.

Hotel Keeper   It's sport and trade, Mr Winston. Progress, an age of industry. The cotton mills, the iron, the furnaces are all fuelled by the trade. And, as I said, it don't be as if some of the niggers don't have it better'n us. Most of them you'll be shipping are either criminals or prisoners or worse. To them it's a proper alternative to death.

Winston   Perhaps.

Hotel Keeper   No 'perhaps' about it. It's about time a gentleman such as yourself stopped worrying over trifles and started thinking on the passage itself. Will you be wanting any more ale?

Winston   No thank you. But if you have a man who could in the morning dispatch a letter for me I would be most grateful.

Hotel Keeper   No sooner said than it will be done. And what time shall I be calling you?

Winston   I believe the company have arranged for a carriage to call on me at seven.

Hotel Keeper   Well, then, there's not much else to be done apart from praying for a good night's rest and a safe passage. I'll be with you in the morning, sir, but meantime you can freely call me if you be needing anything.

Pause as he moves to leave the room.

It's a pity there's no girlie to see you off. I'm quite used to sneaking them in for the odd copper.

Winston   No thank you, Mr Squires, I don't think that will be necessary but I'm obliged to you for the thought.

Hotel Keeper   Well, maybe next time, sir. Good night.

Winston   Good night, Mr Squires.

*The **Hotel Keeper** leaves and closes the door behind him. There is a deafening silence. Then the bells of St Paul's start to ring out. There is no crescendo. They begin climactically. Mix through to light African drumming.*

African   On the first day I did not understand. It was difficult for any of us to understand. 400, maybe 450 of us.

Screams of capture and burning.

Slavery, the capture and subjugation of one people by another, was something we understood. The greater the numbers you capture, the greater your chance of eventual victory. The greater your power. But this was something different.

The sound of the sea lapping up against the side of a ship at anchor.

The numbers were endless. Surely the white man did not intend to try and empty the whole of our land. And if this was his aim, why did he not people it with those like himself?

Pause.

Those among us who collaborated, who quickly learned the language of these intruders, who ate with them, these men changed. They walked differently. Purposefully. With arrogance. Women who slept with the collaborators said these men now smelt strangely. Our people who mixed with them suddenly knew both more and less at the same time. They knew how to handle the guns the white men gave to them. But they knew not who they were anymore.

The interior of a slave ship. Creaking wood. Sickness. Vomit. Aches and moans. We can also hear the sound of sailors overhead.

Brother   I cannot survive not knowing what it is that we are expected to endure.

African   But if you give up you hand to them the victory. We will simply cease to exist. You are my youngest brother and I order you to survive.

Pause.

Is there any here that knows the Hausa language?

Some answer 'Yes'.

Good. Is there any here that knows the language of the white man?

Silence.

Or to where it is that we are to be taken?

Silence.

Voice # 1   Your brother is right. There is more nobility in our death than in this uncertain shame.

Fade to the sound of the sea lapping up against the side of the ship at anchor.

African   And so we lay tea-spooned, one behind the other, chained, one on top of the other, shackled, like goat, believing any voice that found the strength to soar above the medley of miserable noises, but fearing the worst, in actual fact speaking only helpful lies to each other knowing that water has no paths and we may never find our way back home.

It is early evening and we are on the deck of the ship. The shouting and activity suggest that it is nearly ready to sail.

Boatswain   Aye, I'll see to it. Right away, sir.

Pause.

Bastard. Worse than the king he is for meddling.

Cabin Boy   Who is?

Boatswain   Who is? First mate is, of course.

Pause.

Don't be looking so scared, lad. First voyage is always the worst. I be reckoning the few hours afore you set upon your first passage be the worst few hours in any white man's life.

Pause.

He been gabbing at you?

Cabin Boy   No.

Boatswain   Come on, Tom. I been at sea since before you be even an 'ard prick in your father's pants. What's he say?

Cabin Boy   He says he wants me to feed the slaves in the aft hold.

Boatswain   And whaas the matter with that? Better'n being down in the main hold. Two days time there'll be no air down there – candle won't be able to burn proper – and you'll be seeing steam rising out of them yonder grates. Main hold'll break a young lad like yourself.

Cabin Boy   I don't want to feed any of 'em.

Boatswain   Now you're being a carrot-head, Tom. You be on a slaver at anchor off the coast of Africa so you got t'expect to be seeing and attending to slaves.

Cabin Boy   Do you like feeding 'em?

Boatswain   No, of course not, and if it weren't for this illness of mine . . .

Coughs and pats his chest.

. . . I'd be right down there with you, but you've got to understand that Mr Hickey be doing you a favour of sorts keeping you out of the dungeon, 'specially as it be a full pack – too full in my opinion.

Cabin Boy   But then they'll die won't they?

Boatswain   Well maybe a third of 'em will, but that's normal reckoning in these conditions.

Cabin Boy   What about the privilege slaves? Will they live?

Boatswain   No reason why not. They're locked away in private quarters. Plenty of room for their hearts to beat. They're the captain's special cargo. He takes a cut of their sale.

Cabin Boy   Can't I feed them?

Boatswain (*laughs*)   You don't be having nothing to be frightened of in the aft hold. Just don't breathe too deep.

Enter the **First Mate***.*

First Mate   Mr Samuel, I told you I want the deck vinegared down before we sail tonight.

Boatswain   I'm just off to see to it, sir.

First Mate   Mr Samuel!

Pause.

What have you been telling this boy?

Boatswain   Nothing, sir.

First Mate   Boy, are you happy with everything?

Cabin Boy   Yes, sir.

First Mate   I can't hear you, boy. Stop mumbling.

Cabin Boy   Yes, sir!

Boatswain   If you don't mind me saying . . .

First Mate   Don't mind you saying what, Mr Samuel?

Boatswain   About the full pack, sir. Does Captain Winston . . .

First Mate   Mr Samuel, the captain knows what I tell him, and you do what I say, understand?

Boatswain   Yes, sir.

First Mate   I want this ship vinegared then you can give the boy a hand feeding the aft hold slaves.

Boatswain   But, Mr Hickey, sir. I be ill, my chest. You said I could . . .

First Mate   Mr Samuel, every last man on this ship is to some degree ill or ailing.

Boatswain   But my chest, sir, you said . . .

First Mate   Just follow instructions, Mr Samuel.

He addresses the boy.

The nigger women are on board, boy. Will you be wanting to come and choose one?

Cabin Boy   No, sir.

First Mate   What about you, Boatswain?

Boatswain   No, sir.

First Mate (*mimics*)   No, sir.

Pause.

You have a job of work, Mr Samuel. Because this is your last passage don't be expecting any special treatment for you'll be finding none. I'll return presently. Attend to your duties the both of you.

Exit **First Mate**.

Boatswain   Bastard, bastard, bastard!

Cabin Boy   Are you going to tell the captain?

Boatswain   What's there to tell him, lad? You think he be the listening sort? He be having as much idea how to run a slaver as I have how to be prime minister of England and president of America all rolled into one.

He coughs and splutters.

Cabin Boy (*unable to hold his relief*)   So does that mean you'll have to help me feed 'em?

Boatswain (*out of breath but curt*)   What do you think, lad?

Pause.

I'm sorry, Tom, but I have to be thinking on my health, especially with a wife and family to meet me at the other side.

Pause. Then almost reflectively.

If everything works out right Mary and the three lads'll be in Boston three or four days ahead of us. There be nothing for me to go back to in England, 'specially in

Norfolk. No work to be had on the land for a labouring man. It's all machines these days.

Cabin Boy   I see.

Boatswain   I'll vinegar the deck after we been and fed 'em.

Cabin Boy   Alright.

Enter **John Winston**.

Winston   Mr Samuel.

Boatswain   Captain, sir.

Winston   I'd like to see Mr Hickey immediately in my cabin.

Boatswain   Yes, sir.

(*To* **Cabin Boy**.) Tom, go ask Mr Hickey to call on the captain in his quarters without delay.

The **Cabin Boy** *goes off.*

Winston   Mr Samuel, is there nothing to be done about this smell?

Boatswain   I'll be vinegaring the deck any moment sir, but I'm telling you it does get worse yet. You'll be finding that most ships sail up to five miles downwind of a slaver, and there's not a boatswain on the face of God's earth who can do a thing about it. It be in the trade, sir.

Winston   I see.

Pause.

I'll be in my cabin. Tell Mr Hickey I'm waiting.

Boatswain   Right you be, sir.

John Winston *goes off leaving the* **Boatswain** *alone on deck. He coughs a little.*

Boatswain   Right you be.

Sound of a ship docking. Harbour noises, etc.

African   We arrived. In America. In the Caribbean. Wherever we arrived, we arrived. In the west. Some of us, my brother included, leapt overboard during the passage believing that if we did so we would return to our native land. Others among us realized more fully what the end result of such action would be. Those who survived were now different. Omaro of the Fon became Thomas of Mr Johnson. Thomas Johnson. Lacunda of the Ashanti became Peter of Mr Williams. Peter Williams. It was strange. The new tongue felt clumsy in our mouths. To speak in one of our own languages was useless for we were deliberately placed with those of other tribes. As a result we had only their clumsy language. Secrets were difficult. But we had secrets. We still have secrets today. The discreet toss of the head in the street. Raising of the eyebrows, or excitable slapping of hands with even the most casual of acquaintances. These are secrets. They mean more than they appear to mean. To you. Like carefully blown wine glasses they contain more than you might initially imagine. They became important when I became Peter Williams and Thomas Johnson. It was some time before I became Mr Peter Williams or Mr Thomas Johnson.

Mix through to the ship's hold. We hear the sound of cramped misery from the captives. Then a bolt is drawn back and a hatch lifted. The slaves begin to panic and shout.

African   Show some dignity, brother. Be brave, as our father would have wished.

Brother   They will not take me alive! I will defy them!

African   Be quiet and have patience.

Cabin Boy   I think I'm going to be sick.

Boatswain   Hold the bucket, Tom, while I get down this ladder. And put your hand to your mouth and nose.

African   There are two of them.

Boatswain   Ah, there we are. Pass me over the bucket.

Cabin Boy   What are they saying?

Brother   I will kill one!

Voice #1   Perhaps we should wait and see if more come.

Boatswain (*bangs a stick*)   Quiet! The lot of you!

The noise dies down a little.

Take the ladle, Tom. Put it in the bucket and pour the food into their mouths. If they won't open them just pour it onto their black faces, for the rats will have it.

Brother   It is poison!

Boatswain   Open your mouth, nigger!

We hear shouting and discontentment among the slaves.

Boatswain   Open!

Cabin Boy   This one won't take it, sir.

Boatswain   On his face and try the next one.

Brother   Brother, do not take the food.

Cabin Boy   He won't take it either.

Boatswain   This one looks fit enough to be a privilege nigger. Fetch a fair price in America.

Cabin Boy   Will you tell the captain?

Brother   Why do they look at you in this way, my brother?

African   Do not be afraid.

Boatswain   I'll tell the captain later. No harm in it. He's built like a cart-horse.

Brother   I am not afraid, but don't take their poison.

Cabin Boy   Well, he won't be a cart-horse for long if he don't eat his food.

Boatswain   He'll eat when he's out of his hole. You mark my words, he'll be different when his folk can't see him. They always are.

Mix through from this business of feeding to the relative peace of Captain **John Winston***'s cabin. There is a knock on the door. He shouts.*

Winston   Enter.

Enter **First Mate***.*

First Mate   You sent for me, Captain.

Winston   I did. Please sit, Mr Hickey.

Pause.

We sail tonight?

First Mate   Aye.

Winston   I see.

Pause.

Is there any danger when the ship first moves?

First Mate   There is, which is why we sail at night. Hope they're more docile then, understand?

Winston   I understand.

Pause.

As to the cargo, Mr Hickey. Tell me, how many Blacks have we aboard?

First Mate   Well, I can't rightly say.

Winston   How many?

First Mate   I reckon about four hundred, may be four hundred and twenty, but all fine pure stock from the Fon, Wolof, Ibibio, Mandinka and Efik tribes who, according to known knowledge that is, be of good disposition being not taken with either melancholy or cannibalism.

Winston   Unless I have made a mistake, Mr Hickey, did I not ask you to make sure, following orders from the company, that this ship was not to be slaved with more than three hundred Blacks.

First Mate   Old *Corinna* can take a tight pack better than any ship I have ever slaved.

Winston   But did I not ask you to do otherwise?

First Mate   Aye, that you did.

Winston   I see.

Pause.

On observing the loading of the ship I did find the near perfect state of nakedness to which you had reduced the Blacks somewhat disturbing, Mr Hickey. Kindly do something about this.

First Mate   Well, Captain, I could give them clothes, but then we'd all die of the sickness it'd cause. You can't be telling me you didn't know that.

Winston   Mr Hickey, given your prolific knowledge of the triangle, which you lost no time in forcing down my throat from the moment I stepped aboard and took command of this ship in London, do you not think that the first requirement of any vessel is respect: law and order.

First Mate   Aye.

Winston (*shouts*)   Well, why then do you persist in going against what I have expressly commanded you to do? Why do you seek to undermine my authority so, why?

First Mate   Because you don't know what the hell you're talking about most of the time.

Pause.

Captain.

Winston (*each word measured in anger*)   I will let that pass, but I never want to hear the ugly clamour of mutiny in your voice again.

First Mate   I never said 'mutiny'.

Winston   We have a ship without a surgeon, already perched on the precipice of fever and you, Mr Hickey, take up over four hundred Blacks.

First Mate   Aye . . . sir.

Winston   It is not too late for us to dispose of some?

First Mate   Aye, well, it's insured cargo so we might as well take the risk and journey with them. If they start to show signs of festering we just throw them over to the sea. We'll be getting rid of some that way.

Winston   We'll be doing what?

First Mate   Throw them over and collect on the insurance. It's standard practice.

Winston   This, Mr Hickey, is a God-fearing ship. Slaving is one thing, murder quite another thing altogether.

First Mate   Through nigger eyes it's all the same.

Winston   I shall hang any man who throws a live slave to the ocean. This is my ship and it will remain my ship, under my command, and any man who wishes to challenge my authority will have to answer to the company, to the King and to God. I hope I've made myself clear.

Noise of screaming and chasing on deck.

Winston   What is that noise, Mr Hickey?

First Mate   Just the crew tasting the women. I've put a couple of tasty niggers aside for you.

Winston   I want no fornication.

First Mate   That's up to you, sir.

Winston   I have just three rules for the middle passage, which you either abide by or suffer the consequences. Firstly, the cargo are to be treated with respect, with no unnecessary suffering inflicted upon them. Secondly, no persons are to be disciplined, cargo or human, without my knowledge. Thirdly, I shall be requiring daily reports as to the state of the ship's business. You may go.

First Mate   You mean you don't intend to come and inspect affairs for yourself?

Winston   I'm not used to the sea, Mr Hickey. I may find it difficult. You may leave.

First Mate   Just one more thing, Captain. Seeing as we sail tomorrow, early Sunday morning, will you be wanting all the niggers baptized too?

Winston   You may leave.

*We hear the **First Mate** slam the door behind him. Mix through to the sound of cane-cutting in the wide open plantation fields.*

African   We came to work. To make money for the landed classes. I was considered a capsule of labour to be worked from dawn till dusk. My six hours' sleep were deemed the only unprofitable aspect of my existence. My sperm and my woman's ovaries, a delightful bonus. And I was to sing to her.

Sings.

    I don't want you to be no slave
    I don't want you to work all day
    I don't want you to be true
    I just want to make love to you

And suddenly the white man wasn't so much of a mystery anymore. From the darkness of the belly of the boat, into the brightness of his agricultural fields. I learnt to know him. To worship his God. He had only the one God. A long-haired man. A white man like himself.

Sound of church singing rising.

Very soon some of us came to worship him with more fervour than those who invented him ever dreamt he could be worshipped.

Beautiful gospel music.

But when the worshipping was over the work began again. Life here was very different from the villages of Africa. And here, in the west, our children spoke the new language and only in small ways did the old world survive. In fact, we soon began to forget what the old ways were. In music and mannerisms only did they live on. In most other things they died. Language can only accommodate so much subversion.

Mix through to the captain's cabin. We hear the rattling of chains.

Boatswain   This is the nigger, Captain. But if you don't mind my saying, it's not right for him to be down here with you.

Winston   Is he tame, Mr Samuel?

Boatswain   Tame, sir?

Winston   Dangerous.

Boatswain   I don't think so, sir. He's chained up anyhow.

Winston   I see.

Pause.

Leave us together for a few moments, Mr Samuel. It will be alright.

Boatswain (*unconvinced*)   Aye, aye, sir.

We hear the door close.

African   I'm not scared of you, white man.

Winston   I'm afraid I don't understand what it is you're trying to say. Do you understand me at all?

African   I will kill you if you attempt to harm me.

Winston   Obviously not.

Pause.

Presumably you have a god that you worship? Many gods, perhaps?

African   I'm not scared of you, white man.

Winston   I wonder if you have family. Or if your people believe in such things as families. A father or a mother? A brother, a sister perhaps?

African   You must be a very stupid man. I cannot understand your words, yet you speak to me as though I am of you – a part of your mind. I think you must also be a very lonely man. A sad man.

Winston   Why are you so proud?

*The **African** moves back. We hear his chains rattle.*

African   Do not come any closer, white man.

Winston   No, I suppose there is no earthly reason why you should trust me. None at all. But I trust you, believe in your honesty and simplicity. Does that sound ridiculous? Am I making a fool of myself?

Two weeks have elapsed. In order to establish the passage of time we hear the sound of the sea crashing and the shouting of the sailors. Then it is quiet. We listen to the monotonous beat of the sea. Fade to silence.

We hear a loud scream, a scuffle and then a splash as something hits the water. Again, scream/scuffle/splash.

First Mate   Mr Samuel, you look like a ghost. A skeleton covered in a piece of tanned leather.

Pause.

What's the matter, can't your ears and mouth work at the same time?

Boatswain   Yes, sir.

First Mate   Mr Samuel, you do want to reach America, don't you? You don't want to die?

Boatswain   No, sir.

First Mate   But you might.

Boatswain   Yes, sir.

First Mate   And if we don't dispatch festering cargo you will die for sure. This way we've all got a chance, especially you, Mr Samuel.

Pause.

You've been on nearly as many slavers as myself.

Boatswain   Sir.

First Mate   Enough to know what a plague can do to a ship without a surgeon.

Boatswain   I've seen it, sir.

First Mate   Aye, and you've lived through it, Mr Samuel. You reckon you'd live through it again?

Boatswain   No, sir.

First Mate   Neither would I. I'm saving both our lives.

Boatswain   I see, sir.

First Mate   You don't like the trade do you?

Boatswain   I be wanting to settle down, sir. Start again. Bring up my family.

First Mate   And how do you feel now?

Boatswain   I be feeling weak, sir.

First Mate   You don't look to me like you're going to make it, Mr Samuel.

Boatswain   I'll make it, sir.

Enter **Cabin Boy**. *He speaks nervously to the* **Boatswain**.

Cabin Boy   I've mended the rigging, Mr Samuel.

Boatswain   Alright, Tom.

First Mate   How are your niggers, boy?

Cabin Boy   Quiet, sir.

First Mate   Aye, too quiet.

(*To* **Boatswain**.) Any trouble from them, Mr Samuel?

Boatswain   No, sir.

First Mate   But do they look alright? I mean, are they happy?

Boatswain   I don't think they be too happy, Mr Hickey.

First Mate   You know what I mean, Mr Samuel.

Boatswain   They be needing some exercise, sir. Two weeks locked in the aft hold be too much for them.

First Mate   Will they need touching up?

Boatswain   Aye, there be a lot of bruising and sore skin.

First Mate   Any more dead, boy?

Cabin Boy   It's hard to tell, sir. It's difficult with them.

First Mate (*laughs*)   Boatswain, have you told him niggers die like us, even if they don't live like us.

Cabin Boy   I know that, sir. What I mean is some are nearly dead. I mean sometimes they look like they're dead.

Pause.

They smell like they're dead.

Boatswain   No more are dead, sir. But some be ailing quite bad.

First Mate   But you think it's safe to let them exercise?

Boatswain   Aye, sir.

First Mate   Boy, I want you to go see to the captain's cabin. Do the boatswain's duties down there.

Cabin Boy   Yes, sir.

Boatswain   He be already doing them regular, what with my illness and everything.

First Mate   Quiet! You can get extra hands and bring the niggers up here to dance if you think it's safe. I'll fetch some muskets.

First Mate *goes off shouting at other sailors.*

Boatswain   Well, you'd best be doing as he says.

Cabin Boy   I just wanted to ask . . .

Boatswain   Well, what is it?

Cabin Boy   I just wanted to ask how long it was before we reached America.

Boatswain   If this wind blows on we should be there in another ten days or so, lad. Why?

Cabin Boy   Nothing, I just wanted to know.

Boatswain   What is it? You be sick of it already?

Cabin Boy   Oh no it's . . .

Boatswain   You'd best be doing the captain's cabin.

Cabin Boy   Aye, aye!

He goes off leaving the **Boatswain** *alone. He coughs deeply, clearly suffering much pain.*

We mix through from the sound of the **Boatswain**'s *coughing, and the sea, to a light, but regular African drum beat. We are outdoors, looking across the plains of West Africa.*

Father   One day, my two sons, this land will be yours, as it was my father's before me, and my father's father before him, and so on for as long as any of our griots can remember. And when this land becomes yours you must tend to it with the same love that you will show your wives and children. It is your ancestral blood that has fed the crops, your sweat that has turned the soil. Those from neighbouring tribes will try to take it from you, but you will resist and fight to the end for what are you without land? Well? My two sons, without land you are little more than chaff that the wind tosses and spins without respect. You are lost, blind, stumbling and ailing. You are nothing, and you will have to begin again a centuries-long struggle to re-assert yourselves. Look hard upon this land and remember my words.

The wind rises. Mix through to the sound of the sea, then to the captain in his cabin reciting from the Bible.

Winston   'Thrice was I beaten with rods, once was I stoned, thrice I suffered shipwreck, a night and a day have I been in the deep; in journeyings often, in perils of water, in perils of robbers, in perils of mine own countrymen, in perils by the heathen, in perils of the city, in perils in the wilderness, in perils in the sea, in perils among false brethren . . .'

Cabin Boy (*knocks and enters*)   Mr Hickey sent me, sir. To clean up.

Winston   What about Mr Samuel? You take orders from him don't you?

Cabin Boy   From everyone, sir.

Winston   Well, get on with it then, boy.

Cabin Boy   Sir.

He begins to sweep the floor.

Winston   What are your people, boy? Do you have any?

Cabin Boy   Not anymore, sir.

Winston   But you used to.

Cabin Boy   Yes, sir.

Winston   Run away?

Cabin Boy   No sir, press-ganged.

Winston   Perhaps that makes us the only two on the ship who have never before sailed the middle passage.

Cabin Boy   The Blacks, sir.

Winston   And the niggers.

Pause.

I don't suppose they count, do they?

Cabin Boy   Suppose not, sir.

Winston   How are your Blacks?

Cabin Boy   Mr Hickey's letting them up today.

Winston   Have they not exercised as yet?

Cabin Boy   No sir.

Winston   Why wasn't I told?

Cabin Boy   I thought you knew, sir.

Winston   You mean they've been trapped in that furnace for two full weeks, without exercise or fresh air.

Cabin Boy   Yes, sir. They're quite weak now, which is why Mr Hickey's being good enough to let them up today.

Winston   Stand up, boy.

Cabin Boy   Sir?

Winston   What's that mark on your face, boy? It's dripping with blood.

Cabin Boy   Nothing sir. Just a rat bite.

Winston   A rat bite?

Cabin Boy   Yes, sir. You can't help it.

Winston   According to Mr Samuel, two days ago three nigger women died of rat bites. Did you know that, boy?

Cabin Boy   Aye, sir, but that's only 'cause there's hundreds of 'em, rats that is, down there. Only the odd one or two gets in our quarters.

Winston   Aren't you scared, boy?

Cabin Boy   No, sir. You only die if it hits a vein or if it's a carrier.

Winston   Boy, you have lice too. Your head's like a breeding ground.

Cabin Boy   I can't help it, sir.

Winston   Are you a Christian, boy?

Cabin Boy   I don't know. I don't think so, sir.

Winston   You don't think so? Christians don't think, boy, they believe.

Cabin Boy   I don't believe so, sir. I've never been instructed proper.

Winston   Would you like to be?

Cabin Boy   I don't know, sir.

Winston   Leave your duties. Tell Mr Hickey I wish to see him after the exercise.

Cabin Boy   Yes, sir.

African   Yes, sir. Yes, sir. Yes, boss. Yes, sir boss. No, sir. No, boss. No, sir boss.

Sounds of cheer and jubilation.

African (*voices sing*)

Slavery chain done broke at last!
Broke at last! Broke at last!
Slavery chain done broke at last!
Gonna praise God till I die!

Emancipation. A big polysyllabic word meaning, for us at least, very little. Wilberforce. Another big polysyllabic word meaning even less. Nothing changed. We could vote. For what? For whom? According to the Constitution of the United States of America we were now legally three-fifths of a man. According to the Constitution of the European powers we were colonial natives.

Laughs.

Theoretically we could determine our own affairs. Some of us did. W. E. B. Du Bois. Frederick Douglass. Marcus Garvey. Pan-Africanists. Always Africa. A sense of home.

Africa like a boll-weevil eating away at the back of our brain. But there was always the huge paradox of our new emancipated status in the west. Of having to fight to be something we knew we already were. Equal. Trying to be something the white man had now admitted we were. Equal. After a fashion. For the evidence of one's life still suggested otherwise. The question we asked ourselves on the ship. Does the white man live on the ocean or does he have a country was now answered. The problem was to try now and ascertain whether that country was also our country. Or were we guilty of cushioning ourselves in a world of self-deception? Pan-Africanist self-deception.

Pause.

I remember my last conversation with my brother.

Sound of slaves exercising on deck. Someone plays the mouth organ. The captives dance and chant. Their chains rattle loudly.

Brother   My brother! We all thought the white man must have killed you.

First Mate   Shut up and dance, nigger!

African   I'm in another part of the ship where, along with ten others, they treat me with some care and attention.

Brother   Why? What is it they want from you?

*We hear the sound of a harsh whiplash, then the scream of the **Brother**.*

First Mate   I said shut up and dance, nigger!

Brother   No! No!

African   Brother, you don't understand. They want us alive. We must simply survive.

First Mate   Stand still or I'll shoot!

Brother (*shouts*)   Only in our death will we return to our lands and our home!

African   No! No!

We hear a gunshot. The slaves stop dancing and singing.

African   No!

We hear a splash.

Cabin Boy   Will he drown, sir?

First Mate (*laughs*)   Drown? He was dead before he hit the water, boy. Take this gun and watch the privilege slaves while I take this filth below deck. Mr Samuel, are you with us?

Boatswain   I'm not feeling too good, Mr Hickey. I think I be quite bad.

First Mate   To your feet, man, or I'll throw you in the hold with the Blacks.

(*To* **Cabin Boy**.) Boy, stay with him while I see these niggers below.

(*To* **Slaves**.) Come on, you stubborn bastards, move!

We hear the **First Mate** *lead off a group of the slaves.*

African   My brother is dead.

Voice # 1   Avenge him! The boy is alone.

Voice # 2   And the other white man is dying.

Cabin Boy   Be quiet! Shut up!

Voice # 1   Your brother has returned to our home.

Cabin Boy   Shut up!

Boatswain   They'll not do anything, Tom. Don't worry.

Cabin Boy   Are you cold, sir?

Boatswain   I'll be colder yet, Tom.

Cabin Boy   I don't understand, sir.

Boatswain   The sea, Tom. Don't be looking so afraid.

Cabin Boy   I don't want you to die.

Boatswain   What you be wanting and what I be getting is different things. But it be happening all the same. You'll be meeting my family in America.

Pause. He begins to sound weaker.

Mary, and the three boys . . .

Cabin Boy   Mr Samuel? Mr Samuel, sir? Can you hear me?

Pause.

Mr Samuel!

We hear a light funereal drum beat.

African   I felt nothing as I watched the white man die. My mind was haunted.

A loud and piercing scream. Then momentary silence.

African   Brother, you must try to dominate your dreams. Turn even your sleeping mind away from our family and home. Turn it towards the future.

Brother   What future?

African   Tomorrow. Think no further than tomorrow.

Father   My two sons, without land you are little more than chaff that the wind tosses and spins without respect. You are lost, blind, stumbling and ailing. You are nothing, and you will have to begin again a centuries-long struggle to re-assert yourselves. Look hard upon this land and remember my words.

Mix through from the sound of the sea, and the light funereal drum beat, to the captain's cabin.

First Mate   The boy said you wish to see me.

Winston   Sit down.

First Mate   I prefer to stand.

Winston   Very well. What I have to say will not take long. I ask of you that you answer me directly and truthfully. That is all.

Pause.

Is it or is it not true that for the past two weeks you have afforded the aft-hold slaves no exercise?

First Mate   No.

Winston   Mr Hickey?

First Mate   I've just finished exercising them myself.

Winston   And before that?

First Mate   Before that what, sir?

Winston   Had they any exercise?

First Mate   No.

Winston   And why was I not informed?

Pause. No answer.

Is it true that there are rats in the quarters of the crew?

First Mate   There's rats everywhere. It's how it should be.

Winston   Why was I not informed?

The **First Mate** *laughs.*

Winston   Thirdly, I have been hearing noises which suggest either punishment or maltreatment of the nigger cargo. Which is it, Mr Hickey, and why have I been hearing these abominable noises?

First Mate   Because you listen too hard . . . sir.

Winston   Why, in the last three days, have I received from you neither daily report nor explanation?

First Mate   I must have forgotten . . . sir.

Winston   Forgotten, Mr Hickey? Forgotten? You and your kind make me sick.

First Mate   What kind might that be, sir?

Winston   Your kind.

First Mate   You mean the lower classes, sir?

Winston   I mean your kind, Mr Hickey and I do not wish to hear the sound of your voice again until I have an explanation of some sort for your behaviour. If your explanation does not suffice, or your behaviour deteriorates any further, upon your arrival in America you will be reported to the agents of the Royal African Company. You will be held on a charge of insubordination, whereafter you will be sentenced in accordance with the laws of England and shipped back to London in order that you might surrender to your fate, so help me God.

The **First Mate** *begins to laugh uncontrollably.*

Winston   This is not the season for merriment.

The **First Mate** *begins to laugh even louder.*

Mix through to the peaceful lapping of the ocean against the hull of a ship crossing the Atlantic in the 1950s.

African   I was on a ship again. This time to England. To complete the third leg of the journey. To complete the triangle two hundred years on. If I was an American I would have stayed. Worked with Dr King or Malcolm X. Burned. Literally burned for my right to a piece of the ever slippery American Constitution. But as I'm now, for our purposes, a colonial native, I am called and pulled by the lure of the motherland.

We hear a West Indian calypso of the 1950s.

To work. To help. To labour. Again. Still travelling. Still speaking a language not my own. Forgetful of the past. Forgetful of the future. Concerned with the present and survival. The world was changing. We had finally learnt that the slave master never changes his mind, never retires. Never tires of being master. Only when we change our mind will the relationship change. And now, for me, perhaps the most crucial of all the battles for self-dignity is to be fought out on his own doorstep. In what we still insist on calling his country, although my sweat built it. I've changed my mind. I have earned my right to be here. Our past and present and future are inextricably interwoven. Perhaps he forgot our wedding? The garland was a rope. The ceremony conducted at the end of the barrel of a gun. The honeymoon is over, I think. Can we not settle down now to the business of learning to live with one another?

We are on deck. The **Cabin Boy** *is scrubbing the deck. Below deck we can faintly hear the slaves singing.*

First Mate   We'll be there in three days, boy.

Cabin Boy   Sir.

First Mate   You don't sound as if you want to see dry land again, boy.

Cabin Boy   I do.

First Mate   You feeling diseased?

Cabin Boy   No more than usual.

First Mate   You sound as if you're blaming me for something.

Cabin Boy   No, sir.

First Mate   Good.

Pause.

You blaming the captain?

Cabin Boy   I'm not blaming anyone.

First Mate   He took a damn fool's risk in leaving the coast without a surgeon. I'd have waited till the last day of God's earth before setting sail without a medical man. That's the main thing you should learn from your first passage. The second is never to set foot on a slaver with a captain who's not in it for the money, and for that alone. Before you know where you are he'll be ordering you to give the niggers knives and forks to eat with.

Pause.

You seen him recently?

Cabin Boy   I went to clean up his cabin yesterday.

First Mate   And did he talk to you?

Cabin Boy   He hasn't said a word since . . .

First Mate   Since when, boy?

Cabin Boy   Since Mr Samuel died.

First Mate   So what's he do then?

Cabin Boy   Nothing.

First Mate   He says nothing?

Cabin Boy   He don't say anything.

First Mate   You've not had an easy first passage, but you've done alright for a lad. And I see you're not so sensitive as you was. No problem in scrubbing up the skin and blood from off the deck. (*Laughs.*) Smallpox is a nasty thing. I'm sure the niggers leave their skin and blood behind on purpose to remind us.

Cabin Boy   They've stopped their singing.

First Mate   They must be getting weaker.

Cabin Boy   The bodies in the main hold need moving before the plague sets in.

First Mate   You're beginning to think like a trader, boy.

Cabin Boy   I can hear 'em moaning most nights, and it's getting worse. They need exercise. But the privilege niggers, they're alright. Not a sore limb among them.

First Mate   So why the toughening up then, boy?

Cabin Boy   Because I want to survive. I don't want to die of scurvy or pox.

First Mate   No reason why you should if you carry on like this. No reason at all. You'll make a good captain yet.

He bursts out laughing.

We mix through to the hold in which the **African** *is being held secure. The sea laps up against the side of the ship. Above we can hear the sailors shouting, and behind the shouting the moans of the slaves in the main hold.*

African   The hurt of having lost my only brother stung me with more ferocity than the pain of the journey. Now I was numb. We, the eleven special ones, sat alone, with companionship from neither family nor friend. My mind was too lame to detect foes. We, the special ones, sat alone, seeing only the boy who brought our food and we waited for the end. There was no longer any conversation. We all knew what the other was thinking, what they would say before they had opened their mouths, what our reply would be. Communication merely reinforced isolation. At least there was a vestige of communion in silence.

The moaning from the main hold becomes more dominant. Hold on it, then fade to silence.

The **First Mate** *knocks and enters the captain's cabin. He stands silently before him. He then laughs slightly and starts to speak.*

First Mate   Mr Winston, you don't be looking too well.

Winston (*weakly*)   Are all my crew wedded to the rum and overfond of these nigger women whose natural hot and lewd temper seems to soon waste what little substance the crew have? And are all my crew bent upon the inflicting of pain on their fellow man? Is this all I'm adrift with, this and a cargo of the blackest niggers.

First Mate   It would seem so wouldn't it, Mr Winston.

Winston   Captain Winston to you!

First Mate   Whatever you wish, Captain.

Pause. **Winston** *sighs deeply.*

Winston   Maybe you were right, Mr Hickey. I care little for wind velocity or squally weather, though it would seem that we've passed through the extremities of both.

First Mate   That we have.

Winston   A Christian man must be better prepared for slavery.

First Mate   It would seem so.

Winston   Better prepared to enter a society of creaking wood which works only by cruelly destroying principles that great men have died for.

First Mate   You're set to make me cry, Captain.

Winston   Mr Hickey, I've been reading, a pastime I suspect you have little acquaintance with. Empire literature, Mr Hickey, pertaining to . . . the pouring of burning wax on arms and shoulders, of boiling sugar on heads. Being tied down to wasps' nests, being buried up to the neck, having the head covered in sugar, and then being eaten alive by ants. Have not these Blacks suffered enough, sir? Is not the tragedy of this ocean journey enough pain for them to endure? Is this not a topic worthy of your attention?

First Mate   What happens to a nigger on land is none of my business and none of yours either. I've met captains like you before, Mr Winston – you don't really care a damn, it's just your conscience that's bothering you. I can smell your conscience. It stinks.

Winston   Yes, Mr Hickey, but I'd rather smell the guilt of my conscience than the filth of your ship.

First Mate   My ship?

Winston   If you so wish. I can think of no other trade or business which has such dreadful effects on the minds of those engaged in it – people like yourself, who would probably be of a more gentle and humane disposition engaged in daylight robbery on the King's highway, or seizing the virtues of young girls, but by Christ, this? This damn trade which secures the mortar, which binds the bricks which have built our country's new industrial wealth, this damn trade shall yet be the downfall of England, Mr Hickey. Or perhaps you care little or nothing for England? Have you nothing to say?

First Mate   Goodnight, Captain.

We hear the sound of the cabin door closing. Then the church bells of St Paul's ring out, and a choir begin to sing evensong.

African   Of course he has nothing to say. He has nothing to say when Asians have their homes fire-bombed in Southall. When Enoch Powell made his 'Rivers of Blood' speech he had nothing to say. When the racist immigration laws were passed he had nothing to say. Of course he has nothing to say. The newspapers and media say it for him. 'Wogs go home'. 'Nigger muggers out'. 'Black mob on rampage'. He had nothing to say then, as he has nothing to say now. The general unwritten, unspoken consensus of society says it for him. Brixton, Liverpool, Bristol go up in flames because the darkies don't know how to behave. It's that simple. (*Laughs.*) How is it that you who were once free are now bound by the same chains that you sought to enslave others with? Chains of ignorance?

Mix through to the sound of the sea. We are on deck.

Cabin Boy   No, I meant the niggers. What are they like?

First Mate   There's nothing I can say to you, boy, that you don't already know if you have two eyes in your head.

Pause. Laughs.

They've all got them flat noses and thick lips 'cause when they're young their mothers carry 'em around like animals on their backs and their faces rub up and squash, you know that? And Blacks from different regions are simple to identify. You go too far up river you get a sleepy type who don't look like he's awake half the time, but this type is the quickest to pounce. And just a little further inland you're really in trouble for you get the type that tends to disformity, distemper and the like. They're big bucks, but weak. You've got to strike a balance when slaving a ship. It's why I sometimes put an old buck in with the privileged slaves. He'll help calm them down. Steady as a rock, encourage 'em to give up, yet he'll be the last to give up himself, but that don't matter for he's older and slower than the rest. Some traders call the niggers black gold. (*Laughs.*) Black shit more like. I'd rather transport shit, it smells better. No better than animals. What kind of a man gets himself trapped like that!

Cabin Boy   But they try and escape.

First Mate   They try, but they're too stupid. They don't have the brain, boy. You need a man's brain to outwit a man.

Cabin Boy   Will they sell?

First Mate   Depends, boy. It depends on how good we can make 'em look. Tomorrow, first thing in the morning, we'll get them up on deck and take a look. Most'll have the flux. Arseholes leaking like open sewers, but we'll block 'em up with tar. If we can't fatten 'em up at least we can freshen 'em up a bit. What do you think, boy?

Cabin Boy   Yes, sir.

First Mate   Aye, yes, sir, yes, sir, yes, sir! Tomorrow we'll reach our United States of America, or rather what used to be ours. Either way she'll just be sitting there, pretty as an Easter bonnet, waiting for us with her legs wide open.

Mix through from the sound of the sea and the noise of an open deck, to drums and festivities on land. Trumpets blare out, and there is a holiday atmosphere of merriment. We then hear an **Auctioneer** *begin to hush the crowd and address them directly. He rings a bell as he starts to do so.*

Auctioneer   Oyez! Oyez! Oyez!

On this wonderful fourth of July in the year of our Lord, seventeen hundred and eighty, at the port of Boston, in the State of Massachusetts, we have here today, shipped by the grace of God in good order and well conditioned by the Royal African Company, owners of the said schooner called *Corinna*, whereof whose masters under God for this present voyage have been one John Winston, deceased, and one Captain William Hickey, grant you the prime slave of the day ready and willing to be set before your eyes, not being above twenty-five years of age, or defective in his lips, eyes or teeth or grown grey, not having venereal disease, smallpox, flux or any other infection. He'll swing from tree to tree and he's yours for life. An African monkey, his monkey and his monkey's monkey are yours too, and every American whether pioneer or long time landowner should have one such as this. Now, then, up here I have a selection of sticks to prod him with so you may poke him, squeeze his parts, flex them, but you mustn't mark him for if you don't want him, there's someone who sure will. He's a good-looking young man from about two hundred miles west of the old Calabar where the finest and most politest niggers are reckoned to come from. Four pounds of pork and a peck of corn a week. There's thirty to forty years' good labour in this nigger.

African   Thirty or forty years' good labour? I can outlive two or three hundred years' good labour. I have done. But I'm leaving the kitchen and the fields. We make our marriage work, you hear. For there can be no divorce. A candle cannot burn in the hold of a slave ship. But a thousand inner-city ghettos can burn. And what is it that this fire illuminates? Poverty? Repression? Oppression? Ignorance? Frustration? Hate? Or just History? An undigested semi-suppressed, woefully ignorant sense of history. From your darkest Africa comes light.

Auctioneer   He is as fine in his manners, and as well built as any buck that ever graced our shores. A sixteen- to seventeen-hour day nigger, a fine breeder as well, and by the look of him a nigger who by the time he's thirty will be as strong as an ox. Behold! I give you the prime nigger heathen of the day. His wages? Christianity. I present to you, the Prince of Africa!

The crowd begin to applaud. Behind the applause we hear flames burning, the dull regular beat of a drum and a choir singing evensong.

Writing Fiction

Broadcast Details

BBC Radio 4, 25 February 1991. Directed by Richard Wortley.

Characters (in order of appearance)

Larry
Sarah
Helen
Saul
Girl
Melvyn Bragg
Paperboy
Radio Announcer
Doris
Nurse
Sadie
Leo
Stan
Pete
Rudy
Lucy
Enid
Roger
Sarah's Mother
Sarah's Father
Barman

Notes on the Play

The main character in this radio play, set in contemporaneous England, is Lawrence Wilson, a writer in his forties who has published six successful novels but whose fame and inspiration have dramatically declined. To make some money, he agrees to run a creative writing seminar, during which he interacts with several would-be authors, including his ex-wife, Sarah. The narrative provides a fascinating satire of the literary world and of the damage that celebrity can wreak on the private life of an individual. These themes are pervasive in the various essays that Caryl Phillips has written on literary figures such as James Baldwin. The play also addresses the difficult relationships within Wilson's family from the perspective of the husband/father figure and therefore contains possible echoes of the situation at the heart of the 2009 novel *In the Falling Snow*.

Bedroom. Alarm blares out. **Larry** *snaps to life.*

Larry Oh no, what's going on?

The radio comes on automatically. The Today *programme. Brian Redhead: 'And the time is now 7 o'clock on Friday the 22nd of January. The news headlines . . .'*

Larry *turns down the volume. Redhead talks on.*

Agh, my head.

Inner Voice 'Agh, my head?' Give me a break, Larry. In the old days you'd have jumped out of bed, made a cup of black coffee, and walked straight to your desk. The wife, or whatever entertainment was by your side, could go hang until you'd got your pre-ordained hours in. But look at you now. No wife, not even a regular woman, and you're floundering. You're only forty-one, man, and you can't make it. Come on, pull yourself together. Where's the fire? Where's your ambition? You're becoming a bloody has-been. Don't let yourself down like this, Larry. Don't go back to sleep.

Sarah I've started to lie to her, Larry. (*Pause.*) Don't you care?

Helen Where are we going, Daddy?

Sarah To make excuses to her for your behaviour.

Larry I think you and Mummy are going to Grandma and Grandpa's. Daddy's going to a conference in Barcelona.

Helen Can I come too?

Larry (*forced laughter*) No, darling, but I'll see you soon.

Sarah Daddy shouts at me, falls over drunk, stays out at night, all because of his work.

Larry

Writer's notebook. September 1971. Writing is a very tactile profession. You tentatively feel your way along, clutching here, groping there, clinging to this, releasing that. (*Pause.*)

Writer's notebook. March 1975. I've been married less than a year. Hardy, Eliot and Scott Fitzgerald all drove their wives mad. But only to stop their wives from driving them mad. Saul still hasn't said anything, but I know he thinks I was wrong to marry Sarah. Maybe he's right.

Bar.

Saul Look, Larry, you need time to write. Money buys time. And I've been thinking. I want the Saul Le Witt Literary Agency to be a small agency of quality. You, maybe two others at the most, and I'll control all the admin. These big agencies with their mega-deal, cross-media, transatlantic garbage ruin writers. It's just going to be Saul Le Witt the agent, Larry Wilson the writer. We're both young; we've got a future in this business. I'll drive hard but fair deals and you'll produce first-class literature. So what do you say?

Larry   Well, I say why not.

Saul   Great. Let's drink to the deal. A partnership of literary quality. Here's to the imminent appearance of the first Larry Wilson novel.

They clink glasses and laugh.

Helen   Daddy?

Sarah   'Daddy is tired, darling'. 'Daddy is not coming back tonight, darling'. 'Daddy's very busy, darling'.

Girl   Look, I know writers need their space. I won't interfere. I'm like you. I don't need many people. I just like being with you, Larry, even when you're nasty. (*Pause.*) But it's your wife, isn't it?

Larry   Writer's notebook. October 1977. I now realize that women have to be regarded as objects of recreation, in much the same way as one views the Odeon or a walk in the park. You engage with such pursuits on your terms and when you have time. (*Pause.*) Unfortunately I'm married.

South Bank Show *music.*

Melvyn Bragg   Good evening. Tonight we feature one of Britain's most successful writers, a young man who although only thirty-three is publishing his sixth novel, *The Autumnal Sun.*

Sarah   Say your prayers, darling, before you get into bed.

Helen   Dear God, thank you for another day. Please be kind to Grandpa and Grandma and to my mummy.

Sarah   Helen, haven't we forgotten somebody?

Helen   No.

Sarah   Helen.

Helen (*reluctantly*)   And Daddy.

Sarah   And who?

Helen   And nobody!

Pause.

Sarah   You're a bastard, Larry. A selfish bastard.

Pause.

Helen   Daddy, I hate you 'cause you hurt Mummy. I hate you! I hate you!

We hear the Radio 4 'pips'. Brian Redhead: 'And the time is now 8 o'clock. The news headlines.' **Larry** *knocks off the radio.*

Larry   Lord, my head!

The doorbell rings.

I'm coming.

We hear **Larry** *getting out of bed.*

Writer's notebook. May 1982. Just read some article about writing by an American novelist. He says that it's a single-minded, selfish activity which demands being emotionally ruthless. He says that you're aware that all the emotions going into your book should really be going into people so you feel guilty. He's right of course, but he must learn to eradicate guilt.

Writer's notebook. May 1969. Just finished my first novel. It's called *Windmill Watching.* I feel able to think of myself as a writer now. I think life is like travelling through a tunnel. You must keep some light in view. But if you temporarily find yourself in the dark, beware! Remember you can grow to see in the dark. The light's your dream, your goal. My dream is not to be good, but to be the best. *Windmill Watching* is a start.

Larry *is walking down the stairs. The doorbell rings out again.*

Okay, I'm coming. Let me get down the bloody stairs.

A bolt is drawn back. The door sticks a little then opens.

Yes, what do you want?

Paperboy   Mr Patel said you owe for eleven weeks at £2.75. That's £30.25.

Larry   Member of MENSA are we?

Boy   I've gotta have £30.25 or I'm not to give you the paper.

Larry   In my day you'd have got a smack around the head for talking like that to your betters.

Boy   You ain't better than me. Our sociology teacher says . . .

Larry   Your what?

Boy   Look mister, £30.25 or no paper.

Larry   Go play in the traffic.

He slams the door. Then the phone rings.

Christ, I feel like I'm under surveillance.

He picks up the phone.

Larry Wilson.

Saul   Hey, Larry. It's Saul. What's the story? You sound terrible.

Larry   I went to Bob Steven's publication party last night. I think I drank too much.

Saul   I hear those new guys, Apex Press, picked him up. Paid him a broad advance.

Larry   I don't want to hear about it.

Saul   Yeah, well. Look, clean up and get down here to the office. Let's talk this thing through once more.

Larry   I'll be over in an hour.

He puts the phone down.

Office. **Larry** *is sipping coffee.*

Saul   Apex Press have some hot girls, even if their distribution's a bit ropey.

Larry   I'm not interested. Not even sure if I'm able.

Saul   Hell, that's bad, Larry. Real bad. Well, let me get straight to the point. We still don't know. I've faxed them and said we want an answer by tomorrow evening or the deal is off. No compromise. You do the screenplay or we withhold the rights.

Larry   You think they'll buy it?

Saul   If they don't it's your own fault. You're a novelist, Larry. You've got no screenplay track-record. I keep telling you, let somebody else adapt the damn novel and you still get fifty grand for the film rights.

Larry   Fifty grand isn't enough. I need the screenplay money too.

Saul   But you don't know how to write a goddamn screenplay.

Larry   You think the men who wrote *Conan the Barbarian* or *Teen Wolf from Outer Space* were geniuses? Any fool can write a film script. And I need the extra twenty-five grand to get out of this hole, Saul. Don't you understand, I'm blocked. Eight years without a novel, I've got a wife who's milking me dry for alimony, I've got a kid to support, a mortgage to pay, and a lifestyle to maintain. I've gotta write something for cash and I thought we'd agreed that the most discreet thing to do was to adapt one of my own books.

Saul   Yeah, it's discreet but it might not be possible.

Larry   Well, you're my bloody agent. Ten per cent in your pocket says make it possible.

Saul   Okay, okay. I'll try, but what are you doing?

Larry   I told you. I'm blocked. (*Pause.*) I'm reading.

Saul   Reading? I can't sell reading.

Larry   And I've got a teaching job. I've got to drive to some godforsaken place in the middle of Wiltshire or Berkshire, I can't even remember. I'm giving a writing programme for £150. That's how badly I need money, Saul, understand? I'm teaching for a living!

Saul   Okay, just cool it a minute. Relax. You need a holiday.

Larry   If you don't get me this deal I'll be getting one in an open prison with insider-dealers and bent accountants.

Saul   Okay, call me tomorrow evening at seven. I'll come into the office and see if there's anything on the answering machine, or if they've sent a fax. You see what I'm doing for you? I'm gonna come into the office on a Saturday and work for you.

Larry   Okay, I'm so grateful. (*Stands up.*) Thanks for the coffee. You should put a Red Cross on your percolator.

Saul   Ring me tomorrow. And Larry, have fun this weekend. I'm sure some fresh air and a change of scenery will do you good. Nature always helps to cleanse the mind.

Larry   You sound like a bloody farmer.

Saul   Hey, don't knock farming. That vet, Herriot, and those rabbits of Watership. That was some heavy-hitting literature. Nature sells, Larry. Ask Thomas Hardy.

Larry   Saul, this isn't funny. If you don't get me this deal I'll have to close up. I figure I'll have five or six thousand pounds to show for nineteen years of writing. A footballer or a sodding policeman earns that much every month.

Saul   Take it easy, Larry. And drive safely, for God's sake. Go on. You know I'll look after you.

Car. Driving up the motorway.

Radio Announcer   Today's morning story is 'The Leaves of Snowdonia' by Brian Gibson.

Larry *turns it off. We hear the following letter.*

Doris   Dear Mr Wilson, We are a privately endowed mansion with self-contained lecture rooms, bar, recreation facilities, library, and catering wing, all set in secluded woodland. Next year we intend to have four Writing Fiction courses with approximately ten pupils per course, and students accepted on a first-come, first-served basis. We were hoping that you might agree to lead a weekend from Friday 22nd of January through until Sunday 24th. For this we can offer you £150 plus 14 pence per mile if you are travelling by car, or second-class return rail fare. I have read all six of your novels and would be honoured to meet you and have you sign them for me. All at Weston Lodge would be delighted if you would consider inaugurating our creative writing programme. Yours sincerely, Doris L. Simmonds (Centre Director)

Inner Voice   Larry, what the hell are you doing ploughing up the motorway to spend a weekend with a bunch of amateurs? You don't need the money that badly. £150 isn't going to help. You've got to learn to discipline yourself again. Come on, how long is it since you even sat at your desk? What are you frightened of? If there's nothing that you're burning to write about, then do some non-fiction. You can't always be spilling your soul. Do something that is technically challenging. Adapt something. Anything, just turn the bloody car around and go back to London. Open the door to the house, close it behind you, and walk straight upstairs and don't come out until you've written three thousand words. Turn the car around, dammit.

Discotheque. We hear the music of 1974. They have to shout to make themselves heard.

Larry   Another drink?

Sarah   No thanks, I'm fine. I didn't know writers went to discotheques.

Larry   I'm not just a writer, Sarah. I'm a twenty-six-year-old man.

Sarah   Who just happens to have written three very successful novels, and who spends all his time talking to me about writing, and literature, and now he doth protest he's just a plain ordinary twenty-six-year-old man. (*Laughs.*)

Larry   Point taken. But I wouldn't mind if we talked about social work.

Sarah   There is nothing glamorous about social work.

Larry   But it's your life and you find it interesting, don't you?

Sarah   Sometimes, but it's not writing, is it.

Larry   Well, you can write. In fact, you write very well. You should take it more seriously.

Sarah   I did take it quite seriously, that's why I came to your workshop last year. But I just haven't had much time recently.

Larry   You should make time. You're damn good.

Sarah   Why thank you, kind teacher.

Larry   Will you marry me?

Sarah   What?

Larry (*shouts*)   I said, will you marry me?

Sarah   Sshh! Don't shout! I can hear. You brought me to a discotheque to ask me to marry you?

Larry   Leo and I used to come here when I worked at the advertising agency. I feel comfortable here. Well?

Sarah   And what kind of a wife do you want?

Larry   A loyal one who understands me.

Sarah   Well, I'm loyal. I don't know if I fully understand you, but I think I'm at least as tolerant as the next person.

Larry   So you will?

Sarah (*laughs*)   And so they both lived happily ever after.

In the car.

Larry   Dear Doris Simmonds, Thank you for your letter. I am replying immediately because if you can confirm the dates, and the fact that I will be able to get away by 1 p.m. on Sunday 24th, then I may well be able to make it. On that same Sunday evening I am due to fly to Los Angeles to finalize arrangements concerning the filming of my novel *The Garden in the City*. Your course sounds very worthwhile, and an ideal antidote (albeit pre-administered) to the vulgarity of Hollywood. Sincerely yours, Lawrence Wilson.

Maternity ward.

Sarah   Larry, is that you?

Larry (*slightly out of breath*)   Of course it's me, darling.

Sarah   Where were you?

Larry   My new German publishers. You know how things can get with them. All beer and babble.

Nurse   Ah, you must be Mr Wilson.

Larry   That's right. (*Pause.*) I'm sorry, Sarah, but I had to dot a few 'i's' and cross a few 't's' on the contract.

Nurse   Mr Wilson, would you like to see your daughter?

Larry   We've had a girl?

Sarah   No! My husband will explain himself to me first.

Nurse   Mrs Wilson, you should rest for a while. I'll show him your beautiful new daughter and then perhaps he can come back later.

Sarah   Dammit, he's *my* husband! He will explain to me why he was not present at the birth of our child!

Nurse   I think you'd better wait outside, Mr Wilson.

Sarah   No, Larry. Don't you dare go anywhere. You bloody well tell me what's more important to you, your German publishers or your family, and tell me now!

Nurse   Outside, Mr Wilson! Doctor! Doctor!

Sarah   Larry, stay where you are! Larry! Larry!

Larry *and the* **Nurse** *move outside. We can still hear* **Sarah** *shouting.*

A shop door bell rings as the door is pushed open. In shop.

Sadie   Afternoon. Can I help you?

Larry   No, it's alright. I'm only browsing.

Sadie   Well, I'm here if you need me.

Radio Announcer   'PM' on Radio 4.

Music, headlines, etc.

Sadie   Is the noise of the transistor disturbing you?

Larry   Not at all. Can I ask, do you have anything by Lawrence Wilson?

Sadie   It's you, isn't it.

Larry (*laughs*)   Afraid so.

Sadie   Leo!

Larry   So this where Leo escaped to.

Sadie   I didn't know he was running.

Leo   Larry, you old dog. What brings you into my neck of the woods?

Larry   It's an old story. I think I'll need a drink to tell it.

Time passes. In the lounge.

Larry   . . . and so I thought, okay a weekend teaching before I go off to Hollywood. It will probably be good for the soul and I'll get a chance to see if Leo really did go back to nature.

Sadie   I wouldn't call owning a small bookstore and health food shop going back to nature.

Leo   But it's hardly the city life Larry and I used to lead when we were . . .

Leo/Larry   . . . advertising executives. 'Do you want a drink, darling? Do you come here often?' (*They both fall about laughing.*)

Sadie   I don't believe that worked on any girl.

Larry   It did, and believe me as far as Leo was concerned any girl would do.

Leo   Steady on, Larry. I'm a married man now. Sadie doesn't want to hear about what went on before I met her.

Sadie   You can say that again.

Leo   Another Scotch, Larry?

Larry   Sure, why not.

Leo *pours.*

Sadie   I've got to lock up the shop and do the till. I'll leave you two juveniles to plough your way down your muddy and unsavoury memory lane.

She goes out.

Larry   Local girl?

Leo   Came to work for me when I opened up. Thought at first she'd be a nice winter-warmer, but she's more than that. Makes me laugh, makes me think, makes me happy. Simple things. But what about you and . . .

Larry   Oh no, I don't want to talk about that.

Leo   I know how it ended. Read about it in the papers.

Larry   Why wedding rings? Why not wedding spears and shields?

Leo   That bad?

Larry   Worse. Without women there would have been eight or ten Lawrence Wilson novels, not the tardy six.

Leo Tardy six! Are you mad? You've done it, Larry. All that college talk about being a writer, and then your dreams when you were at the agency, you've made them real. You're the biggest success story I know, or I'll ever know. Just one novel and I'd die a happy man and you talk about a tardy six.

Larry You haven't stopped writing have you?

Leo As far as writing is concerned forget me. I was always a dreamer, you were the man of action.

Sadie *returns.*

Sadie You two figured out how many you scored in the summer of '72 yet?

Leo More than Geoff Boycott, that's for sure. (*They both laugh.*)

Sadie I'm not chasing you out, Larry, but it's gone six. I thought you said you'd a course to teach, or is it all done by computers these days?

Larry Oh my God!

Leo One for the road?

Larry You must be joking. They'll be burning copies of my books in another ten minutes.

Leo We will see you again, won't we? We don't lock the door, so just drop by any time.

Larry Thanks. This could be a long weekend. You might be saving a man's life. Ciao!

Corridor. Sound of footsteps.

Inner Voice So this is it, Larry. You didn't turn the car around, and you've seen for yourself how happy Leo is. Now you've got to earn your £150. But you don't care though do you? Go on, admit it, it's easier to be a literary celebrity than it is to be a writer. Being a writer involves solitary, sometimes unrewarding work, doesn't it, Larry? Book signings, lectures, conferences, hotels, 747s, adoring faces, the double-takes in bookshops, the awards, the honorary degrees, these things make you feel good. This is what it's about for you, isn't it Larry? Christ, who needs all that fruitless thinking, and typing, and rewriting, and thinking, and re-writing and typing. Nothing bloody glamorous and ego-warming about that is there? Well, go on, Larry, open the door. Take the easy route. Meet your fans.

Footsteps stop.

By the way, Larry, can you still see the light at the end of the tunnel? Do you remember your dream?

Lecture room. Door opens and closes. Murmuring dies down as **Larry** *enters.*

Larry Hi, I'm Lawrence Wilson. Sorry I'm a few moments late. (*Pause as he walks to the head of the room.*) I feel a little uneasy standing at the head of this table, like I'm about to carve a chicken or something.

Silence.

Well, these are the jokes, folks. Now, most people call me Larry so feel free to call me that, at least to my face.

Small laughter.

Hey, we're getting there. You're alive. Put your nerves back into your pencil cases and let's just talk for a minute. First of all, names. I'll go round the table left to right. So you're . . .

Voices   Stan . . . Elizabeth . . . Rudy . . . Roger . . . Lucy . . . Nick . . . Mrs Reid, Enid . . . Pete . . .

Larry   Great, we'll make a start. Now, there are some audiovisual aids and a xerox machine in the office. The only rule of thumb I have about writing is this: use your eyes. But also watch with your ears, fingers, nose, lips and mouth. Writing is about total inner and outer observation. Are there any immediate questions?

Stan   Can you tell us what's happening tonight?

Larry   Sure. Now I assume Mrs Simmonds has given you an introduction to the geography of the lodge and where you will be staying and everything.

Pete   Those huts in the woods are freezing.

Rudy   Yeah, there's no heating, man.

Larry   I'll have a word with Mrs Simmonds.

Lucy   Honestly, anyone would think it was *The Gulag Archipelago*.

Stan   What about this evening then? Do we have 'owt to do or can we just lurk about?

Larry   Certainly not. There's no time to waste. Now, I'm going to go into the seminar room and you will all come in for a quick four or five minutes' chat with me alone. Then we will have a general question and answer session in the bar.

He goes to open the door.

So, I'll take the first one when you're ready.

Seminar room. Sound of a light being switched on and a chair scraping.

Larry   Writer's notebook. December 1985. Tonight Sarah left me. Four years without a novel. I've always known that writing was a way of controlling the chaotic and dangerous thoughts that lie within. Without writing I don't know if I can endure what I see and feel. But I'm not sure what I see and feel anymore.

Seminar room. We hear an attempt to ignite a gas fire.

Lucy   Hi!

Larry   Oh hi! I'm just trying to light the fire. It's a bit nippy in here. There! (*Stands.*) It's Lucy, isn't it?

Lucy   You've got a good memory.

Larry   Well, I try. Now what can I do for you this weekend?

Lucy   Well, where to begin. I'm trying to do a second draft of my novel but I'm really getting bogged down? You know, not sure if I'm throwing out the good with the bad, unsure which bits to expand and which to leave alone. And I'm having trouble with the incidental characters. Tolstoy was so brilliant at incidentals, but I don't seem to be able to get them. It's probably more editorial work than anything else, but I really don't want to show it to my publishers as yet in case I get a better offer from somewhere else when it's finished.

Larry   I see, you're already published.

Lucy   Yes, *The Vegetarian Cookbook*. In fact, its full title is *The Vegetarian Cookbook for Women*, but I hate it so I just call it *The Vegetarian Cookbook*.

Larry   Would you like me to read part of your novel?

Lucy   Please. These are the first two chapters. It's called *A Russian Winter*.

Larry   Nice title.

Fade out.

Fade up.

Larry   Shall I help you?

Enid   No, I can manage thank you. (*Sits noisily. Out of breath.*) Now then, young man, just who are you? I was under the impression that Leonard Wilson would be speaking here this weekend. And I know you're not dear old Lenny, you're too young for a start, and you speak like a layabout. Lenny has such a wonderful rich baritone.

Larry   You must mean Leonard Wilson of *Love's High Price* and *Dishonourable Bride*.

Enid   Why has Leonard never won the Nobel Prize, you tell me that? They give it to all this foreign muck, even gave it to a darkie a few years ago. Leonard beautifies our tongue. It's only right that he should be rewarded.

Larry   I'm afraid Leonard Wilson is dead.

Enid   Leonard's dead? He can't be. If he's dead what are you doing here?

Larry   I'm Larry Wilson. Lawrence Wilson.

Enid   I've never heard of you. (*Stands.*) I shall have to think about this. And what do you mean by calling this weekend 'Writing Fiction'? You are encouraging people to propagate untruths.

Larry   Surely you want to write something this weekend. Wouldn't you like to talk to me about what we might do?

Enid   You're a foul-mouthed pup aren't you?

She goes out. Pause. Then **Larry** *goes to the door.*

Larry   Can I have the next writer, please.

Inner Voice   Turn the car around, Larry. I told you to turn the damn thing around and go home.

He sits back down.

Stan   Alright, I'm Stan.

Larry   Take a seat, Stan. How would you like to spend the weekend?

Stan   Well, I'd like to stop writing for a start-off. I don't seem to be able to stop writing. It started out as a hobby, you know a spot of recreation of the local writers' circle. We meet in Barnsley Town Hall of a Friday night. It's dead convenient for me for I work there in local government like. First there was the odd short story. I used to specialize in whippets. All my stories were about whippets but I never kept none. I'm a ferret man. But whippets is a way of extending the imagination cos there's not much kith nor kin between whippets and ferrets. Any road Mr McManus, the teacher like, he suggested to us that I try doing something historical so I've got this book set in the year nought in Tasmania. All the action parallels the birth and early years of Christ, but it's about heathens in Australia.

Fade out.

Fade up.

Larry   Sit down, Pete. What's the guitar for?

Pete   I'm glad you spotted that. I do song-novels. I used to be into music. Well, I still am, but then I got into a heavy trip reading novels so I put them together. Listen. (*He sings to the tune of 'Heartbreak Hotel'.*)

> Gregor Samsa looked into the mirror
> And what did he see
> He saw two long antennae
> Lord he'd turned into a bee
> I say now
> Don't look in the mirror baby
> Don't look at your self
> The next stage is you'll turn
> Into an elf.

What do you reckon? I've done the same to *Oliver Twist*, and I read another book the other day that I thought I could adapt. It's a Russian book called *Crime and Punishment*. (*He sings to the tune of 'Jailhouse Rock'.*)

> I say one for a rouble
> Two for a dime
> Rashkolnikov you're a low dirty swine

Larry   Alright! Alright!

Pete   The name's Pete.

Larry   I think we might be getting ourselves in a copyright tangle here, but we can talk about this later. First of all what would you like to do this weekend?

Pete   Just play. I want you to suggest some markets for me. You know, people I might send demo tapes to.

Larry   I'll rack my brain and see what I can come up with.

Pete   Okay, that's cool. I don't want to burn off your clock. There's still one more to come.

Larry   Yes, I know.

Pete   Okay, keep it in your pants, Larry.

Larry   Thank you. I'll try.

Pete *goes out. Pause.*

Sarah   Hello, Larry. (*Shuts the door.*) Well, aren't you going to say anything. It's not like you to be lost for words.

Larry   What are you doing here?

Sarah   Whoa, hold on a minute. This is an open course. I saw nothing in the brochure barring ex-wives. In fact, I saw nothing in the brochure about anybody being barred. (*Laughs.*) You really drew a fistful of short straws, didn't you, Larry. I think the last lad lost his way en route to Woodstock. (*Laughs.*) Larry, stop looking at me like that. I've come on the course to write. Or, to be more honest, I've written. I would like you to read something.

Larry   Something you've written?

Sarah   Of course it's something I've written.

Larry   How is my daughter?

Sarah   Helen's fine. She's growing up to be a strong-minded little woman. (*Pause.*) I'm sorry, Larry, but if she doesn't want to see you there's nothing I can do about it. Eventually she'll grow out of it. I shouldn't worry.

Larry   I shouldn't worry! You poison the mind of my only child against me and then tell me that I shouldn't worry. Have you come here in an attempt to humiliate me?

Sarah   Larry, stop! Keep your voice down. Nobody's come here to humiliate you. (*Pause.*) I've written a book, Larry. My agent and publisher . . .

Larry   Oh, you're a writer now are you? Social worker not good enough for you anymore.

Sarah   Larry! Where did we meet for heaven's sake?

Larry   Inner circle of Dante's Hell?

Sarah   At a writers' workshop. Only I wasn't very good at it then. But in the last couple of years, I've managed to get down to it with Brian's help.

Larry   Who the hell is Brian?

Sarah   A man. A friend, he helps with Helen and around the house.

Larry   Yes, I'll bet he does.

Sarah   I've written a novel, Larry and it's going to be published in September. I'd like you to read it.

Larry   For Christ's sake, you've got an agent, a publisher, a finished manuscript, why should I read it, apart from the fact that it's probably some kind of embarrassing exposé of our marriage, and I really don't know if I can face that along with everything else that's going on in my life right now.

Sarah   Larry, I'd like you to read at least a part of it. (*Pause.*) Don't worry, I won't let on to anyone here that we're historically intertwined. (*Pause.*) Larry, are you really shocked or just being bull-headed? Look at me, for God's sake.

Larry   Get out, Sarah. Please.

Sarah   Alright, Larry, but I really do want to talk. I'll see you later.

She leaves. Door closes.

Larry (*sighs*)   Oh, no.

Party.

Sarah   Larry, I want a divorce.

Larry   Jesus, not now at Saul's Christmas party.

Sarah   Yes now!

Voice   Larry, how you doing? You're sure taking your time over your new masterpiece. But I hear it's great. Is this Mrs Wilson?

Larry   Sarah, meet Mike Summers from Random House. He's the Senior Fiction Editor.

Voice   Pleased to meet you, Mrs Wilson. Try and hurry him up a little, will you. We're all waiting for this new book. (*Laughs and moves off.*)

Sarah   I'm leaving you, Larry.

Larry   Why, for Christ's sake? What have I done?

Sarah   It's not so much the adultery. (*Pause.*) Larry, please wipe that self-righteous indignation off your face. (*Pause.*) I said wipe it off!

Conversation around them dies.

Larry   Sarah, please.

Saul   Hey, everything alright over here?

Larry   Yes, Saul, everything's fine.

Sarah   Leave us alone.

Saul   Anything you say.

Sarah   I'm used to your bedding every wet-knickered girl in town who asks you to scribble your name on the title page of one of your books. I don't like to admit it, but I've grown to live with it. But I don't want Helen to grow up and be like me.

Larry   What are you talking about?

Sarah   I've started to lie to her, Larry. To make excuses to her for your behaviour. Daddy shouts at me, falls over drunk, stays out at night, all because of his work. 'Daddy is tired, darling'. 'Daddy is not coming back tonight, darling'. 'Daddy is very busy, darling'. The truth is, Helen, that Daddy is probably doing some publicity tart in her Acton bedsit.

Larry   Sarah, please.

Sarah   No, Larry. Not anymore. I'm tired. And in case you hadn't noticed, your daughter is beginning to dislike you. We're leaving tomorrow. You'll have the relevant separation papers as soon as I can speak with a lawyer.

Larry   You can't do this, Sarah.

Sarah   I can, Larry. And I intend to.

Larry   No, you can't! You can't leave me!

Saul   Hey, you two, take it easy. This is a Christmas party. Enjoy!

Sarah   Goodnight, Larry. Saul.

Larry   Hey! You wait where you are! Don't you dare! Sarah! Sarah!

Bar. The bar is busy. There is laughter in the background.

Lucy   You mean, *The Autumnal Sun* wasn't based on personal experience?

Larry   Hardly. You see it's far more usual for a writer's early works to be based on their own lives. That's why *Windmill Watching* and *Love in a Secret Zone* are my most autobiographical books.

Lucy   I tried to get hold of them for the course. Well, not exactly for the course, but so that I'd read everything of yours before we met.

Larry   Well, I'm afraid, Lucy, that they're both out of print now.

Pete   I didn't know we had to read your books to come on this course.

Larry   You don't.

Stan   Good job really seeing as you can't get hold of half of them.

Larry   I wouldn't go so far as to say half. *Freedom Train, The Garden in the City, Moonshadow* and *The Autumnal Sun* are still in print.

Lucy   But it's a few years since you've published now, isn't it, Larry?

Larry   Well, I've been busy doing lecturing and working on a few film projects. In fact, I have to take off on Sunday night and fly to LA. Hollywood are doing a movie of *The Garden in the City*.

Rudy   Who's in it, man?

Larry   Well, I don't know yet. These things are always up to the director.

Rudy   Who's the director?

Larry   That's something else that's yet to be settled. Hollywood loves keeping writers in the dark.

Lucy   But what about a new novel, Larry. Something completely original.

Larry   Well, I'm working on something, but I can't really talk about it.

Roger   You've got to understand that all writers are private animals with different gestation periods. You shouldn't push him too much.

Rudy   What do you know about it, man?

Pete   Yeah, what have you written then?

Roger   I've not spent £40 to come here and be challenged by the likes of you. I'm simply making a general point.

Stan   Are there any of your books, Lawrence, that might be suitable for my two grandsons?

Larry   Well, they're all a bit adult, I guess. (*Pause.*) Maybe *Windmill Watching*.

Stan   But you can't get that book. Can't you get it back into print?

Larry   Well, I can try. Or rather my agent can.

Roger   And if your agent can't then nobody's can. Larry's represented by Saul Le Witt. Probably the biggest, definitely the best.

Rudy   Who represents you then? Rent-a-mouth?

Pete *and* **Rudy** *laugh.*

Larry   Listen, I've a few things to do before tomorrow so I'll leave you all to it. I hope you sleep well. Goodnight.

All   Goodnight! Goodnight, Larry.

Bedroom. Door closes.

Inner Voice   You liked that didn't you Larry? All that rubbish about flying to LA on Sunday. You should be spending Sunday afternoon with your wife and child shouldn't you, kicking a ball in the park, or walking around some museum. Flying to LA? You've barely got the petrol to make it back to London.

Larry   Jesus, don't remind me.

He pours a large measure of Scotch. There is a knock at the door.

Come in.

Door opens.

Doris   You weren't going to sleep, were you? I thought you might like a drink. Oh, you've got one already. And I hoped you'd be kind enough to sign my books for me. Or rather, your books.

Larry   Of course. Sit down, Mrs Simmonds. There's not much room but make yourself at home.

Door closes.

Doris   Are you sure I've not interrupted the muse?

Larry   No, the muse has already fled for the day. She's left me here all alone. Let me pour you a drink.

He pours.

Say when.

Doris   When! I think I've maybe had a touch too much already. A bit of Dutch courage before I approached the famous writer.

Larry   Cheers.

Doris   Cheers. Would you mind awfully signing these?

Larry   Very impressive. All first editions. I'll make them out 'To Doris', shall I?

Doris   Please (*Pause.*) Gerald, my husband, he's left me.

Larry   I'm sorry to hear that.

Doris   It's only temporary. He does this every weekend. He has a fancy woman working over at Bordley market. She sells silk and the like.

Larry   That's very sad. I'm sorry.

Doris   Larry?

Larry   I'd forgotten how handsome these volumes are. I'm generally only asked to scrawl in the paperback edition. There we are, all signed. (*Pause.*) Sorry, I thought you were asking me a question.

Doris   I'm afraid I'd better go now. I'm a little bit ashamed.

Larry   There's nothing to be ashamed of.

Doris   Yes there is. (*Pause.*) Thank you for signing the books. If there's anything I can do to make . . .

Larry   Everything's fine.

Doris   Goodnight, Mr Wilson.

She leaves. Door closes.

Larry   Oh Lord have mercy.

He pours himself another large drink.

Bedroom. We hear a telephone being dialled.

Girl   Larry, come back to bed. What are you doing?

Somebody answers the other end.

Sarah's Mother (*very county*)   336721. Hello.

Larry   I want to speak with my wife.

Sarah's Mother   Larry, Sarah's asleep. It's 2.30 in the morning and quite frankly both her father and I have just about had enough of your antics.

Larry   I've got a right to speak to her.

Sarah's Mother   We're trying to be reasonable with you, Larry, but you're not helping things. (*Aside.*) It's him again.

Girl   Larry, who are you talking to?

Sarah's Father (*military gruff*)   Dammit, Larry. You're a grown man. This is getting beyond a joke. She doesn't want to speak to you, and especially at such an uncivil hour. Goodnight.

The phone is slammed down.

Girl   Did you do that on purpose?

Larry   Do what?

Girl   Try to humiliate me.

Larry   I'm sorry. (*Pause.*) Look, I can't work because of the damn woman. She's always on my mind.

Girl   But you said you couldn't work when she was around you.

Larry   That's true as well. The bloody woman's destroying my life. I'm getting left behind. Soon people will be writing me off as a 'has-been'.

Girl   No they won't, Larry.

Larry   Of course they will. Anyway, what the hell do you know about it? BBC PAs are supposed to obey, not question.

Girl   Is that why I'm here?

Larry   You're here because I want you to be here.

Girl   I see.

Larry   Do you? A man in my position has all kinds of commitments from lecturing to attending conferences, opening the local bloody bazaar to making documentaries with you lot. Over the years time for work has shrunk. Do you understand that?

Girl   I understand, Larry. You need someone to protect you.

Larry   She couldn't wait to get out, always pestering me about her independence as though I had her tied to a rack in the kitchen. So she leaves, and what happens. She starts up, bloody hounding me about alimony and child support for Helen. That plus my other commitments, no wonder I can't write anymore.

Girl   Can I help? (*Pause.*) Look, I know writers need their space. I won't interfere. I'm like you, I don't need many people. I just like being with you, Larry, even when you're nasty. (*Pause.*) But it's your wife, isn't it? Do you still feel you've got unfinished business with her? (*Pause.*) I take it that means 'yes'. (*Pause.*) Larry, I'm not just another pie-eyed floozy you can bang and put down at will. I think I can help. (*Pause.*) Well, don't you have anything to say? (*Pause.*) I'm going home, Larry.

Larry   I'll call you a mini-cab.

Leo's house. Sound of a drunken **Larry** *stumbling through a room. He mutters to himself.*

Larry   Can't see a bloody thing.

He knocks over a milk bottle.

Oh Lord!

Light switch snaps on.

Leo   Alright, don't move. I'm armed.

Larry   Good God, Leo. What's that? A poker?

Sadie   I might have known.

Leo   Larry, what in hell's name are you doing here? It's nearly two in the morning.

Sadie   I'll put the kettle on.

Larry   Nope. No need, my fine woman. I've brought refreshment enough with me. The finest malt whisky. The gift of a slightly frustrated grand dame.

Sadie   I'm not your fine woman.

Leo   Come through here and sit down, Larry. Sadie, go back to bed, darling. I'll stay with Larry.

Larry   You did say I was to consider the place my own. To drop by any time.

Leo   Yes, but two in the morning, Larry.

Larry   What time do you stop serving your muesli burgers and wholemeal bakes? I mean, what's wrong with a damn good raw steak dripping lightly with a little rosé-coloured blood, now tell me that? Eh?

Sadie   Goodnight, and tell him to keep his voice down.

Larry   Goodnight, my darling. Mixed grill for breakfast. Heavy on the kidneys and fried bread.

Sadie *goes out.* **Larry** *is laughing.*

Larry   Leo, I'm trapped up the road with a bunch of crazy bastards. Are we near Broadmoor? (*Drinks.*) Listen, the asylum runs courses in Japanese flower arrangement and advanced knitting design! You'd have thought that 'Writing Fiction' would be reasonably safe, but oh no. The loony quota is well up to what I've come to expect. Last one of these things I did a woman told me that in a previous life I'd made her pregnant.

Leo   I wouldn't put anything past you.

Larry   It's not looking good, Leo, and . . . I've got no money. Well, don't stare like that, it's hardly surprising. I haven't written a bloody thing in years – I can't.

Leo   I did wonder.

Larry   And worst of all. (*Pause.*) You're never going to believe this.

Leo   Try me.

Larry   Well, my pain-in-the-neck ex-wife is on the course as a bloody student of mine.

Leo   I know.

Larry   What do you mean, you know? What in God's name is going on around here?

Leo   Ssshh! Keep your voice down. I know because she called in to ask the way. I didn't speak to her, I was here in the back, but I recognized her voice and stole a look. She's in very good nick.

Larry   Never mind about that. You were only the best man, I was the bridegroom, remember. I'm the one who says what nick she's in and, yes, she's in very good nick. And she's a writer. She's written a book and she wants me to read it.

Leo   Well, is that bad news?

Larry   Of course it's bad news. She's got some man as well, some big bare-chested bronzed buck called Brian. They probably make love on animal skins and walk around the house in the nude.

Leo   Well, Sadie and I sometimes . . .

Larry   Oh for Christ's sake don't tell me. What's the matter with clothes and bedrooms? I thought we gave up all that baloney when we got beaten up at Grosvenor Square, and part-exchanged our Joan Baez albums.

Leo   The nearest you came to Grosvenor Square was if a taxi took a short cut to the pub, and the only Joan you ever had was a secretary or a bank teller. Grow up, Larry, she's a big woman. She can do what she likes.

Larry   What? Are you on her side now?

Leo   I'm on nobody's side but . . . but it's nearly twenty years since you first published a novel and you've changed. Actually, you changed even before you were published.

Larry   What do you mean by that, Leo?

Leo   Oh come on, I don't want to rake over all this old ground again.

Larry   What old ground?

Leo   You know full well what old ground. You stole the plot of your first novel from me, it's as simple as that. I don't hold it against you, it's just that . . . well, it's just that I wish you'd admit it. Be man enough to say, 'Yes, I did', and then we could be . . . well, perhaps we could be . . .

Larry   Go on, say it, perhaps we could be friends again. Well, let me tell you something, Leo, the amount of time we spent together it was inevitable that were one of us to sit down and write anything it would contain some part of the other's creative mind. Take a look at our advertising copy. Well? We were the Galton and Simpson of the company. Couldn't come up with a slogan or text without the other one. And then when one of us did sit down and drill out a novel, and a damn fine novel it was too, old *Windmill Watching*, what did you have to say to me? Not 'Congratulations, old man, I didn't know you had it in you'; or, 'This mysterious filly you've been dating is actually a book'. Well, come on, Leo, Mr Pal, Mr Drinking Partner, what did you say to me? I'll tell you, you said bugger all and sent me a solicitor's letter, some bloody friend you turned out to be.

Leo   I'm sorry, Larry, but you have to understand how I felt.

Larry   I did. You were cucumber-green with jealousy, that's how you felt. I think it was decent of me to continue to consider you as a friend, and then to ask you to be my best man, and then what happens? You just leave.

Leo   Leave? When you married Sarah you had three novels behind you, enough money to pack in advertising, and you'd just bought a bloody posh flat in Kensington. Don't you understand, you were flying too high for me. I *was* green with envy, but Jesus I was also proud. I found myself unconsciously elevating my social status by mentioning you. You were the only person I knew who'd actually made it. You were my goddamn hero not my friend anymore and I knew, even if you didn't, that if I were to continue to see you and have to slot into your life around agents, publishers, foreign literature festivals and famous celebrities I'd eventually come to hate you, but look at us now. We're sitting down talking, we still like each other, we've got memories, we can laugh and joke, that's what I wanted to preserve, Larry, and that's why I 'left' as you put it. I knew that when things calmed down we'd occasionally get back together and, well, here we are, and you're no longer burning the furious early fuse, you're calmer and more collected, and maybe I am too.

Larry (*laughs*)   Calmer, more collected! Leo, I'm sloshed. And didn't you hear me, I'm broke, I'm washed up as a writer.

Leo   I don't believe you. You feel tired, and life has become repetitive. Accept it, Larry, for it's quite common. I've read a book about it. You are trying to dramatize it, to make it appear a crisis. In fact, the greatest crisis in a writer's life is to begin to write. That's the ultimate act of courage and I lacked conviction. I envied you for you made me realize how conventional I was.

Larry   Damn, Leo, let's not talk about it.

Leo   Whatever you say, Larry. I just hope I haven't made things worse for you.

Larry (*laughs*)   I wish I had you to talk to more often. You talk sense. I don't know how you've managed to . . .

Leo   To keep the common touch. Easy, I never had any success. (*Stands.*) Listen, you better get some sleep. I'll fetch you some blankets. You just stretch out there.

Larry   No, don't worry about the blankets, I'll be fine. I'll snooze a while then drive back to Broadmoor. I'll see you either tomorrow or Sunday, depending on when I can get parole. And please apologize to Sadie. She's a good woman.

Leo   I know. I'm lucky.

Larry   You deserve it, Leo. You knew your limitations and didn't trouble fate.

Leo   'Night, Larry.

Larry   Sleep well.

He pours himself the rest of the Scotch and lies out on the settee.

Inner Voice   So you believe that, do you, Larry? That it's as simple as never ever having had any success? Rubbish. Lots of people have been successful and managed to keep their wife and children. No, I'm afraid there's something the matter with you, isn't there. I'll tell you what it is. Blind, burning, uncaring ambition, that you can pass off as a vocational necessity. Well, you can't kick two footballs at once, you should know that. Any fool could have told you that. If you must play with two footballs then one has to take priority.

Noisy bar.

Saul   Sorry to drag you away from your desk, Larry.

Larry   That's okay. I felt like a drink anyway.

Saul   How's it going? (*Pause.*) The novel, how's it going?

Larry   Slowly. Look Saul, what's the matter with you? Do you have some bad news?

Saul   No. It's just that I wanted to tell you before it got into the trade rags.

Larry   Tell me what?

Saul   I've taken on Paul Jenson, Alan Briers and Jane Summerton. But I want you to know that you're still my number one client.

Larry   Well, they're three big authors, Saul. Congratulations.

Saul   Well, there is a bit more to it than that. You see I've managed to get them pretty big advances from William Johnson.

Larry   And me?

Saul   You've not written anything since *The Autumnal Sun*, Larry. When you've done the next novel I'll try and move you too.

Larry   I see.

Saul   Hey, don't feel bad about it. I know how competitive you guys are over advances and stuff, but I've got to have a product to sell. When do you think you'll be ready?

Larry   Hell, Saul. I don't know. It's difficult. I've got Sarah chewing me up, and I've got commitments all over the place. I don't know. I'm trying.

Saul   Well, if you need to talk anything over, just call. You know where to reach me.

Larry   Yeah, I'll call you.

Bathroom. **Larry** *is brushing his teeth.*

Sarah   But I can't believe that Saul would do that to you. It's you who really got him going as an agent, and it's your success that's attracting other writers to him. These three make a dozen in the last year alone. He's going to have no time left for you. Larry, you've got to put your foot down. Threaten to go to another agent.

Larry   Who? Saul's the biggest now. Anywhere else is a step down.

Sarah   Larry, Saul's taking you for granted. They all are. You've got to say 'no' to some of these people. They're not interested in you or your peace of mind. It's just who you appear to be and what you can do for them. Tell them all to take a running jump.

Larry   Please, Sarah. I'm tired and I've got a plane to catch in the morning.

Sarah   Don't go.

Larry   I've got to. It's a big conference and I've never been to Turkey. I don't see why I shouldn't go.

Sarah   Because, Larry, you promised to take Helen and I to Devon, that's why.

Larry   Did I? (*Pause.*) I'm sorry.

Larry   Writer's notebook. December 1987. My New Year resolution is simple. No more PAs, actresses, journalists. I've got to work. Six years, nearly seven, without a novel. It's the novel form that will ensure my reputation. All else is just evasiveness. It was Thomas Hardy who said, 'it is not the vulgar applause at the outset – that comes to all – but the general feeling at the exit.' Well, I'm still a long way from the exit, even though I'm a little tired. Alright, a short rest, then on with the long-awaited seventh Larry Wilson novel.

An envelope is ripped open.

Sarah   Dear Larry, Thank you for the kind letter, and Happy New Year to you as well. I'm glad to hear that your seventh novel (do you have a title as yet?) is almost complete and that Saul has negotiated a large advance for you. You seem pleased with the work you have done, and it goes without saying that I look forward to reading the book. I'm afraid that Helen still does not ask after you, and when I raise the subject of her father she refuses to listen. Try not to worry, Larry. It seems to me indicative of how much she loves you. If she displayed indifference that, I think, would be cause for worry. Mummy and Daddy are very sad about what has happened, but want it to be known that you should still consider them your friends. Take care of yourself, Larry, and write well. I'm extremely pleased that you are back at your desk and hope that it will all continue to go smoothly. Regards, Sarah.

In car. Car drawing to a halt.

Inner Voice   Remember the letter to Sarah, Larry? Tremendous fiction. Seventh novel? Big advance? You've got to be joking. You should be grateful she's too well-bred to ask you about it. You've made a royal ass of yourself, haven't you?

Car stops. Car door opens and slams. **Larry** *starts to walk across the car park.*

Inner Voice   And now what? Back to this nonsense. You've got a headache, you feel and look terrible, and you've got to spend the whole day in this asylum. Well, I tried, but you wouldn't listen, would you.

Larry *stands in the corridor. He sighs deeply.*

Lucy   No peace for the wicked, eh?

Larry   Morning, Lucy. I'm afraid I'm not feeling my best. I've even forgotten where the seminar rooms are.

Lucy   Yes, you do seem a little lost. Fancy a coffee?

Larry   Lead the way.

Noisy dining room.

Lucy   You sit down. I'll get it. Sugar? Milk?

Larry   Just black coffee. And strong.

Lucy   Like that is it?

Larry   'Fraid so.

He moves across the dining hall.

Sarah   Morning, Larry.

Larry   Sarah.

Rudy   What about a good morning for me, man? Or is it just the girls you're dealing with.

Sarah   Sit down and join us, Larry.

Rudy   Yeah, man. Take the pressure off your fountain pen.

Larry   I'm having a coffee and a quick chat with someone else.

Rudy   Crucial move. That blonde chick looks sweet.

Lucy   Hi! Shall we all sit down here?

Larry   No, let's sit over there and finish what we were talking about.

Lucy   Oh, alright then. (*To* **Rudy** *and* **Sarah**.) See you later.

They move over and sit.

Larry   I find these things work better if I get to know you as individuals as soon as possible. Later on today we can break up into more sociable groups.

Lucy   That's okay, whatever you say. Did you get a chance to look at *A Russian Winter*?

Larry   Well, actually, I was anxious to talk about it with you. It's quite a remarkably optimistic piece of work.

Lucy (*laughs*)   You find it optimistic! My agent said it's so depressing that they might have to issue razor blades with the book.

Larry   Well, obviously, I've only read the opening two chapters, but it's still not that morbid. Have you ever tried Beckett?

Lucy   No, but I'm glad you don't find it depressing. Can I give the rest to you?

Larry   You must. I'm not sure if I'll be able to read it all this weekend, but I could always post it back to you, or if you live in London . . .

Lucy   I live in Notting Hill Gate.

Larry   Well, perhaps we can meet for a drink and I'll give it back to you then.

Lucy   I'd like that.

Larry   Good.

Lucy   Shall I bring the rest around to you this evening after the readings?

Larry   That's an idea. (*Pause.*) I think I'd better go and talk to these two.

Lucy   Okay. I'll see you later, Larry.

Larry *crosses to where* **Sarah** *and* **Rudy** *are sitting.*

Larry   I'm not going to interrupt. Just checking that you're both fine.

Rudy   Yes, man, I'm working on breaking down my script for you.

Larry   Excellent. Look, does anyone know where I might find a phone box?

Sarah   Well, why not just phone from the front office.

Larry   No, well, it's a private call.

Rudy   There's one by the toilets outside the bar. But it's not a phonecard phone. They don't have them out here in the wilds.

Phone box. **Larry** *is waiting for somebody to pick up the phone at the other end of the line.*

Larry   Oh for Christ's sake, come on.

An answering machine clicks on.

Saul   This is the Saul Le Witt Literary Agency. If we can do anything to help you then leave your name, number and time and date of calling . . . Beep!

Larry   Saul, this is Larry. I'm at this place called Weston Lodge. I'll try you again, but things are closing in on me. I'll explain later.

He puts down the phone.

Roger   Oh, Larry, they said I might find you here. Can we step into the bar for a quick drink? I'd like to talk over a few things with you.

Bar.

Larry   And a sherry for you, Roger.

Roger   I know it's quite unusual to drink sherry before lunch but it's an old habit I picked up from my father.

Larry   I haven't got much time. You said you wanted to talk.

Roger   Yes, about my career.

Larry   What career?

Roger (*laughs*)   What career! Well, I don't mean my one as a captain of industry.

Larry   You still don't want to show me anything you've written?

Roger   I've got a letter here from a drama producer, Mike De Lissier. I told you, he's at Broadcasting House, sorry, BH. He likes my stuff a lot, but feels that the longer descriptive pieces, the bits between the dialogue, are the best parts of my plays. That's led me to think more and more of the novel. What do you think?

Larry   Look, Roger, I don't know who this man is. If you want me to tell you how to write, then you'll have to show me something. I'm not a clairvoyant.

Roger   But, Larry, I know I can write. I just need an agent. I was wondering if I could maybe use your name. I mean, I know it's not everything it was but . . .

Larry   I beg your pardon.

Roger   Well, you have gone down a bit of late.

Larry   Roger, why don't you crawl back to your room and hang yourself?

Roger   Now steady on, old man. I didn't mean to be offensive.

Larry   No-hopers like you don't have to try to be offensive, you just are.

Roger   No-hopers? I think you're a bit sloshed if you don't mind my saying.

Larry   Do you honestly think I've got time to waste listening to you prattling on about some BBC hack who was in all likelihood trying not to hurt your feelings? I've met idiots like you in every conceivable corner of this country, the fool who thinks he can become a writer overnight. The fool who half-envies, half-abhors the man who has made a living out of it. Why don't you go away and write something, or just shut up. Go on, sod off, I've had enough of you. I've got my business to sort out. And I need another drink.

Gets up and crosses to the bar.

Large Scotch and ice. No, make it a double double.

Barman   Double ice?

Larry   Double bloody everything. And some change for the phone.

Phone box. **Larry** *is waiting for somebody to pick up the phone at the other end of the line. An answering machine clicks on.*

Saul   This is the Saul Le Witt Literary Agency. If we can do anything to help you then leave your name, number and time and date of calling . . . Beep!

Larry   Saul, for Christ's sake, where are you?

Doris   Mr. Wilson?

Larry   Gotta go now. Call you later.

He puts down the phone.

Doris   I'm afraid you've missed lunch. Can I get you a sandwich?

Larry   No thanks, Mrs Simmonds. I'll manage.

Doris   Gerald's just the same. Never stops to think of his stomach. Well, anyway, the video is all set up and they're waiting.

Larry   I'll be right over. I'll just finish my drink.

Doris   Would you like a black coffee?

Larry   No thanks. I won't be a minute.

Doris   Well, we'll be waiting. I'll see you in the television lounge.

She walks off. **Larry** *goes back to the bar.*

Barman   Another double double?

Larry   No, it'll have to be quick. A single. No, make it a double single.

Barman   A double?

Larry   Whatever you like.

Television lounge. We hear a VCR click on. Then South Bank Show *music.*

Melvyn Bragg   Good evening. Tonight we feature one of Britain's most successful writers, a young man who although only thirty-three is publishing his sixth novel, *The Autumnal Sun*. Incredibly enough it was over a decade ago that we were first introduced to the name of Lawrence Wilson, his cherubic face peering out from the dust jacket of his first and award-winning novel, *Windmill Watching*. Today Lawrence Wilson lives in London with his wife and small daughter, and I caught up with him before he began a nationwide tour to promote the novel that many feel will, in four weeks' time, result in his being the youngest recipient of the Booker Prize.

Pete   Did you win it, Larry?

Lucy   Wasn't it Iris Murdoch? Or V. S. Naipaul? It usually is.

Melvyn Bragg   Larry, tell me a little about the genesis of *Windmill Watching*. After all it seems to be a remarkably assured novel for such a young man, and despite its coming at the end of the sixties it avoids being categorized as a hippie tome. In fact, it looks forward to the meaner, but rather more practical seventies.

Doris (*whispers*)   You look very handsome there.

Larry   Thank you.

Rudy   Don't look like there's too much action in this movie, baby.

Doris   Can you be quiet please. We're trying to watch Larry.

Larry (*whispers*)   Perhaps you might send somebody to knock on my door at four. I've got some reading to do before the next therapy session.

Doris   Yes, I'll do that, Larry.

Larry (*gets to his feet*)   Thanks.

Bedroom. Door closes. The sound of a drink being poured.

Inner Voice   That's it, take a drink. You can't look at that tape can you, Larry. And I don't blame you. That film was the beginning of the end. You really thought you'd arrived.

Larry   But it's form that's the 'sine qua non' of writing. How one deals with form will ultimately determine how you'll be judged. Am I making sense?

Director   Okay, cut! That's a good out.

Melvyn Bragg   Thanks, Larry. I really enjoyed interviewing you. I think Ron will need some shots of us walking in your garden then we can wrap.

Larry   Maybe we can keep in touch. Have dinner occasionally.

Melvyn Bragg   I'd like that, but it'll have to be after this series. I'm away to America for a Vonnegut special, then down to Argentina to do a documentary on the legacy of Borges. But I'll call you.

Larry   Well, whatever. No rush.

Melvyn Bragg   I think you're the one who'll be busy though. Ladbrokes have you down as the Booker favourite.

Larry   Come on, Melvyn, what are we, greyhounds? You know the score with all that crap.

Melvyn Bragg   Well, I wouldn't be surprised if you won. *The Autumnal Sun* is a damn good novel.

Larry   Thanks, but I'm not sure if I need all that media overkill.

Melvyn Bragg (*laughs*)   You've got it already. After all, what are we doing here? And believe me, once the serious attention arrives it won't go away unless you hide from it, and somewhere where we can't find you.

Inner Voice   Did you hide, Larry? No way, not Lawrence Wilson. Never occurred to you. Never gave yourself any time to think, did you, old man. Stopped reading, just skimmed books; watched video films and television programmes on fast forward; couldn't go to the cinema for there were no intermissions to leave in; theatre? Forget it, too slow. You didn't need to earn £100 for the odd *Guardian* or *Kaleidoscope* review, but you did them for you worried that your public might forget you, and you're still worried, aren't you?

Larry   Writer's notebook. September 1981. Melvyn Bragg has just left. He thinks *The Autumnal Sun* might win the Booker. It occurs to me that literature in the late twentieth century is a business, like football or modelling. I'm a performer. There's no use saying Shakespeare, or Van Gogh, or Michaelangelo didn't have agents. They would have today. Can you see anybody missing out on ten per cent of the Sistine Chapel?

Shop doorbell rings.

Sadie   Don't tell me you still haven't found the place?

Sarah   No, I found it alright. It's just that . . . tell me, are you married to Leo?

Sadie   Yes, I am. And you're Sarah, aren't you. Larry Wilson's ex-wife.

Sarah   That's me alright.

Sadie   I thought so. I'll get Leo for you.

Lounge.

Leo   Sarah, of course you were going to upset him. It's a hell of a shock for him to see you again after three years.

Sarah   But what was I supposed to do? Publish without letting him at least have a chance to read it and talk to me about it?

Leo   But will it make any difference what he says?

Silence.

No, of course not. Sarah, just go ahead and publish. If it's the truth and it hurts him then that's tough. It's your art, be true to it.

Sarah   I know. (*Pause.*) Leo, later this evening I'm going to catch a train back to London. I just wanted to say 'hi' before I left.

Leo   Well, for what it's worth I think you're doing the right thing. Larry will just have to work this one out for himself. He's jealous, proud, hurt, all of these things. Your presence is just confusing him even further.

Sarah   I know. I really don't want to be another problem for him.

Leo   Well you're his ex-wife and the mother of his child. You've got no choice in the matter. You'll always be a problem.

Sarah   I suppose you're right.

Leo   I am right. But tell me. Are you happy? Is life without Larry making you happier?

Sarah   Listen, I still feel for him. It's only natural, I can't help it.

Leo   He needs help, Sarah. He turned up here drunk at two o'clock this morning.

Sarah   Two o'clock?

Leo   You go back to London and I'll talk to him.

Sarah   Did he ask about us? I wondered if the three of us being together again would bring out his old suspicions.

Leo   He doesn't know, Sarah. And it was . . . well, it was . . .

Sarah   You don't have to say it, I know. It was a short, pleasant, but meaningless affair. I once half-confessed to him and told him I was friendly with a child psychologist called Theo.

Leo   Theo?

Sarah (*laughs*)   It's the best I could come up with. I suppose it's almost Leo.

Leo (*laughs*)   Pretty damned close, I'd say.

Sarah   Are *you* happy, Leo?

Leo   Sadie is a wonderful girl. And I'm sure your Brian's a wonderful man.

Sarah   Which just leaves Larry. Typical Larry. Always the centre of attention.

Leo   Don't worry, I'll speak with him.

They kiss.

Take care, Sarah.

Lecture room.

Larry   Okay, who's first to read?

Silence.

Well, come on, one of you must have something that you want to share with the others. I told you yesterday, writing's a very lonely profession. It's good to interchange ideas with others. Shall I nominate somebody?

Rudy   I'll start. I've got this idea for a film. A movie called *The Avenger* and Larry's suggested that I turn it into a story first. It's about a guy called Winston whose brother gets beaten up bad by the cops and dies so he goes out to avenge his death in Handsworth and blows away a dozen Feds before they catch up with him.

Roger   It sounds like childish nonsense.

Sarah   Shouldn't we all give Rudy a chance to read some. I heard a little in the dining room this afternoon and it's actually very good.

Rudy   I'm not sure I want to read it out. It's not ready yet. But I've got a poem. I wrote it last year. It goes like this.

> Do you know how it feels to be away
> Away from those who love you
> Do you know how it feels to know
> To know that they'll never see you again.
> They said the streets were paved with gold
> That the buildings would be magnificent and old
> That although the winter wasn't good
> A man could and would
> Make a life in this place
> And my mom believed every word.
> Do you know how it feels to be away
> Away from those who know you
> Do you know how it feels.

Stan   Is that it?

Rudy   Yeah.

Stan   Well, I liked it a lot. Much better than *The Avenger*.

Rudy   It's about my mum. She died last year.

Sarah   It's very moving, Rudy. Excellent.

Larry   Anybody else have anything else to say about it?

Lucy   Can I have a copy?

Rudy   Yeah, I'll write you one out.

Roger   It's a limerick more than a poem, isn't it?

Pete   Why don't you shut your face.

Lucy   Can I read something now? It's from my novel, *A Russian Winter*. All you have to know is that Masha, a nineteen-year-old peasant girl, has just been raped by Sacha, a landowner. She's sad.

Stan   I'll bet she bloody is.

Lucy   'Masha touched herself and felt the blood oozing thick down the inside of . . .'

Roger   Alright! Just wait a minute, I've had enough.

Rudy   What do you mean you've had enough?

Lucy   How dare you interrupt!

Roger   I'm sick to death of women and Blacks getting away with third-rate tripe just because they're supposed to be under-privileged. They're no worse off than I was, and I've made something of my life coming from a poor north-eastern background. And don't anybody dare call me a fascist; I was at Aldermaston, but why should I have to listen to this filth, this violence and menopausal nonsense?

Pete   I told you once and I ain't gonna tell you again.

Roger   What are you going to do? Serenade me with your guitar or bash me over the head with it? Oh, yes, very mature indeed. I heard you this afternoon trying to set *The Waste Land* to music, very commendable. If Eliot had wanted to write musicals he'd have rung up Rodgers and Hammerstein and got a proper songwriter to do it.

Rudy   You're a goddamn racist, man. Come on, call me a name and make my day.

Roger   There we go, appropriating the easy slogan as usual. (*Laughs.*) Me, a racist? Do you know how many of your people I employ from Pakistan, Africa, West Indies, all over the place.

Rudy   I've never been anywhere near the West Indies. I'm from the Midlands.

Roger   Well, then, talk like a Brummie instead of some chocolate John Wayne.

Stan   I wanted to read my whippet stories out but I'm not sure I do now.

Lucy   I'm not even sure I want to be in the same room as you, Roger.

Larry   Well, that's it then. Everyone is going home now are they?

Sarah   I'm sorry, Larry, but you'll just have to do something about that man.

Larry   Sarah, don't you dare tell me what to do! Especially in that whingeing tone of voice.

Rudy   I told you it was her in the film, man.

Sarah   Larry, please.

Pete   That's his wife?

Roger   Well, it's her I feel sorry for.

Sarah   I'm sorry, Larry, but he's spoiling the weekend for everybody. Why don't you ask him to leave?

Larry   Well, seeing as you know so much about it, Sarah, and seeing as you're a bloody professional writer now, you take over the damn weekend. I've had it, understand? I'm the one who is leaving.

He goes. He slams the door.

Stan   Don't cry, love.

Lucy   I'm not crying, but if I want to cry I'll bloody well cry.

She slams the door as she leaves.

Pete   If somebody had just had the sense to smack that prat over there in the gob we could have saved all this bother.

Bedroom. We hear a knock on the door.

Larry   It's open.

The door opens and closes.

Lucy   I'm sorry about what happened back there. It was my fault, I should never have started to read *A Russian Winter*.

Larry   It's not your fault, it's mine. I'm supposed to be in control of everything but I'm not in the right frame of mind for this.

Lucy   I'm sorry.

Larry   I told you, don't be sorry. It's nothing to do with you.

Lucy   I know you don't want to read my novel. It's not that great, but I can send you a copy of *The Vegetarian Cookbook*. Or bring you a copy.

Larry   I don't think that's a good idea.

Lucy   No? (*Pause.*) Oh well. I hope everything works out for you. You were excellent on the Melvyn Bragg show.

Larry   That was eight years ago.

Lucy   So what?

Larry   So everything.

Lucy   So nothing. Take care of yourself. If you're ever by Notting Hill Gate you know what to do.

Larry   I know.

Lucy *closes the door as she leaves.*

Goodbye.

Larry   Writer's notebook. February 1972. Just read *Wuthering Heights*. It's a novel pregnant with love. One day I would like to write a novel like that. I wonder if Emily Brontë was in love, or did she simply imagine the passion? My two novels, and this new one, *Freedom Train*, are a bit thin where it comes to emotions of the heart. I'll have to research this area later.

Car park. Car engine turns over but does not fire.

Larry   Damn!

Knock on the window. He rolls down the glass.

Sarah   Going my way?

Larry   I've been there before, remember?

Sarah   Well, then, you know what to expect.

She opens the door and throws her stuff onto the back seat. The engine starts and the car pulls away. We hear it fade into the distance.

Motorway. Car driving along.

Larry   Would you like to stop for a cup of tea or coffee? There's a service station in a few miles. Should be clear of Saturday night football hooligans by now.

Sarah   That would be nice. (*Pause.*) Leo was looking in fine shape, wasn't he? Told me he'd taken up jogging.

Larry   So you went to see Leo as well. I did wonder if you'd remember.

Sarah   Of course, I remember. He was your best man.

Larry   Had a good old chat about the literary wreck, did you?

Sarah   Why do you persist in seeing yourself in just literary terms? There's you, Larry the writer, and there's the more important you, Larry the man. I couldn't stomach a repeat viewing of that awful *South Bank Show* with you trying to be cool and impressive – and I might add succeeding. But you tried to kill Larry the man, didn't you?

Larry   Maybe I was afraid to nurture him. Afraid that I might not be able to write if I wasted time over him.

Sarah   And look what happened. You're just left with Larry the writer. Can he write? (*Pause.*) Well? What about the seventh novel? That was a lie, wasn't it, Larry?

Larry   Sarah, I told you I need a peaceful journey after the last twenty-four hours. In fact, after the last eight years. Just let me drive myself quietly down the motorway for the last time.

Sarah   What do you mean for the last time? You said for the last time, Larry.

Larry   I don't know. I didn't mean anything by it.

Sarah   Are you seeing anyone?

Larry   You mean like a shrink, a head doctor or something?

Sarah   No, I mean a girl. A woman. Have you got anyone?

Larry   What in hell's name has that got to do with you?

Sarah   Nothing. I suppose I'm just interested.

Larry   Well, I haven't. There, satisfied?

Sarah   Oh, Larry, come on, you're too good to be on your own. You're funny and kind underneath all that angst and self-flagellation. If you can't write at the moment then it's not the end of the world. Do something else until you straighten yourself out. You're a very fine teacher.

Larry   Are you trying to be funny?

Sarah   I'm not talking about that nonsense back there, although even there you were very good with most of them. Anyhow, if you don't want to teach then just do something else. Anything. Find Larry the man again. It's crazy to smother him, but it's unforgivable to not bother to try and revive him.

Larry   You sound like Leo.

Sarah   I sound like Sarah.

Larry   You imagine I don't know about you and Leo?

Sarah   Know what? I don't know what you're talking about.

Larry   It doesn't matter. I suppose I brought you together in a sense. As with most things it's my own fault. And then you ask me if I'm happy. (*Laughs.*) I haven't been happy in years.

Sarah   You were happy once.

Larry   Like hell I was.

Sarah   Yes, you were happy because you had something to say, but you'd also saved a little corner of your soul for me and Helen and a few others. But then you began to believe more and more in the competitive side of literature, and we weren't important any more. (*Pause.*) Has it ever occurred to you, Larry, that you became more interested in being a writer than in writing.

Larry   Maybe.

Sarah   Those people back there disturb you because, however ineptly they might express it, however ridiculous they might be, they actually think they have something to say. Their writing comes from real desire. That fool Roger, on the other hand, is just interested in becoming a writer; he's you without the curse of talent.

Larry *pulls up the car.*

Larry   I'm not sure about this service station. They vary a lot.

Sarah   Oh, Larry, for God's sake.

They get out of the car. **Larry** *speaks above the noise of the traffic.*

Larry   I've a quick phone call to make. I'll see you upstairs in the cafe.

Sarah   Alright.

Phone box. We hear a phone ringing out. Then somebody picks up at the other end.

Saul   Larry, where are you? Brands Hatch?

Larry   I'm on the motorway on my way back to London.

Saul   Didn't you get the message to ring me? I left it with some bozo woman.

Larry   No, I didn't. Anyway, what's the score.

Saul   No dice, Larry. You know to tell you the truth, they don't even know if they can make the picture at all now. Seems like the new Redford film has bombed. It's taken the bottom out of this year's new movie allocation. (*Pause.*) Are you there, Larry?

Larry   Yeah, I hear you. So they may pull altogether?

Saul   Looks that way. (*Pause.*) Look, I'm sorry but these LA film bastards are impossible. They tell even bigger lies than us, and in less sophisticated English.

Larry   Forget it, Saul. I'll talk to you Monday.

Saul   Okay, I'm sorry, Larry. I tried my best.

Larry *puts down the telephone and stands alone in silence.*

Voice   Hey, come on, mate! It's cold out here. Make another call or move out!

Motorway cafe. Noise of traffic whipping by.

Sarah   I got you tea, is that alright?

Larry   Thanks.

Sarah   Bad news.

Larry   I think I'll have to sell the house. Everything in fact. I'm bankrupt.

Sarah   Isn't there any other way?

Larry   Only the Mishima route.

Sarah   I wanted to talk to you about money, Larry. You see Brian and I are getting married. And I've got quite a large advance for my novel. You'll no longer have to pay me any alimony or child support.

Larry   Well, my, my. How things change. You were always the one knocking agents and publishing and large advances, and that kind of life.

Sarah   Larry, they're just people who work for me. I don't socialize with them. I'm polite, they're polite, they oil the wheels, they know their place. I know mine.

Larry   I see. (*Pause.*) I don't know why I pay any damned child support. I never see Helen.

Sarah   Helen is twelve now and . . .

Larry   I know how old she is!

Sarah   Keep your voice down! I think things will change when she realizes Brian and I are serious. She'll be interested in her real father again, and you can see her as often as you like.

Larry   Planning to drive her out by breeding with this buck are you?

Sarah   I *am* having a baby, Larry.

Larry   Oh for heaven's sake, at your age?

Sarah   I'm thirty-eight, Larry. I'm trying to be reasonable with you. I loved you. That means something, to me at least. I'd like you to be happy again.

Larry   Happy, happy, happy. What the hell is this happy? (*Pause.*) What's your novel called?

Sarah   *That Dizzy Feeling.* I know it's not very good. You were always the one for titles. *Freedom Train* was my favourite.

Larry   We met that year. At the writers' workshop I was giving. God you were . . .

Sarah   Ripe for the picking? I wasn't, but I soon was. 'Writing Fiction', a workshop with Lawrence Wilson. (*Pause.*) Will you do something for me, Larry.

Larry   What?

Sarah   You'll have some money left over from selling the house. Take it and travel. Blow it all, you deserve to, then come back and start all over again. I've got faith in you as a man, Larry. If you want to know the truth, it was the writer I divorced, the part of you that grew to need constant massaging, and heavy spotlights shone on it. The part of you that loved being lied to by Saul and all those other hangers-on, the part of you that glowed in the company of sycophants and phonies. (*Pause.*) Don't look at me like that. It's not too late. If it's literary races you believe in then you're well ahead of the field. You can afford to slow down to a standstill. Believe me, you owe it to yourself. And to Helen. And if you never start up writing again, well, that's a chance you'll have to take. A risk, but a risk I'm sure Helen would appreciate. Another tea?

Larry   Please.

Sarah *gets up.*

Larry   Sarah. (*Pause.*) I would like to read your book.

Sarah   You would?

Larry   You weren't the only one with that dizzy feeling.

Sarah   I'm glad to hear it. (*Pause.*) Larry, why don't you come down to see Helen next weekend. Surprise her.

Larry   You think she'd want that?

Sarah   I'll send Brian off somewhere. Just turn up as though you've come to collect the manuscript.

Larry   Next weekend?

Sarah   We'll be waiting for you. Here.

She opens her purse.

I meant to give this to you. It's a photograph of Helen taken at last year's pantomime. She played Aladdin. She's got your nose and mouth, Larry.

Larry   She's always had my nose and mouth. And don't talk to me as though I've never clapped eyes on her. She's my daughter, not some Vietnamese boat-child I'm about to adopt.

Sarah   You did say tea didn't you?

Larry   Yes, tea.

Sarah *goes off.*

Bedroom

Helen   Where are we going, Daddy?

Larry   I think you and Mummy are going to Grandma and Grandpa's. Daddy's going to a conference in Barcelona.

Helen   Can I come too?

Larry (*forced laughter*)   No, darling, but I'll see you soon.

Larry   Writer's notebook. January 1986. I sense Sarah is going to leave me. I don't know when, but the situation is becoming intolerable. Quote. Lawrence Durrell. 'The Artist's work constitutes the only satisfactory relationship he can have with his fellow men since he seeks his real friends among the dead and the unborn.' Unquote.

Sarah *returns and sits.*

Sarah   Tea. One sugar.

Larry   Lawrence Durrell. He knows the price of the ticket.

Sarah   Lawrence Durrell? What on earth are you talking about? You always said Lawrence Durrell wrote garbage.

Larry   Did I? (*Pause.*) Yes, I did, didn't I.

Sarah   Larry, you really do need a break.

Larry   Don't worry. I'll get one. (*Pause.*) Yes, he did. He wrote rubbish. What the hell does he mean 'among the dead and the unborn'? What are we, gravediggers?

Sarah   Larry, I can't follow what you're talking about, but remember if you want to impress Helen next week ask for coffee. She hates tea.

Larry   Coffee, not tea.

Sarah   It'll be a good start. (*Pause.*) Larry, you are listening to me, aren't you? You will come?

Larry   Okay, I'll be there alright. I won't forget. Coffee not tea. Send me another picture, Sarah. I want to see the child as she is, not dressed up in some make-believe garb with her face plastered in muck.

Sarah   I'll send you another picture. I'll send it off on Monday.

Larry   Good. (*Pause.*) Good. (*Pause.*) Good. 'Making real friends among the dead and the unborn'? He's got to be joking.

Noise of motorway traffic whipping by.

A Kind of Home: James Baldwin in Paris

Broadcast Details

BBC Radio 4, 9 January 2004. Directed by Ned Chaillet.

Characters (in order of appearance)

Jean-Claude
Interviewer
Jimmy
Mother
Alice
Eugene
Richard Wright
Mrs Wilkes
Theo
Gina
Barman
Man
Nurse
French Female Voice
French Male Voice
Hotel Owner
Clerk
Waiter
American men
Agent

Notes on the Play

As its title indicates, this play revolves around James Baldwin, a writer who has had a major influence on Caryl Phillips's work. The narrative focuses on the decisive years that the Harlem-born artist spent in Paris at the beginning of his writing career, hoping to escape racist America. Told by Jean-Claude, Baldwin's lover at the time, *A Kind of Home* evokes Baldwin's interactions with several people, including famous writer Richard Wright.

Together with *A Long Way from Home*, Phillips's 2008 radio drama devoted to Marvin Gaye, and *Dinner in the Village*, his 2011 radio play dramatizing the relationships between Richard Wright and C. L. R. James, and their respective wives, this play crystallizes his interest in illuminating the lives of artists from the African diaspora, a concern also central to his 2005 novel *Dancing in the Dark*, centring on Broadway artiste Bert Williams. *A Kind of Home* also provides a compelling insight into Phillips's way of approaching biographical fiction, which he most recently illustrated again in his 2018 novel *A View of the Empire at Sunset*, a narrative that dramatizes the early life of the famous Caribbean-born writer Jean Rhys.

Scene One

Ext. Street. Paris. Day.

The high, rich sound of an African-American choir singing gospel music mixes through until we hear the noise of street traffic. Cars swish by. Raised French voices. The occasional pair of stilettos against the sidewalk. The blaring of car horns. **Jean-Claude** *is sitting at a Left Bank cafe.*

Jean-Claude   It's a different Paris today. Louder. Perhaps less charming. But it's still Paris. Turn back the clock half a century and I'd recognize the same buildings. The same cafes, the same bars. Hell, in fact, almost the same faces. I was a younger man then, and so was he. (*Laughs.*) Okay, I was a teenager. I was seventeen. And he was in his mid-twenties. We met, of course, in a bar. That was how it began, two lonely boys in Paris trying to find their way in the world. And now he's gone, and I'm a grandfather living . . . well, living a different life. What you might call a more conventional life. What he would call the life of a 'square'. (*Laughs.*) If he were here today he would look at me with those big eyes of his and say, 'Baby, but why are you living like them? You're better than them. We both are.' It would be half plea, half accusation, but he'd say, 'Baby, don't be a square.' There are people in this city who might still recognize his name. James Baldwin. The famous Black American author. The man who wrote *Go Tell It on the Mountain. The Fire Next Time. Another Country. No Name in the Street.* In his time the social and literary conscience of Black America. And then there are others.

He mimics a French man.

'James who?' (*Laughs.*) James who? Let me tell you 'who'. A small, skinny pop-eyed Negro boy from New York City, James Baldwin. All the way from New York City, US of A. Back then I had no idea of the kind of world that he came from. He used to say 'cats around here don't understand me, but it doesn't matter as long as I understand them'. (*Muses.*) That was pretty much Jimmy's philosophy of life. 'Ignorant mothers.' I can still hear him whispering it under his breath, and then he'd laugh and life would go on. But that laughter came from a difficult place. It came from a place so dark, so deep that it took great courage to find it. Behind Jimmy's laughter there was great hurt, and in the end he let me see it. In the end he trusted me. This great writer . . . this great man . . . this lonely Negro boy in Paris . . . he trusted me. (*Pause.*) He loved me.

Scene Two

Ext. New York office. Day.

An **Interviewer** *sits behind a desk, onto which he tosses a file. He sighs.*

Interviewer   So you've waited tables, you've been an elevator boy, and you've worked in a munitions factory. These are coloured boys' jobs. I take it you've also shined shoes, been a Pullman car porter and served drinks at the Cotton Club.

(*Laughs. There is silence.*) Son, you do realize that none of this so-called 'experience' prepares you for white-collar work in a Manhattan office.

Jimmy   But I can do the job, sir. All I need is a chance.

Interviewer (*laughs*)   Boy, what do you think this is. 'Be nice to coloured people' week? Maybe you're thinking that I should sit you by the door so that everybody can see that we've got us a Negro boy on the payroll. Is that what you think?

Jimmy   No, sir.

Interviewer   You sweet on some white girl in the office? You know you can tell me, son. Which one is it?

Jimmy   Nothing like that, sir.

Interviewer   Maybe you think of her at night and touch yourself.

Jimmy   Maybe you should just get yourself some extra help to pick up this goddamn desk!

He tips up the **Interviewer**'s *desk and we hear the man cry out as he falls back out of his seat.*

Interviewer   Goddamn you, nigger.

We hear the door open and then slam. **Jimmy** *begins to run off up the street.*

Interviewer (*trying to get to his feet*)   Boy, you come back here, you hear me? Stop!

Scene Three

Int. Harlem apartment. Day.

Jimmy   I'm sorry, Momma, but I didn't get the job. Which means I don't have no money to help out with the kids.

Mother   Son, it don't matter. You'll get something. The main thing is that you don't give up.

Jimmy   You mean like my father.

Mother   Jimmy, your father didn't give up. He simply woke up one morning and he couldn't take it no more. We all have a breaking point, but some people don't see it until it's passed them by and it's too late. I don't want you to end up like your father, Jimmy. Crazy, shouting, angry.

Jimmy   Momma, I mean to be a writer. It's what I want, but I also know that I got to help you out. I don't want you scrubbing white people's floors forever.

Mother   Child, if I got to scrub the white man's floor from now until doomsday then I'll scrub. What I don't want is you putting your life on hold on account of me and the rest of the kids. You understand?

Jimmy   I hear you, Momma.

Mother   The oldest one always shoulders a lot of responsibility, Jimmy, and I'm proud of how you've taken it on. But enough is enough. You've got your own life too. You're not just a son and a brother. You're also a man, and don't you forget it.

Scene Four

Int. Greenwich Village bar. Night.

Light jazz music is playing and we are in a crowded, smoky bar.

Alice   What's the matter, Jimmy? Don't you want to meet my parents?

Jimmy   Do they want to meet me? Tell me, how many Negroes have they ever had in their Connecticut house? And baby, I'm talking about Negroes who don't clean or cook.

Alice   Why are you talking like this? Has something happened?

Jimmy   Baby, America happened.

Alice   Put down the glass, Jimmy. Look at me. Did something happen today? You can tell me.

Jimmy   I'm sorry. It's nothing. (*Pause.*) Your parents haven't done anything to me, it's just . . .

Alice   I understand, Jimmy. You can say it. It's just white people. But only some white people, Jimmy and you mustn't turn me into one of those people. (*Pause.*) Look, maybe you *should* go and see Richard Wright.

Jimmy   You mean because he has a white wife and maybe he can talk some sense into me?

Alice   No! Because you've sent him your work. He's the most famous Black writer in the world, you said so yourself. Everybody's read *Native Son* and *Black Boy*. Even my lily white Connecticut parents have read Richard Wright. Maybe he can help you find a publisher, or an agent, or something.

Jimmy   He can begin by helping me to get a decent job so that I can help my mother to feed my brother and sisters.

Alice   Here.

She opens her purse and takes out some money.

Take it, please. (*Pause.*) Jimmy, take the money. Just until you get a job. I'm not offering you charity.

Jimmy   Thanks. I'll pay you back.

Alice   I know you will. But it's okay. One day they'll be my family too. (*Pause.*) Jimmy?

Jimmy   Alice, I have to do something with my life. I can't live like this. America is turning me into an angry, bitter man. The type of person my father became. I don't want to live my whole life reacting to a country that is supposed to be my home, fighting everything and everybody. That simply ain't no way to live.

Alice   I know, Jimmy, I know.

Jimmy   But that's the thing, Alice. You don't know. I'm sorry but you can't know.

Alice   Isn't that your friend coming over here?

Eugene (*softly spoken*)   Hi. Jimmy. Alice. I thought I might find you here.

Alice   Sit down, Eugene. Let's get you a drink.

Eugene   Thanks. I'll just use the bathroom first. I won't be long.

He walks away.

Alice   What's the matter with him? He never likes it down here with us.

Jimmy   With us?

Alice   I mean he doesn't like it down here in the Village where *we* live – you and I, Jimmy – not where white people live. For God's sake stop trying to turn me into something I'm not.

Jimmy   I'm sorry.

Alice   When he comes back I think you should take him to where he feels more comfortable. He obviously needs to talk to you. I mean, he's not come down here to see me.

Jimmy   You want me to take him away? Like he's some kind of stray dog, is that it?

Alice   I want you to take him to where he'll feel more comfortable. For his sake. I'm thinking of Eugene, Jimmy.

Jimmy   Okay.

Alice   Jimmy, try to remember that we love each other. We're supposed to find strength in each other's presence.

Jimmy   I know, Alice. I know.

Scene Five

Ext. George Washington Bridge. Night.

Jimmy   Eugene, man, I love standing on the George Washington Bridge. You're in New York City, but you're also out of it. Like you can admire the city and still breathe.

Eugene   It's so quiet here, Jimmy. I wish it could be like this all the time.

Jimmy   Take it easy, Eugene. We're both going to be writers. I keep telling you that, but if it's going to happen then we've got to be patient.

Eugene   Jimmy, I don't have no place to live. The landlord threw my stuff out in the street and I'm back in Harlem living in one room with my mother. Truth is, I'm running out of patience. I can't afford no more patience, Jimmy, everything is getting me down.

Jimmy   Baby, you got to keep on going and keep your eyes on the prize.

Eugene   What prize? I got no place to live, and I can't get no job. I'm a grown man and my own country don't got no use for me, or for you, Jimmy. In this world all I got is my momma and you, Jimmy. (*Pause.*) Hold me, Jimmy.

Jimmy   Hey, knock it off, Eugene. How many times I told you, man. You gotta keep your hands to yourself.

Eugene   Jimmy, why can't the two of us go off some place together? I know we can make it work.

Jimmy   Eugene, Eugene, Eugene. (*Pause.*) Tomorrow I'm gonna come by and see you at your momma's place. Trust me we're both gonna find jobs, and you'll find some place to stay and we'll write our books. It's all gonna be just fine. But you have to learn to go a little easy on yourself.

Scene Six

Int. New York House. Day.

We hear a doorbell ring out. A beat of silence and then we hear footsteps scurrying down some stairs.

Wright   Hold on, I'm coming.

We hear the sound of the door opening.

Ah, young Mr Baldwin, I presume. Come in. Come in.

Jimmy   Thank you, Mr Wright. I'm sorry for bothering you.

Wright   Little man, there's no need to apologize. Sit down. Sit down. As you can see I'm packing for Paris so you just caught me in time. A little extended visit to the land of liberty, equality, fraternity. The other day my daughter needed to use the bathroom, but one of those fancy department stores on Fifth refused to let her. Didn't matter that I was Richard Wright, that I could have bought half the place. The poor little girl had to suffer physically and emotionally. Little man, we can't do this to our own children. What we're living through is painful enough for us. So hello, Paris for this boy.

Jimmy   I see.

*We hear **Wright** continuing to pack. Moving boxes, etc.*

Wright   I was beginning to think that you'd abandoned your manuscript. It's good, little man. It's got potential.

Jimmy   I'm trying to write about our condition without any . . . without any . . .

Wright (*laughs*)   Protest. Isn't that what you're trying to say. You want to write without hollering your message from the rooftops like me. Richard Wright, world-famous author of *Native Son*. Protest writer.

Jimmy   Well, not exactly.

Wright   You want to be an artist, not a protest writer. It's all over your manuscript. And actually, that's what's wrong with it. All this artsy, sensitive stuff is not what our people need right now. Commitment, little man, that's what it's all about. You following me?

Jimmy   Yes, sir.

Wright (*laughs*)   I got you a fellowship. Not much, but enough money so that you can do some more work on your book.

Jimmy   Thank you, Mr Wright. I didn't expect this.

Wright   I know you didn't expect it, which is why I got it for you. But you don't let me down now. You make sure you articulate our people's situation. We need young brothers like you to tell it like it is. Nothing wrong with writing because you're angry and hurt. Nothing wrong with letting the man know that we're not happy with our lot.

Jimmy   Yes, sir. I understand.

Wright   Guess while I'm over there in Paris I'll have to keep my eyes open and check out the literary pages of the *Trib*. (*Laughs*.) Little man's coming right up behind me ready to knock me off my perch.

Scene Seven

Int. Greenwich Village bar. Night.

Light jazz music is playing.

Jimmy   But I thought you'd be happy that I won a fellowship.

Alice   But, Jimmy, you don't like his work. You can't take money from him. I wanted you to go to him for ideas and encouragement. Not charity.

Jimmy   It's not money from him, it's a fellowship from a foundation. You wanted me to show him my work, and he liked it enough to get me a fellowship. It's not *his* money! Dammit, I thought you'd be pleased. You want to control me, Alice? Is that it? You want to be my white fairy godmother?

Alice   You're always so angry, Jimmy. No wonder my parents don't want to meet you. (*Pause*.) I was going to tell you.

Jimmy   Your parents don't want to meet me, then to hell with your parents.

Alice   Excuse me.

Jimmy   I said to hell with your parents and everybody like them. I don't need to meet your goddamn stupid parents.

Alice   How dare you . . .

Jimmy   I need money, and I won this fellowship through the evidence of my work and I don't give a damn if Richard Wright or Satan himself recommended me, the money will help me get away from people like you. Yes, you!

Alice   Then you better be going on your way, Jimmy, because you don't even treat me like a woman. I've no idea what it is you think we're doing together anyway.

She stands.

My father's right. I don't need an unemployed Greenwich Village dreamer in my life.

She moves to leave.

You need to join the army, Jimmy. Or get a trade. You need to do something with your sad little life before you end up as little more than a lonely coloured dreamer.

Jimmy (*pointedly*)   I won a fellowship.

Alice   Jimmy, take control of your life. Stop dreaming. Stop waiting for handouts. Prizes, grants. I love you enough to tell you, that's no life for you. You're a bigger man than this, Jimmy, and despite everything, I want only the best for you.

Jimmy   I know you do, Alice. I know you do.

Scene Eight

Int. Rooming house in Harlem. Day.

Jimmy *is standing in a stairwell and knocking on a door.*

Jimmy (*shouts*)   Mrs Wilkes! (*Pause.*) Mrs Wilkes!

We hear a door slowly opening.

Mrs Wilkes   Boy, I'm not deaf. Where have you been? For a whole week my Eugene looked for you. Every day. Morning, noon and night. Every day my Eugene looked for you.

Jimmy   I'm sorry but I had to solve some problems downtown. Where's Eugene? He find a place?

Mrs Wilkes (*snaps*)   Where's Eugene? Where's Eugene? Everybody left my boy and he's gone. Does that matter to you, son? Eugene jumped off the George Washington Bridge. He's gone. My boy's gone from me while you had to solve some problems downtown!

Jimmy   Eugene's dead?

Mrs Wilkes   How many more young men are we going to lose? Is your momma ready to lose you? My Eugene's gone! Gone, child. He felt like every one had given up on him.

Jimmy   Mrs Wilkes . . .

Mrs Wilkes   Son, I know it ain't your fault. But my heart can't take no more talk of Eugene. You hear me? No more. No more. You better go now, boy. You go along.

She shuts the door and we hear it echo in the silence.

Eugene   Jimmy, for a moment I was flying. I could see the lights of the city, Jimmy, spread out all in front of me like lights twinkling on a Christmas tree. It was real pretty. Then when I looked down before me I could see the lights reflected in the black water, all silver and sparkling and beautiful. I was flying, Jimmy, and I was free. At last I was free, and I was thinking of how much I wanted you to be there flying with me, Jimmy. Arms spread out, raggedy clothes blowing and flapping in the wind, big watermelon-eating smile on my face, I was flying, Jimmy, and I was free.

Scene Nine

Ext. Street. Paris. Day.

We hear the noise of traffic. **Jean-Claude** *is still sitting at the Left Bank cafe.*

Jean-Claude   After Eugene's suicide Jimmy left New York for Paris. He took the money from his fellowship and the twenty-four-year-old James Baldwin bought a one-way ticket for France. He arrived in Paris in November 1948 with just $40 in his pocket. Jimmy brought with him his unfinished book and a great desire to succeed. He was hungry in all senses of the word. He was also lonely and disoriented for he had left behind his family and his friends. Here, in Paris, Jimmy immediately sought out the only person that he knew.

Scene Ten

Ext. Paris cafe. Day.

Wright   Hey, boy! You speak French yet? *Parlez-vous français?*

Jimmy   No, Mr Wright. I've just arrived in Paris.

Wright   Call me Richard. What's with this Mr Wright label? The French air is full of equality. Go on, boy. Breathe it. Fill up your lungs. How's that novel of yours? You still trying to write like a white man?

Jimmy   I don't think that . . .

Wright Aw, come on. I'm only joking, boy. Sit down, sit down. You found a nice hotel, I take it? Now all you got to do is get some food in that scrawny little body of yours, and find yourself a nice girl to give you some stability so you can write. You hear me, boy?

Jimmy Yes, sir.

Wright Some good solid female companionship, that's what you need. You don't need to be tom-catting about these boulevards like the other coloureds in France. I want to see you settled down. Now, my wife knows how to cook, clean and provide me with the comforts that a writer needs in order to write the books that will change the world. Now, you do want to change the white man's world, don't you?

Jimmy I suppose so.

Wright Turn it up on its goddamn head and shake some sense into it. But in order to do that you need some tranquillity, and only a solid ordered life with a good wife to support you is going to give that to you. This bohemian, drifting, easy style of living is just going to make things harder for you, boy. You mark my words.

Scene Eleven

Int. Hotel. Night.

Jimmy *is asleep in a dingy hotel room. He hears the sound of loud banging on his door and shouting from the hallway.*

Theo Hey, Jimmy, baby. That you?

Jimmy Theo?

He climbs from his bed and opens the door.

Theo Jimmy, baby. Where's Alice, man?

Jimmy We're finished. She's back in the Village.

Theo Oh man, Greenwich Village. Don't remind me of the past. That's over. That's old. Paris, this is where it's at. It's real here, cool people all hanging out together. I've got a beautiful Swedish chick named Gina who's over here learning French, man. They all speak it. But you don't really need anything except bedroom French. And, man, if you don't want to bother with the language thing then there's always co-eds, or English girls. I mean this place is like heaven, baby.

Jimmy I gotta get out of this hotel. It's too expensive.

Theo Man's gotta watch his money in Paris. Too much good living then bam!, suddenly ain't got no bread for a few days. I got my pop sending me a monthly cheque and I'm only just getting by. We'll get you a cheaper place, but first you gotta come and meet Gina. Hang with us, man. Swing with us, Jimmy.

Scene Twelve

Int. Paris bar. Night.

Jimmy, **Theo** *and* **Gina** *are partying in a noisy Paris bar on the Left Bank. Their voices are raised to make themselves heard.*

Jimmy   Theo, I don't give a damn what Mr Richard Wright says, this protest literature don't make no goddamn sense.

Theo   But that's what people want to hear from you coloured writers. I mean what's your problem, man? Do the '*Uncle Tom's Cabin* thing', make some money, then you can go back to your real work.

Jimmy (*pounds the table*)   I do *not* need money that badly. How much do you think my soul is worth, Theo? I got a starving family in America – they're America's family – but I cannot debase my art, not even for them. Literature is too beautiful to be hijacked by that kind of semi-political bullshit.

Theo   Take it easy, man. It's just a suggestion.

Gina   I have a typewriter that Jimmy can use. I don't see why coloured people should have to write only this protest.

Theo   Gina, it's the fashion, baby. It's an American thing. Me, I'm gonna write a book that will blow this capitalist bullshit right out of the water. Karl Marx and FDR are on a desert island. Gradually they get so that they're digging each other.

He starts to laugh. Then **Jimmy** *and* **Gina** *start to laugh.*

Theo   Baby, love begins to blossom on my little desert island.

Gina   Theo, why are you always so silly? Why are you never serious about anything?

Theo   I'm serious about you, honey. (*Kisses her.*) Maybe you got a friend for Jimmy? He's got a broken heart that needs mending. Double quick. Ain't that right, Jimmy?

Jimmy   I'm learning to live with my broken heart, Theo. There are people all around us living with broken hearts. We just don't notice them, my friend. We just don't see them.

Scene Thirteen

Int. Working men's cafe. Dawn.

Jimmy, **Theo** *and* **Gina** *are in a working men's cafe having breakfast. They are tired after a long night drinking.* **Gina** *is ordering some more coffee in French.*

Jimmy   *Café* is coffee, right?

Gina   That's right, Jimmy. Theo doesn't want to even make an effort to learn.

Theo   We saved these people in two wars. If it wasn't for us they'd all be speaking German so the least they can do is learn English.

Gina (*irritated*)   You are so bloody American sometimes.

Jimmy   Who are the people in this cafe?

Theo   The dispossessed, brother. The French working masses, and the Arabs. Those that the system chewed up and spat out. They don't have the American system over here. You know 'give me your huddled masses'. It's all messed up.

Jimmy   You think we're better than them? That our 'system' is better?

Theo   Hell, yes. We're Americans, Jimmy.

Jimmy   And some of us are more American than others.

Gina   Jimmy is right. Not everything in America is good. Surely there are some bad things about your country.

Theo   But when we're good, we're better than everybody else. Ain't that true, Jimmy?

Jimmy (*laughs*)   Theo, life isn't that simple my friend. There's no winners and losers. Only pain, suffering and a little loss, and love, who knows what's next on the agenda. It's difficult to tell. It's what makes the whole thing so beautiful, my friend. Really beautiful.

Scene Fourteen

Int. Hotel room. Day.

We hear the sound of typewriter keys clacking away.

Gina   You're always working, Jimmy. Locked up in this silly hotel room. Everybody is asking after you.

Pause. **Jimmy** *continues to type.*

Gina   Am I disturbing you?

Jimmy   Gina, I don't mind if you sit here, but I need to write. I don't have no rich daddy to go back to; a man who'll give me a job at the bank and pretend that my bohemian days in Paris were just a game.

Gina   Has Theo done something to offend you? Is that why you're hiding out here working on your novel?

Jimmy (*laughs*)   Baby, I'm not hiding out. I'm just trying to feed myself and my family. And this, my dear, is not my novel. This is an essay about Mr Richard Wright.

Gina   You're writing about him?

Jimmy   No, no, no. You can't read it until it's finished.

He starts to type again. He pauses.

Gina, don't you have anywhere else to go?

Gina   I like you, Jimmy. I came to this country so that I didn't have to settle for being just a wife and a mother, and hate myself back in Sweden. Here, in Paris, I can hide in another language, drink too much, be who I want to be. Like you, Jimmy, I'm escaping towards me – whoever that might be. But, Jimmy, have you told Theo that you don't like girls? That you like boys. (*Pause.*) No, I didn't think so. Perhaps you should tell him. It's no big thing. I'm not here because I want anything from you, Jimmy. Like I said, I like you. That's okay, isn't it?

Scene Fifteen

Int. Studio. **Jimmy** *reading.*

Jimmy   'For Bigger's tragedy is not that he is cold or Black or hungry, not even that he is American, Black; but that he has accepted a theology that denies him life, that he admits the possibility of his being sub-human and feels constrained, therefore, to battle for his humanity according to those criteria bequeathed him at his birth. But your humanity is our burden, our life; we need not battle for we need only do what is infinitely more difficult – that is, accept it . . .'

Scene Sixteen

Ext. Street cafe. Day.

Theo *is sitting at the cafe reading from* **Jimmy***'s piece.*

Theo   '. . . the failure of the protest novel lies in its rejection of life, the human being, the denial of his beauty, dread, power, in its insistence that it is his categorization alone which is real and which cannot be transcended.' Man, this shit is heavy, Jimmy.

Jimmy   You got a problem with 'heavy'?

Theo   I mean, this is an all-out attack on Wright, man. We came here to work on our novels and live in peace with each other. You can't be writing stuff like this.

Jimmy (*shouts and bangs the table*)   Don't you ever tell me what I can and what I can't write!

Theo   Hey, take it easy, Jimmy.

Jimmy   I left America because too many people wanted to tell me what I should be doing and what I should not be doing. I refuse to live in your silly little box! I refuse to be defined by you!

He scrapes back his chair and stands up.

Theo   Hey, Jimmy! Jimmy, come on, man. Take it easy for heaven's sake.

Jimmy   You're all on the run, Theo. All of you so-called American artists here in Paris. Running from yourselves. Using Paris as a playground. Well, I never had the luxury of running from myself, and I'm not about to start now.

He begins to walk out.

Theo   Hey, Jimmy. Don't go. Why are you bringing all this racial heaviness into things. It was never like this in the Village.

Jimmy   It was always like this, Theo, it's just that you had the luxury of not noticing. I didn't travel across the Atlantic to continue the same discussion with Americans too blind to see the man beneath my skin, or too blind to see beyond the skin that masks their own corrupt manhood. Do not, Theo, talk to me about 'racial heaviness'. On this subject I am the teacher and you are the student.

Theo   Man, maybe you need to just stay clear of Americans, Jimmy. Seems like we just set you off.

Jimmy   Some Americans, my friend. Indeed some Americans do set me off. It's a terrible burden, don't you think?

Scene Seventeen

Int. Gay bar. Night.

Barman   Monsieur, I think that maybe you should not have another drink. You look terrible.

Jimmy   But that's how we, the wretched of the earth, are supposed to feel.

Barman (*laughs*)   You must sleep or your exotic charm will begin to abandon you.

*A **Man** approaches the bar.*

Man   Vin blanc, s'il vous plait.

(*To* **Jimmy**.) Can I buy you a drink?

Jimmy   That would be beautiful, baby.

Man   Do you call everybody baby?

Jimmy   Only those I can hold in my arms.

Man   Then you can call me baby.

Barman   Monsieur Baldwin, a Johnnie Walker?

Jimmy   Make that a large one. (*Laughs.*) My friend and I have a long night ahead of us.

Scene Eighteen

Int. Hotel bedroom. Night.

We hear **Jimmy** *being slapped and then kicked.* **Jimmy** *winces in pain.*

Jimmy   Please, no more. I can't take no more.

Man   You ask me for money like I am some cheap sugar daddy, isn't that what you Americans call it?

Jimmy   Baby, I did everything you wanted me to do.

Man   I should report you to the police so they will take away your residency card. We do not need filth like you in our country.

Jimmy   Where are you going? I cannot pay for this hotel room.

The door slams shut.

Please, don't leave me here.

Scene Nineteen

Int. Paris bar. Night.

The jazz is 'hot' and loud. **Theo** *sees* **Jimmy** *coming across the bar towards him.*

Theo   Jimmy! Over here.

Jimmy *comes closer.*

Theo   Oh my God, what happened to you?

Jimmy   Life in the Fourth Republic is not all liberty and equality for the darker brother. Any chance of a whiskey, Theo?

Theo (*to* **Waiter**)   Monsieur, another beer and a large Scotch.

Jimmy (*laughs*)   Still avoiding French?

Theo   I'm sorry about the things I said, Jimmy. You're right. I'm just wasting my time here.

Jimmy   You've got talent, Theo, if you apply yourself properly. You *can* write but you just . . .

Theo   Just love to party. I know. You're right.

Jimmy   You've got to do anything, absolutely anything, to get the book done and get it out the house. You know that, Theo.

Theo   I know, but I've had it with this place. The game's over for me. Pop's cut off the cash flow and so Gina and I are going back to the States. To settle down, I guess.

Jimmy   Gina's going to the States? With you?

Theo   Something wrong with that? I mean you and Gina, you haven't been . . .

Jimmy (*laughs*)   Don't worry, man. I haven't been with Gina.

Theo   I've been hearing some things, Jimmy. About your preferences. People are talking.

Jimmy   Well, man that's what people will do. I don't have time, Theo, to sit around in cafes all day talking about being a writer. I got no trust fund. I gotta get cash where and how I can, otherwise I'm treading a path that's gonna take me right back to the George Washington Bridge.

Theo   I don't understand.

Jimmy   You go on back to America, Theo. You be my Huck Finn growing up into his American adulthood. But don't forget your Jim who you left behind on the river.

Theo   What's going to happen to you, Jimmy?

Jimmy   Don't you worry about me, baby. I can take care of myself. I promised my momma that I wouldn't let Paris or France or Europe harm her boy and I intend to keep that promise. I'll be fine, Theo. Don't you worry yourself.

Scene Twenty

Ext. By the river Seine. Night.

Jimmy *is walking by the Seine. We hear the soft lapping of the river, and the echo of his footsteps. Then we hear another set of footsteps.*

Man   Monsieur, do you have a light?

Jimmy   Sure.

Jimmy *strikes a match.*

Man   Ah, so you are an American. I was hoping you might be an African.

Jimmy   You like Africans?

Man   Can you be my African?

Jimmy   Baby, I'm as American as momma's apple pie and if you don't like it you can kiss my Black ass.

The **Man** *grabs* **Jimmy**.

Hey, you take your goddamn hands off of me! Stop that shit!

We hear the man punch **Jimmy** *and* **Jimmy** *cry out in pain.*

Scene Twenty-one

Int. Hospital. Day.

Gina *and* **Jimmy** *are laughing. We hear whiskey being noisily poured into two glasses.*

Jimmy   Gina, hide the bottle. They'll kill me if they think we've been drinking.

Gina   But this is a hospital. They can't kill you

They both laugh.

Jimmy   So Theo has really gone back to the land of the free and the home of the brave?

Gina   You didn't think that I would marry him and go to live in America did you? (*Pause.*) Jimmy, Theo's a square. You know that.

Jimmy   But what's going to become of you, Gina? You going back to Sweden?

Gina (*laughs*)   Women like me were meant to watch over men like you. Artists, Jimmy. I'll watch over you as you write your novel.

Jimmy   I've got to make some money, Gina, which is how I got into this mess in the first place. Magazines pay me for essays and men pay me for company. (*Laughs.*) That's what I do.

Gina   That's not what you do. You're a novelist and you have to take care of yourself and get down to work.

Jimmy   They don't believe I can do it.

Gina   Who's 'they'? And 'they' don't believe you can do what?

Jimmy   A coloured man who thinks he can write is nothing but a dancing dog to them. I dance for my supper, Gina, but that's how I take care of myself. Either in their bedrooms or in their salons. But what else can I do? I have to eat.

Nurse   Monsieur Baldwin. What is that you are drinking?

Jimmy   American apple juice, nurse. It's a present from my fiancée, Gina. I don't believe you've met, have you?

Nurse   Monsieur Baldwin, please.

Gina *and* **Jimmy** *both burst into laughter.*

Scene Twenty-two

Int. Literary salon. Evening.

We listen to the hub-hub of an upper-class French literary salon in which voices are raised in competing conversations. Gradually one conversation becomes dominant.

Jimmy   But we do not *come* to Europe, we are escaping America. That is what you don't understand.

French Female Voice   But Henry James loved Europe. And all American writers come here to Paris to grow up and mature.

Jimmy   I was living under the belief that the French Republic was a country, not a finishing school.

French Male Voice   It is not just the writers, and not just the Americans. It is all the artists of the world who love Paris, even the Negroes who try with their simple music.

Jimmy   If you consider the music of Bessie Smith and Louis Armstrong to be 'simple music' then we are, my sophisticated friends, in rather deep trouble.

French Female Voice   But other Negroes come with their protest writing. Let us not forget that Mr Baldwin is a writer.

French Male Voice   Mr Baldwin, I am afraid I am not familiar with your work. Perhaps you might entertain us with a recitation.

Jimmy   Entertain you? With my writing?

French Female Voice   Oh yes, please, would you, Mr Baldwin?

Silence.

French Male Voice   I fear we may have offended our guest.

We hear the sound of a glass being smashed against a wall, and then an almighty crash as though a table has been turned over.

French Female Voice   Mr Baldwin! What are you doing?

Jimmy   I know you people. I've been inside your kitchens all my life. Now it's your turn to do some cleaning up.

Scene Twenty-three

Int. Hotel room. Day.

We hear the sound of typing. Then we hear footsteps climbing some stairs and getting closer to us. There is a loud banging on the door. **Jimmy** *stops typing.*

Hotel Owner   Mr Baldwin!

He knocks again.

Mr Baldwin, I know you are in the room. (*Pause.*) Mr Baldwin, I can let you stay to the end of the week, then either you pay me the rent or you will have to leave. Do you hear me? (*Pause.*) Mr Baldwin, you will pay me or you will go. That is all I have to say.

We listen to the **Hotel Owner** *as he turns to leave. We hear him tramp slowly down the stairs. Then the noise of typing starts again.*

Scene Twenty-four

Ext. Cafe. Day.

Wright   But I don't understand you, little man. First, you attack me in print, then you come to me asking for money?

Jimmy   I'll pay you back if that's what's worrying you.

Wright (*laughs*)   No, that's not what's worrying me, boy. What's worrying me is you. Seems like you don't want to mix with your fellow coloured artists, and you're running around town with that Scandinavian girl, and all types of inverts and fags. You gotta get yourself sorted out, boy. That Gina's got some serious alcohol problems and she's sleeping with every Black cat in town.

Jimmy   But all your so-called 'coloured artists' do is buy a beret and call themselves a painter or a writer or an actor. Shit, what they gonna act in? How many productions of *Othello* you think these people can produce at one time? Only thing your coloured artist friends have in common is that they all want to see their faces in *Ebony Magazine*, and inside of themselves they all want to go home once they've had their five minutes of fun over here. They're no more artists than you and I are United States senators.

Wright   Boy, you're one angry little brother.

Jimmy   And I don't want you talking about Gina like that. She saved my life.

Wright   Saved your life, my ass. We got a word for chicks like that, and we got another word for the type of people you like to hang with.

Jimmy (*stands up*)   You know you can keep your money. I don't need anything from you.

Wright   Well, that's mighty big talk, boy. But I didn't offer to give you any money now did I?

He laughs.

Jimmy   I used to respect you.

Wright   I do something to lose your respect?

Jimmy   Nothing in particular, Mr Wright. More like everything in general.

Wright   Well, little man, I guess there ain't much that I can do to fix that now, is there?

Scene Twenty-five

Ext. Paris cafe. Day.

We can still hear the noise of the traffic and people rushing by.

Jean-Claude   The Jimmy that I met that night looked like a confused and hurt little boy. I was only seventeen and God knows what I must have looked like. Lost, for sure. Perhaps a little frightened, but I always tried to look tough. That was my only means of survival. I always looked as though I was ready to fight, but inside I too was a confused and hurt little boy.

Scene Twenty-six

Int. Paris bar. Night.

We hear the sound of piano music that is playing quietly in the bar. We hear the door open and close, and then the footsteps of somebody walking into the bar.

Barman   Monsieur, how old are you?

Jean-Claude   I am twenty-two. How old are you?

Jimmy (*laughs*)   That's a good question. He's old enough to know better than to ask such a vulgar question.

(*To* **Jean-Claude**.) Please sit down.

Jean-Claude   Are you going to buy me a drink?

Barman   Now that's the funniest thing I've heard in a long time.

Jimmy   Same again, and whatever my friend would like.

Jean-Claude   So you have money?

Jimmy   I have credit. I am Jimmy Baldwin, their local American charity case. I write, I go to collect my mail, I avoid people. I come to this bar, meet people, then I write again. It is not a very glamorous life. And you? No, let me guess. You are a sportsman. An athlete.

Jean-Claude   I am a painter. Or rather, I would like to be a painter.

Jimmy   Then that's what you will be. Look at that man in the corner with the wine. What is he?

Jean-Claude   He want us to believe that he is a businessman. But . . . but he is not honest.

Jimmy   Good. I like that. He is not honest. That's good. Are you honest?

Jean-Claude   I am too young to be honest. It would be a waste of my youth.

Jimmy (*laughs*)   Here's a toast to your youth . . .

Jean-Claude   Jean-Claude.

Jimmy   To Jean-Claude, and youth.

Scene Twenty-seven

Int. Amex office at Odeon. Day.

We hear the noisy hustle and bustle of the American Express office at Odeon. People are shouting out names.

Jimmy   Baldwin! You got anything for Baldwin!

Clerk   Yeah, we got something for you today. Here you go, pal.

Gradually the sound of the hustle and bustle begins to fade and we hear a single voice.

Mother's Voice   Dear Jimmy, just a short letter to let you know that we are well. The children are so proud of their brother all the way over there in Paris, France doing whatever it is you're doing. Since I stopped working scrubbing floors I've begun to get some help from the church, but things are difficult. If you have any spare money then we would welcome it like a blessing, but you must take care of yourself first. I'm sorry to have to tell you that Eugene's mama, Mrs Wilkes, passed. Seems like her body just ran out of nourishment and in his infinite wisdom the Lord took her up and unto him. She always asked after you and I know she regarded you as another son. Son, write to me when you get a moment, but most important you take care of yourself. Remember you're all we've got. Your loving momma.

Scene Twenty-eight

Int. Hotel. Day.

Jimmy *is typing. He hears somebody slump against the door. Then he hears a loud noise as the person tries to get up and fails, and then a moan. He gets to his feet and opens the door. We hear something fall to the ground.*

Jimmy   Gina! Oh Jesus, girl, you've got to quit the juice.

Gina   I hear you're in love with a boy. Is it true? Is that why I don't hear nothing from you no more?

Jimmy   Gina, baby. Let me help you up.

Gina   It's not supposed to be like this, Jimmy. You're supposed to be the artist that I'm saving. But it's me that needs saving, isn't it, Jimmy? I'm a fallen woman.

She laughs.

Jimmy   Please, Gina. You've got to wise up. There's a lot of Negroes in this town using street skills to stay one step ahead of a vagrancy charge or deportation. Gina, to them it's all a game. They're hustling money and they'll happily service white co-eds who don't feel they can graduate from Europe until they've had 'that' experience, and they'll use you in the same way. Gina, you've got to pull yourself together. I don't want to hear people saying bad things about you.

Gina   Don't be ashamed of me, Jimmy. Paris isn't good for everybody. But at least I'm living. Back home, that was no place for me, Jimmy. I couldn't make it there.

She starts to cry.

Jimmy   Oh Jesus, Gina. Don't cry, girl. You gotta keep fighting if you're gonna make it in this world. How many times have I told you that?

Gina   The concierge reported me to the authorities for not having my passport with me. I think I will have to go, Jimmy. I think I have to go home. Why do these people hate us so much?

She continues to cry.

I don't belong but I feel safe in Paris, but now it is finished. It is all over for me.

Scene Twenty-nine

Int. Hotel bedroom. Night.

Jean-Claude *sneezes. We hear the noise of traffic and shouting in the street.*

Jean-Claude   Please, Jimmy. Come back to bed. It is cold and I cannot sleep with all this noise and shouting in the streets. (*Pause.*) How many times are you going to read your letter?

Jimmy   I don't know if Momma and the kids are going to make it through the winter. I've got to send them some money.

We hear **Jimmy** *get back into bed.*

Jean-Claude   Jimmy, I am very sorry but I have no money. Whatever I have you know I will give it to you.

Jimmy   Baby, I know you have no money. I'm not asking you.

Jean-Claude   But I want to help. You are not sleeping at night, you are not eating, you are not writing. Jimmy you are not even going to the stupid salons that you love to hate.

Jimmy   These people do not want me anymore. They say I am too 'difficult'.

Jean-Claude   Good. You do not need to be their exotic entertainment for the evening.

Jimmy   I need their money.

Jean-Claude   You always have magazines or newspapers that will pay you to write for them.

Jimmy   But Jean-Claude, I can't go on like this just writing articles for the money. My novel is getting away from me.

Jean-Claude   You have to write your book, and that is all that matters.

Jimmy   You really believe this don't you, baby?

Jean-Claude   I'm not going to make it as a painter, so one of us has to succeed. (*Laughs.*) Jimmy, it's time for your book.

Jimmy   But I'm worried that maybe I've forgotten how.

Jean-Claude   You haven't forgotten. I will find a way for you to write your novel. I promise you, I will find a way.

Scene Thirty

Ext. Cafe. Day.

We hear the loud raucous laughter of a group of **American Men** *who are drinking and talking. The* **Waiter** *approaches* **Jimmy**.

Waiter   The Negro Americans, they would like you to join them.

American Man #1   Brother Baldwin, get over here with us.

Jimmy   I got some reading to do. I'll catch up with you guys later.

American Man #2   Hey, sister Baldwin!

The **American Men** *all fall about laughing.*

Waiter   Every day you come in here. You sit by yourself and read your book, and write. You must not be so lonely. It is sad.

Jimmy (*laughs*)   If I'm going to save my family back home, then I have to work. These guys, well, I guess they've got other things on their minds that a poor coloured boy like me can't afford.

Waiter   I don't understand.

Jimmy   In order to avoid sitting in judgement on himself, a man often pays a very high price. I refuse to pay this price.

Waiter   You believe these men to be wasting their time.

Jimmy   My brother, one soon learns that what they do with their time is none of my business; when they attempt to abuse my time then it is my responsibility to defend myself.

Waiter   I understand. You are a very wise man.

Jimmy   Baby, I'm trying. I'm trying.

Scene Thirty-one

Int. Hotel room. Day.

Jimmy   No! You are offering me charity! Jean-Claude, I don't need charity from you, not now, not ever!

Jean-Claude   What charity? My parents have a small chalet in Switzerland and we can go there for the winter. We can live and you can write. Where is the charity?

Jimmy   I am an American man with hundreds of years of pride and history. To go with a young boy to his Swiss village and live from his money. What do you think I am?

Jean-Claude   But, Jimmy, you are so angry.

Jimmy   Baby, I'm angry with myself at what I've allowed myself to become. You mean well, I know that, but enough is enough. I have to go now, baby. You go your way and I'll go mine and we'll just remember this as a beautiful interlude.

Jimmy *kisses* **Jean-Claude**.

Ciao, baby.

Jean-Claude   Where are you going?

Jimmy   To where I can get the work done, Jean-Claude. To where I can work without depressing myself.

Jean-Claude   But you are being stupid, Jimmy. If you do not wish to go to Switzerland that is one thing. But to walk out like this into the night.

Jimmy   I love you, baby, but I guess we're all only one stop away from the George Washington Bridge.

Jean-Claude   But now you are not making any sense. What is this bridge you are talking of?

Jimmy   I love you.

Jean-Claude   No, Jimmy, please. Come back. Jimmy, Please!

Scene Thirty-two

Ext. Paris cafe. Day.

Jean-Claude   But Jimmy had nowhere to go, and he came back to me that same night. A week later we were in Switzerland. Jimmy came back to me because he knew that being with me was the only way that he was going to get his work done. And Jimmy came back to me because, of course, he loved me. I didn't need him to tell me this, I knew he loved me. (*Pause.*) And I loved him, more than I ever dared to tell him. Jimmy was my idol. And seeing him at work that winter taught me everything that I needed to know about love, dedication and purpose. Jimmy lived for his novel.

Scene Thirty-three

Int. Cabin in Switzerland. Day.

Jimmy   What's the matter, baby? I've mailed the book to my agent. *Go Tell It On the Mountain* is finished and out of the house, and now we will go back to Paris in the spring to see the flowers bloom and the city come to life again.

Jean-Claude   Jimmy, I have told you, I can't be with you. You don't need me now, and I understand.

Jimmy   But we're going back to Paris, and then we're going to the States together when I get a publisher. Come on, Jean-Claude. This is your book too, baby. You lived it.

Jean-Claude   It's your book, Jimmy, and you will get a publisher, and all the attention and fame and money that you deserve. I love you, but I've only done what any friend would do.

Jimmy   You want to stay here? You don't even want to come back to Paris?

Jean-Claude   I'll come to Paris, Jimmy. But it will be different now. You'll see. You're on your way, and you don't need me.

Jimmy   But that's *not* how I treat people.

Jean-Claude   We met each other at a time when we needed each other. In a silly little bar on a beautiful night. But Jimmy, I knew then that you were a man whose journey through life would be remarkable. It is too early for you to be accumulating luggage. To be with you, Jimmy, to love you, is to know that there is only a brief window of time with you. One has to respect this and let you move on. Please don't say anything. Already too many words. Love needs fewer words. Or none at all.

Scene Thirty-four

Int. Paris bar. Day.

Jimmy *walks into a Paris bar that is quiet. Suggests the afternoon. The pinball machine is being played.* **Jimmy** *walks towards it.*

Jimmy   Mr Wright?

Wright   Little man. I thought you'd gone back to the States?

Jimmy   I'm still here. But where is everybody? I went to the old cafe but people don't seem to be around anymore.

Wright (*laughs*)   I guess this winter finally killed off a lot of dreams. A few moved on to Germany or Sweden with their girls, but most have gone back to the States. Holiday's over. (*Laughs.*) And you, little man? Still pleasing the white man with that gentle pen of yours?

Jimmy   I'm just pleasing myself. You see, you'll always be a Negro writer, but that's not for me.

Wright   No, but the fact that you'll always be a Negro is obviously troubling you.

Jimmy   You think so? You know what I like about Paris is that at least if I'm starving in this city, it's Jimmy who's starving, not some poor coloured man. Back home I walk into a place and people look at me hard because I'm coloured. It's only just dawned on me that over here they might be looking at me because I'm a good-looking cat. (*Laughs.*) Smooth and clean. Just smooth and clean.

Wright   Well, I have to hand it to you, you ain't changed your crazy-ass tune one lick, boy. Not one lick. (*Pause.*) Don't you ever miss home? I mean grits, greens and gravy. A plate of ribs? You ever miss down-home food, boy?

Jimmy   I miss my family. And I guess I miss New York.

Wright   I hear you. Paris sure is beautiful, but you can't find everything in Paris. Certain things they just don't stock over here.

Jimmy   Certain people too.

Wright   Well, ain't that the truth.

Jimmy   You ready to go back home?

Wright   To what? A fading reputation? People telling me that I don't really understand America anymore because I've been away too long? Reckon I'll just stay here and keep on writing. And you, little man? You going home? You going back to where you're from?

Scene Thirty-five

Int. Amex office. Day.

Jimmy *is at the busy Amex office at Odeon.*

Clerk   Baldwin!

Jimmy   That's me.

Jean-Claude   Is it the letter?

Jimmy *tears open the envelope.*

Jean-Claude   Well, Jimmy? Is it the letter?

Jimmy   My agent says they want the book. Knopf. The biggest publisher in America. Oh my God, we've done it, baby. They want *Go Tell It on the Mountain*.

Jean-Claude   That's fantastic, Jimmy! Fantastic! Now we must go for Champagne.

Jimmy   And then to New York. We're going home!

Jean-Claude   Jimmy, you are going home. And I too am going home.

Jimmy   But, Jean-Claude . . .

Jean-Claude   No 'but'. I do not want to hear this 'but' anymore. Tonight we must have a nice time and not argue for tomorrow is the first day of the rest of our lives. You said it yourself, that in America I will be a white man, and you will be a coloured man, and nothing will ever be the same. I am going back to my home, Jimmy. And you are going to your glorious future. But first, *mon ami*, Champagne.

Scene Thirty-six

Int. Agent's office in New York. Day.

Agent   And when they get finished copies of the book where should I tell Knopf to send them?

Jimmy   Paris. The American Express office.

Agent   You're going back? I'm your agent, Jimmy, and I'm telling you there's so much that's going on in this country that needs talking about. People are marching, things are changing. You're in a great position to be a spokesman, Jimmy. Your people need to hear from you.

Jimmy   I'm going back so I can write. I don't think I'm ready to be a spokesman.

Agent   Is it a girl?

Jimmy (*laughs*)   If only.

Agent   Well, if it's not a girl, then for Pete's sake stay. We need you here, Jimmy.

Jimmy (*laughs*)   Today, when I got to the lobby of this building, they asked me if I had a package to deliver.

Agent   Who asked you that? I'll have his goddamn job.

Jimmy (*laughs*)   Doesn't look to me like too much has changed around here. The truth is, Paris has become a kind of home to me. A place where I could grow up and write without all of this bullshit to deal with. I'm not leaving home now, I'm just going to another kind of home.

Agent   But what you don't understand is that here in America, with all these civil rights issues, you're a part of the solution, Jimmy. I don't want you to fade from the scene like Wright. But if people can't see you then they forget you, whether you go to Paris, London, Madrid, you name it. You fast become yesterday's man and I don't want that for you, Jimmy. Just think about it a little. You're an American and America needs you. It needs to see you, feel you participating in the country.

Scene Thirty-seven

Int. Harlem. Day.

The sound of excitable children playing. Music in the background. **Jimmy** *sits with his* **Mother**.

Mother   Jimmy, you shouldn't spend all this money on presents for the children. They need clothes and food, not play things.

Jimmy (*laughs*)   Look at them. You don't think they need play things?

Mother   You're too good to us, Jimmy.

Jimmy   That ain't possible. I'm only sorry that I didn't have more money to give you before. But things were pretty rough back there in France. It wasn't always easy.

Mother   But why are you going back then, Jimmy? Why not stay here with us?

Jimmy   Momma, I want to tell you about who I am.

Mother (*laughs*)   You think there's anything about you that your momma doesn't already know? I knew who you were before you did, child, and I don't want to hear no excuses, not now, not ever. You got only one thing you have to do for me, and that's make sure that you don't end up jumping off no George Washington Bridge. You're my boy no matter who or what you are so don't you be starting with any explanations.

Jimmy   Thank you, Momma.

Mother   You go on back to your Paris, France or whatever you call it, and we know we'll hear from you when you're able. Whatever you got to write, say, or do, we're your family and don't you forget it.

Jimmy   I won't ever forget it. (*Pause.*) I'll never forget.

Scene Thirty-eight

Ext. Paris cafe. Day.

Jean-Claude   Thirty-four years later James Baldwin died in France. In the years in between he went back and forth between the United States and his other home, France, and, yes, I even went with him a few times. We loved each other but I did go back to my life, and eventually to a wife and child. My wife understood when I named our second child James after the man who saved a seventeen-year-old boy who, one night, wandered into an awful bar in Paris. *Go Tell It on the Mountain* was a success, as were the books that followed, and Jimmy became a famous man. As I knew he would. As he knew he would. Jimmy eventually became James Baldwin. Writer, essayist, spokesman. A colossus of American literature, a little man with a heart the size of Africa; my friend, my lover, my heart. A man who understood Black and white, man and woman, Europe and America, a man whose work spoke eloquently of the connections between these different states. A man of supreme understanding whose writing helped us to understand ourselves. Inevitably, he did for a time find himself 'protesting' wrongs in the world. He was a responsible writer. But Jimmy's books were ultimately always about love, family, sexuality and friendship. He died peacefully in France surrounded by friends and family. And was buried in his other home. New York City. It's a different Paris today. Louder, perhaps less charming. But it's still Paris. And, of course to me, it will always be Jimmy's Paris.

Scene Thirty-nine

James Baldwin on tape.

[From *No Complaints: James Baldwin at 60*. Written and presented by Caryl Phillips. BBC Radio 4, 23 March 1985]

Jimmy   'It turns out that I've lived half of my life in Europe. And I sometimes wonder what's become of me. Whereas Americans, as I said before, are condemned to think of the ocean as dividing them, I don't think of it that way at all. I've crossed that ocean enough and paid enough for the passage to see to what extent it connects if you are not afraid of the connection, if you see what I mean. You see, in any case in the time of my life I've watched the doctrine of white supremacy with which I was born on the other side of the ocean . . . (which in principle when I was twenty-four, though I was never quite that stupid, but in principle . . .) but the doctrine of white supremacy was born in Europe and it is having the same effect in all the European cities that it had in all the cities that I grew up in when I was in America – before I left America – what is happening in London, Amsterdam, Berlin, Paris, is what was happening in America when I was a little boy. The doctrine has come home to roost and no one knows what's happening now, but the circle has closed. Does this make sense to you?'

Mix through to high, rich gospel music.

Hotel Cristobel

Broadcast Details

BBC Radio 3, 13 March 2005. Directed by Ned Chaillet.

Characters (in order of appearance)

Kathleen, *late seventies*
John, *thirtyish*
Schultz, *early forties*

Notes on the Play

Like Caryl Phillips's second novel, *A State of Independence* (1986), this radio play in two acts, which was first meant to be a stage drama, is entirely set on an unnamed, newly independent, Caribbean island that very much resembles the author's native St Kitts. Taking place in an old-fashioned hotel, it concentrates on the interaction between three characters – the white English proprietress, the Black local waiter and a white American tourist. These are not only allegorical figures but also finely delineated individuals with their own existential issues. *Hotel Cristobel* is an important text for readers of Phillips's work for it offers a pithy, yet insightful, investigation into the way the region of his birth is still shaped by its links with former colonial and neo-colonial powers.

Act One

Scene One

Evening. We are on the gallery of the Hotel Cristobel. The hotel is a wooden, two-storey, slightly weather-beaten colonial building. The gallery is at the back of the hotel, and it overlooks the sea. The hotel is fringed by palm trees. We hear the wind whistling through the trees and mixing with the sound of the sea.

On the gallery there are creaky wooden steps that lead down to the beach. On the gallery itself there is a hammock, and three wicker chairs that surround a small wooden table. On a separate table there is an old-fashioned wireless. On the floor is an ice-box. The shuttered windows are open, and the small 'mosquito net' curtains are being blown in the breeze. We hear the occasional shutter bang closed.

Kathleen *is standing at the front of the gallery and looking out to sea. She is dressed in a full-length, white linen dress. Around her shoulders she has a shawl to protect her from the evening breeze. Her hair is up, her feet clad in flat and sensible shoes. We hear her walk as the planking for the gallery is old and somewhat eroded by the sea.*

John *sits in one of the chairs. He is bent double over a writing pad. He is wearing a 'loud' shirt and easy slacks. He has on open leather sandals. He leans forward, then backwards. He taps his foot.* **Kathleen** *paces about a little, then continues to dictate her letter.*

Kathleen   A hotel is not a . . .

She pauses

John   Is not a . . .

He looks up, but she is looking dreamily out to sea.

Yes, Mrs K. A hotel is not a . . .

Kathleen (*she looks back at him*)   John, have you taken to relaxing your hair?

John   To relaxing what, Mrs K?

Kathleen   To relaxing your hair. Isn't that what you call it? Putting all that grease on it, or whatever it is that you village boys do.

John   I had a fellar take a look at it, and he give it a rubdown. It's a 'go-ahead' type of hairstyle. You like it, Mrs K?

Kathleen   It looks like a wet sponge.

John   So you don't like it?

Kathleen *looks at* **John** *and then crosses towards him. She runs a hand gingerly across the top of his hair.*

Kathleen   Good Lord, John, it's all wet. Quite disgusting.

Her hand is now slightly damp.

John   Mrs K, it don't be nothing but afro-sheen.

Kathleen   You had better fetch me a towel.

John   So what happen? You got a problem with my culture?

Kathleen   A towel, John. I need a towel.

John   Alright, Mrs K, alright. I'm not deaf. I heard you.

He goes off into the house. **Kathleen** *looks up at the stars, then she continues to dictate to herself.*

Kathleen   A hotel is not an easy place to manage these days. And taking into consideration the speed at which things on this island appear to be changing, with these large all-inclusive monstrosities, these con-domin-iums, these apartment blocks . . .

John *comes back onto the gallery with a towel and an envelope. He stands and looks at her.*

John   Mrs K, you want me to take down the letter or you want me to bring you a towel? You must make up your mind for I can't do two things at once.

Kathleen   Oh, for heaven's sake, John. I was only practising.

He stares at her.

Come along, the towel.

John *hands her the towel.* **Kathleen** *wipes her hand.* **John** *fingers the envelope.*

John   Mrs K, Denmark Smith send a fellar around with some kind of letter for the new guest, Mr Schultz. I have the letter here. You want me to give it to Mr Schultz when he arrive?

Kathleen   No, just leave it on the table. I shall attend to it later.

John   But Mrs K, Denmark Smith mark the envelope 'urgent'.

Kathleen   Which is why I will deal with it, John, and not you. Obviously Mr Denmark Smith would like his communication to be handled with some grace and expediency. (*Pause.*) John, would you care to explain the somewhat childish pouting that is decorating your face? (*Pause.*) No? Well, suffice to say you have been acting rather strangely of late.

John   Strange like how? I've done something to upset you, is that it?

Kathleen   You seem anxious. A trifle impatient with me.

John   Mrs K, I'm impatient with the situation. The hotel is in big trouble, but you're acting like nothing is the matter.

Kathleen   I think you'll find that the future of Hotel Cristobel is my concern and not yours. Now, how is your wife?

John   Marva's not too well. She's ready to have our fifth child at any moment, but we need more money.

Kathleen   For what?

John   For food. She's got to keep up her strength. A pregnant woman is an expensive woman. She's eating like a damn horse!

Kathleen   I know things are difficult, but she must eat properly.

John   I know that, and that's what I'm telling you. I need more money so I can buy food. Me and the four children are starving to death.

Kathleen   Starving to death? (*Laughs.*) I think not.

John   Okay, okay, maybe not starving, but hungry.

Kathleen   Well, you'll simply have to make some personal sacrifices and cut back.

John   Cut back on what? You ain't paying me enough to cut back. I don't smoke, and I drink only in moderation. I cut back any more then I can't afford to put clothes on my back. You want me to come to work naked, is that it, Mrs K?

Kathleen   Don't be stupid.

John   You want my children, my lovely children, to expire? Mrs K, you want people to remember you as a murdering oppressor of Black people?

Kathleen   I hardly think . . .

John (*he clutches his stomach and groans*)   Oh, God. Oh, Jesus the pain bad, bad, bad.

Kathleen   What's the matter?

She comes to him.

John? John!

John   Mrs K. You must help me. (*Pause. He gets his breath.*) Malnutrition.

Kathleen (*annoyed*)   Don't be so damn ignorant. You're simply not funny. You amuse nobody but yourself with your infantile theatrics.

She looks at him. Then she turns and walks some distance. **John** *realizes it's a bad joke. He gets up.*

John   Mrs K, I just making a joke.

She says nothing.

Okay, I sorry, okay? I'm just making a stupid joke.

She says nothing.

Mrs K, just listen to me, please. If the bank takes back the hotel then we both lose out. You lose a home and I lose a job. We have to do something about this situation, and we have to do it now.

Kathleen   I think we had better press on with my letter.

John   Mrs K, I'm serious.

Kathleen   Please. Enough of your impudence. My letter!

John *sits. He picks up the pad and is ready to continue.*

Kathleen   Where were we?

John   Mrs K, about this letter. We writing begging your brother in England for cash?

Kathleen   Well, actually, John, we are trying to be a little more discreet than that.

John   But we begging him for cash all the same.

Kathleen   Is that any of your business?

John   I think so. What happens to Hotel Cristobel concerns me, too. I work here, this is my job.

Pause. They stare at each other.

Mrs K, I beg you don't look at me so brutish. I telling you, I worried. You seriously think your brother going to give you cash?

Kathleen   There are an infinite number of causes to which we might put a little money.

John   I know. Like paying me a decent wage.

Kathleen   This really is becoming rather bothersome. (*Sighs.*) John, I am well aware of the fact that you have been due a pay rise for the last two years.

John   Three years.

Kathleen   Three years?

John   At least three years.

Kathleen   I see. (*Pause.*) Perhaps the guests might appreciate a touch of redecoration. We might even . . .

John   Mrs K!

Kathleen   Yes, John. What is it? And might I ask you to keep your voice down. I am not deaf.

John   I have a suggestion that I feel moved to make to you.

Kathleen   Yes, well, I suppose I'm listening.

John *puts down the pad. We hear him stand and begin to walk around a little.*

John   Mrs K, we don't get that many guests that you should be worrying your head over what they want. They like what they see and that is the end of that. That's for number one. And for number two, you know your brother does never bother with these letters. I'm just wasting off your ink.

Kathleen   John, these are statements indicative of your perception of how I might best organize my hotel and my life. Suggestions they most certainly are not.

John   I'm sorry, but I have to say something for this situation is long past foolish, and I have some ideas as to how we can change things up a little around this place.

Kathleen   Some ideas?

John   Yes, Mrs K, I got some ideas.

Kathleen   John, are you actually in possession of independently conceived ideas?

John   Mrs K, I don't see why you feel you have to blasted well patronize me. I'm not stupid, you know.

Kathleen   So you say.

We hear her sit. Pause.

Well, I'm all ears.

John   Mrs K, my idea goes like so.

He gestures to the hotel.

If you can imagine this place.

Kathleen   This place? You mean Hotel Cristobel?

John   Sure, the hotel.

Kathleen   Well over fifty years as owner and proprietress of Hotel Cristobel have fused the reality of 'this place' into my mind. No, I'm afraid I cannot imagine it.

John   What I mean is if you can imagine this place with a lick of paint and a few party lights. You know, if you can imagine it niced-up.

Kathleen   When Alfred was alive, we had party lights, and a victrola.

John   Well, we getting there now. You really getting the idea.

Kathleen   I hate to disappoint you, John, but I'm not entirely sure that I am 'getting there', wherever 'there' may be.

John   A nightclub, Mrs K. 'John's Place'.

Kathleen   'John's Place'?

John   Well, I must tell you the truth, Mrs K. I've been planning more along the lines of 'John's Hideaway Bar and Bistro', for then Marva can come and do some 'roots' cooking. If I knock out the walls in between the downstairs rooms, it can make a real nice disco-dine space. Upstairs I'll still keep the guest rooms, but out here on the gallery I want to build an extension towards the sea, get a set of speakers rigged up, and put on a little rush-matting roof covering. Then I can book the Texaco Steel Band, for they're the hardest now, and they can come down here and play, say every Thursday and Saturday: no Tuesday and Thursday, for Saturday can fill without no attraction. Mrs K, I got a serious head for business.

Kathleen   Well, I can see that you consider yourself to be gifted with the Midas touch.

John   The what?

Kathleen   The ability to turn chaff into wheat.

John *looks puzzled*

Kathleen   The supposedly worthless into the profitable.

John   I think so, Mrs K. This place needs shaking up, bad, bad, bad. And me, well, I'm the man with the plan. Village rum shops is one thing, Mrs K, but what I'm talking about is something respectable. A kind of wining and dining place where a man can sit down with a nice lady and have a drink and look at the sea and the beauty of nature. The kind of place where you might even want to, how you say, pop the question to a girl. We don't have nothing like this on the island but I think we ready now. It's the twenty-first century, man, and I don't see no reason why we can't carry it off. Mrs K, we can start to make money again.

Kathleen   We?

John   I can run this place like a proper business.

Suddenly, in the distance, we hear fireworks begin to shoot off into the night sky.

Kathleen   What on earth is that commotion?

John   You didn't hear on the radio, Mrs K? Tonight they giving out a little firework thing to celebrate the independence anniversary. Don't tell me you forget that today is Independence Day, and that it's ten years since we get our freedom from you.

Kathleen   From me?

John   You know, from England. Downing Street and all that thing.

Kathleen   What an unruly clamour. It would have cost them little to have provided us with some form of warning.

John   They did, on the radio, but if you insist on having that thing tuned into the BBC World Service day and night, then how do you expect to catch the local news? We must support the young nation.

Kathleen   I'm not sure that I'm fully appreciative of your tone, John.

John   Mrs K, you have to start living for here and now. With the people, for the people. That England thing is dead, man. That BBC thing is old style. (*Demonstrates.*) Let me show you. You gotta wind your hip and move with the times. What you say, Mrs K. I got a steel band bottom for true, eh?

Kathleen   I don't need the likes of you telling me what I should or should not be doing with my life. I trust I am making myself clear.

She appeals to him.

For heaven's sake, stop your vulgar gyrations.

Silence. He stops. For a moment they both watch as the fireworks continue to explode.

John   Mrs K?

Kathleen   I can hear you, John.

John   What about my idea then?

Kathleen   You are seriously asking me to turn my Cristobel over to you?

John   Mrs K, you can put up your feet and leave things to Marva and me, for we going do all the work. I promise you that the only thing you must do is relax and gaze out to sea. I'm not going to charge you any rent or anything.

Kathleen   John, please don't disappoint me by talking in this fashion.

John   Mrs K, the hotel don't make money anymore. But I can't blame you. I mean how you supposed to know that they going to build a new airport, and a nine-storey beach hotel club, and all the other things.

Kathleen   Alfred knew.

John   Well, he don't be here no more, but I sure he bound to come pleased if he could see this place make a big comeback to what it used to be like: the swankiest, brightest, enviablest place on this island, man. Come night, I used to stand up over there by the trees and listen to the music and parties. All of we schoolchildren did. And a real serious bet was to see who could crawl past the gallery without being seen. We used to use our elbows and knees like so. (*He goes down onto the beach and demonstrates.*) Once in a while some guest would see one of us and point and shout. 'Good God, there's something out there', or some words like that, and we would jump to our feet and run like hell, but you all never catch us. (*Laughs.*) However, you know me, Mrs K; how blasted stupid I can be sometimes, for the only time anyone ever spy me off this gallery I get so frighten that I just jump up and run the wrong way straight into the sea. (*Laughs. He gets up and brushes himself down.*) Jesus Christ, I nearly drown that night. When I get home my mother give me such a lashing for coming in so wet and stinking. Boy, Hotel Cristobel was the hardest place on the island in them days, and nobody dare dream that one day they might end up working here – it's true, nobody did imagine that one day they might ever set foot in Hotel Cristobel, and look at me now, I'm here, and you know I might just be the saviour for this place, the man who can really bring it right back to what it was, so what you say, Mrs K? You feel it's destiny?

Kathleen   I feel that perhaps you ought to go and prepare Mr Schultz's room.

Pause. **John** *is stung.*

John   Mrs K, let me ask you something. How many more begging letters you going to send to England?

Kathleen *ignores him.*

John   Mrs K, you don't have no more time.

Kathleen   Are you planning on poisoning me, John? Or do you intend to smother me in my sleep?

John   Mrs K, I can fix you up a little room at the back of the hotel, but you say 'no' then this is the last you going to hear of any such offer.

Kathleen   You impudent monkey!

John   Mrs K, I offer you a room and you wilfully belittle me.

Kathleen   Who the blazes are you to offer me a room in my own hotel!

John   Woman, face facts! You're just sitting here on your backside with your body in this century and your head in the last. This is a business, not a damn rest home.

Kathleen   I know exactly what it is, now get out!

John   Mrs K . . .

Kathleen (*shouts*)   Get out!

John   Why the hell you can't face facts? Mrs K, the hotel is bankrupt! You want the bank to evict you, is that it?

Kathleen   How dare you speak to me this way?

John   And why the hell you bother writing your brother Gerald when you know that all he's going to do is send back the same message – 'sell up and return to Somerset' – which means the man is old now and he needs somebody to cook for him.

Kathleen (*points*)   Leave.

John (*sighs and shakes his head*)   Mrs K, I gone. I finish trying to help you.

John *starts to slowly walk off.*

Kathleen   Get out of here!

John   Don't worry. I'm going. If you lose the hotel to the bank then you've only got your stubborn self to blame, Mrs K. Nobody else. Just yourself and your foolish pride. I take it we finish with this letter to your brother?

Kathleen   Just put it down there! Put it down, and now leave me alone! Go away! Go away!

John *walks off into the house.*

Kathleen *goes across to the table and rips the letter that she was dictating to* **John** *out of the pad. She tears the page into shreds and scatters it onto the table. She comes to the front of the gallery and looks up at the sky as the firework display starts up again. She sobs a little and is clearly distressed.*

Scene Two

Afternoon. **Schultz** *is in his mid-forties and dressed in jeans, sneakers and a polo shirt. He stands on the gallery and looks out to sea. He seems relaxed. He turns and ambles over to the ice-box, where we hear him take out a beer, open it and begin to drink. He perches up on the gallery fencing and once again looks out to sea.*

Kathleen *appears from inside the house.* **Schultz** *jumps down as though he knows he shouldn't be sitting on the fence.*

Kathleen   Here we are. I found the postcards.

She hands **Schultz** *some postcards.*

Schultz   Thanks.

Kathleen   I hoard everything. And then, of course, when I need something I can't find it.

Schultz   Well, thanks for taking the trouble to . . .

Kathleen   We are a small island people, Mr Schultz.

She sits.

A sea and mountain people. You can view both from any point on the island. A small jewel in the crown is how we like to think of ourselves.

Schultz   A jewel in the English crown. Like India.

Kathleen *looks puzzled.*

Schultz   That's what you Brits used to call India.

Kathleen   Did we, indeed?

Schultz   Sure did. Interesting period, the Raj. But I always thought it obvious that the English and the Indians would get on. After all, there's not that much difference between the English class system and the Indian caste system. Although there is some mobility in the class system that the caste system can never tolerate.

Kathleen   Are you familiar with India?

Schultz   Sure. At the end of my junior year at college I went backpacking in Southern India. You know, back then everyone was into that mystic thing. I headed for Kerala and Tamil Nadu. It was great getting close to the people, but the poverty kind of left an impression on me. No matter how much you read and prepare, it always gets to you. It was like that in India, in Mexico, in Africa, in fact in every place I've been.

Kathleen   So you're a third-world wallah?

Schultz   I don't know about that, but I like to bond with people who are in touch with their environment. You know, people who've not been warped by CNN, Oprah Winfrey and McDonald's.

Kathleen   Well, you've certainly lost me. Opera who?

Schultz   Oprah Winfrey. She's a talk-show host. Well, she's more like an industry these days with her magazine and businesses.

Kathleen   Yes, well, I'm afraid that such things, talk shows or whatever they are called, are not my cup of tea.

Schultz   Well, I sort of agree with you. All I'm trying to say is I like to bond with people who are pure.

Kathleen   Come, come. Romantic tosh.

Schultz   Well, isn't this what you're doing here?

Kathleen   I'm not sure that I'm following you.

Schultz   You know, getting to know the names of their fresh fruits and vegetables? Figuring out the local customs and celebrating their local festival days?

Kathleen   Mr Schultz, you cannot be serious?

Schultz   Of course I'm serious. We can learn a lot from these people.

Kathleen   From these people?

Schultz   Absolutely. The baggage handler at the airport had scars on his cheeks. And he was tall, like a Masai. I'm sure that up in the hills some remnants of old African religions are still practised.

Kathleen   Mr Schultz, until very recently this island was blessed with the good fortune of dwelling under the jolly Union Jack. You will no doubt be horrified to learn that we eat apples and oranges, potatoes and carrots. Our local customs involve going to church and the reading of superior novels. Our festival days? Christmas, Easter and Whitsuntide. Am I making myself clear?

Schultz   But that's you.

Kathleen   No, Mr Schultz, that is us. (*Pause.*) Until recently we formed a rather sizeable expatriate community.

Schultz   But what about the Black people?

Kathleen   They can speak for themselves. We gave them a language. Now pay attention to the postcards. They will provide you with some insight into the former, and in my opinion, more acceptable times in these parts.

She gets up and begins to mix herself a drink. **Schultz** *continues to look through the postcards.*

Schultz   Say, listen. I hope you don't mind but I helped myself to a beer.

Kathleen   Of course not. It is what they are there for. Tropical heat demands that you regularly slake your thirst.

Schultz   Okay. Thanks. (*Laughs.*) I didn't know whether it was self-service or what?

Kathleen *ignores him.* **Schultz** *is rather uncomfortable.*

Kathleen   We have about 40,000 people, overwhelmingly Negro in origin.

Schultz   Black.

Kathleen   I beg your pardon.

Schultz   Black people. Negro is two stages back. Negro came first. Well, there were some things before that, but it's best not to talk about them. Then came coloured. And now it's Black. Although these days many like to talk about being 'of African origin'. However, I think you'll find most prefer the term Black.

Kathleen   I must admit I find the term a little too aggressive.

Schultz   But it's what they prefer.

Kathleen   Well, Mr Schultz, there are many things that they prefer, but they can't have everything. We wouldn't want to spoil them now, would we?

Pause. **Schultz** *puts down the cards.* **Kathleen** *stands.*

Kathleen   I take it you've finished perusing my postcards.

She takes them up.

Schultz   Thanks. They're something else. You don't see many black and white prints these days.

Kathleen   Views of this island as it was thirty or forty years ago are becoming increasingly rare.

Schultz   Well, that's my main thing: history.

Kathleen   Your 'main thing'? Are you a history don?

Schultz   No, not exactly. I'm a businessman. In New York City. Here's my card.

He hands **Kathleen** *a card. She scrutinizes it.*

Kathleen   Vice-President of Newman Incorporated?

She puts the card down as though she might catch something from it.

Schultz   Yes, I know. Vice-President. It sounds impressive, but in the States everyone's got a title of some sort.

Kathleen   Yes, I imagine it helps you Americans to feel as though you are important.

Schultz (*laughs*)   Something like that. But like I was saying, in my spare time I read a lot of history.

Kathleen   And your period?

Schultz   My period?

Kathleen   Your field of speciality?

Schultz   I guess I don't have one. Although, I am interested in Native American history. Have you read Dee Brown?

Kathleen   Dee Brown?

Schultz   *Bury My Heart at Wounded Knee*? It's a great book. It inspired the Costner film *Dances with Wolves*. It's an ugly part of our history, but I really think we're coming to terms with it now. You know, finally taking some responsibility for what we did, rather than this cowboys and Indians stuff. You know, the Westerns, in which they were always bloodthirsty and we were always the poor trembling palefaces.

Kathleen   I see. Tea?

She rings a small bell.

Schultz   That would be just fine. Real English tea.

Kathleen   You are not married, are you, Mr Schultz?

Schultz (*laughs nervously*)   No, I'm not married. You ready to fix me up?

Kathleen   But you have someone in mind? Someone to whom you might one day propose?

Schultz   Well, not exactly.

Kathleen   No? How sad.

John *enters. He has on a smart blazer. He holds a tray, and he has a towel draped over one arm.*

Kathleen   Ah, John. This is Mr Schultz, our American guest. He is on the island taking a short weekend vacation from . . . which city is it that you said you originated from, Mr Schultz?

Schultz   Well, I work in New York City, but I was actually born in upstate New York. In Buffalo.

Kathleen   Oh, dear. Such unusual names. I don't believe either of us have ever visited New York, have we, John?

John   I can't remember. Maybe. Maybe not.

Kathleen   John has never left the island, but he is forever trying to impress the guests.

John   Mrs K, that's not fair.

Kathleen   Now then, John, you have told me yourself that you have never visited even the closest of our neighbouring islands. And what's more, you have spoken to me about this in a manner which made it clear that you were rather proud of this sad little fact.

John   Mrs K, it's not fair to say that I'm forever trying to impress the guests.

Kathleen (*ignores* **John**)   Now, Mr Schultz. New York. I believe you also have a Greenwich, a Birmingham, a Plymouth, a Leeds, a Manchester, a New London, a

New Hampshire and even a New England. You Americans really are quite bereft of a convincing imagination, aren't you? I blame it all on an excess of televisual entertainment.

John   You get cable in here then you soon going to see how fast business will pick up.

Schultz   But you've got cable down here, right?

John   Not in this establishment, man.

Kathleen (*to* **Schultz**)   I won't have it in Hotel Cristobel. I find the square monster in the corner kills the art of conversing, don't you?

Schultz   Well, sure, to some extent, but people seem to like it.

Kathleen   Would that include yourself, Mr Schultz?

Schultz   Well, for the news. You know, despite its bias, CNN can help you keep up with the rest of the world.

Kathleen   Really? We have managed quite well with the BBC for over half a century. All this cable fuss is beyond me. (*Laughs.*) Perhaps it's my age.

Schultz   Well, you're not that . . .

Kathleen   John, we would like to take tea out here, please. (*To* **Schultz**.) Would you like some scones? They're homemade, of course.

Schultz   Scones?

Kathleen   Little cakes. Pa-stries.

She pronounces the word with contempt.

Schultz   Sure. Thanks. That sounds great.

John *starts noting down their order on a little pad.*

John   You'll be wanting milk and sugar, Mr Schultz?

Schultz   Thanks.

Kathleen   For heaven's sake, whatever has got into you, John? Why are you writing everything down? Just bring everything on a large tray as you always do. We can discuss the permutations of milk and sugar on your return.

John   Alright, Mrs K. (*To* **Schultz**.) Excuse me, Mr Schultz.

They both watch as **John** *goes back inside the house.*

Kathleen   They really can be quite trying.

Schultz   Seems a pleasant-enough guy.

Kathleen   His real name is Johnstone, but I find it a ridiculous mouthful. They have a very curious tradition of name-giving down here. Keethon, lthbert, Wilfur. I must say I've had the strangest-named Negroes working for me over the years.

Schultz   You know, I think Johnstone's quite a noble name.

Kathleen   Do you really? How interesting.

Schultz   Does he like it?

Kathleen   I really have not the foggiest.

Schultz   What do his friends call him?

Kathleen   Again, I really have no idea.

Schultz   His wife?

Kathleen   Marva.

Schultz   Marva?

Kathleen   That is her name, not his. You see what I mean? Such an odd name. I believe she is expecting yet another child; her fifth.

Schultz   I imagine she calls him Johnstone. Seems fair enough to me.

Kathleen   She's a queer little fish. Sitting at home surrounded by her horde of piccannies. But I've never been one to probe. My husband always used to say, the less you know, the better prepared you are.

Schultz   For what?

Kathleen   Success, I daresay. He truly believed that discretion was the most important aspect of our business. See nothing, hear nothing, and they will always come back. Although we have not been doing so well of late. We are becoming a little dominated by the larger hotels. They are in league with the airlines, you know. I believe this form of tourism is known as a 'package arrangement'. Straight from the airport for a week of besporting oneself by the hotel swimming pool, a little malingering in some ghastly casino, and then back to airport. I do hope that I am not sounding bitter.

Schultz   Not at all. But I think they've got every reason to envy you.

Kathleen   And why might that be?

Schultz   Come on, there's nothing authentic about the Hilton or the Sheraton. They've got nothing to do with the local culture.

Kathleen   I see. (*Pause.*) Is this your first visit to the island, Mr Schultz?

Schultz   Sure. First time.

Kathleen   Then I take it you have no acquaintances hereabouts?

Schultz   Well, no. Like I said, I've never been here before.

Kathleen   I see. (*Pause.*) Mr Schultz, you mentioned 'local culture'. During your visit, do you hope to find evidence of some ancient people, such as the Greeks or Romans? Or is it parchment, old hieroglyphics, or tombs that you are searching for?

Schultz   I'm not searching for anything. I'm just talking about the people's culture. The Black people's culture.

Kathleen   Mr Schultz, you have not arrived in your beloved India, nor in China, nor even in Africa. You have arrived, Mr Schultz, on a mongrel scrap of island which having had the temerity to demand independence from us has now spurned the only culture it ever had.

Schultz   But there's a slave history down here – a plantation history much like the South. You can't pretend that this never happened. Hell, this place is jumping with history.

Kathleen   History, yes. Culture, no.

Schultz   But you can't take away their culture.

Kathleen   Whose culture?

Schultz   The Black people.

Kathleen   They have no culture except that which we gave to them. And now they're telling us they don't want it. I say let them swing from the bloody trees if that's what they want to do.

Schultz   I have to say, ma'am, you're kind of harsh.

Kathleen   Yes, the truth can be difficult.

Pause. **Schultz** *shuffles nervously.*

Schultz   If you'll excuse me I think I'd better take a little afternoon siesta. I had to get up early this morning. Then there was all that hanging about and changing flights in Puerto Rico.

Kathleen   As you wish. Will you be requiring dinner this evening?

Schultz   Well, I was thinking that I might go into the town.

Kathleen   As you please.

Schultz   Well, there's only me here so I don't want you to have to open up the kitchen. I was thinking there might be a nice place where I could relax and drink up some of the action.

Kathleen   Action?

Schultz   You know, maybe meet some locals. Find out what's going on around here.

Kathleen   You appear to be a man in search of companionship.

Schultz   Excuse me?

Kathleen   Believe me, I understand your predicament.

Pause. They both look at each other. Then **Schultz** *breaks the silence and laughs nervously.*

Schultz   I mean, all I want to do is chill out a little with the local guys. You know it's almost polite, if you know what I mean, when you come to a place like this to do a little acknowledging of the other. But you make it seem kind of suspect. (*Laughs again*.) You're something else, ma'am.

Kathleen   Sadly, Mr Schultz, I am becoming something else. There was a time that being who I am meant that I was somebody here. However pitiful my status in England. I might inflate it many times over by merely arriving in such parts. (*Pause*.) But these are modern times.

Pause. She speaks with quiet resignation.

I am becoming something else. (*Pause*.) And now for that siesta of yours. I shall have John bring you your tea to your room.

Schultz   Please don't go to any trouble.

Kathleen   It's no trouble.

Schultz   Well . . . thank you.

Kathleen   I don't care what you do in town, Mr Schultz. As long as you confine your mixing to the world beyond my Hotel Cristobel.

Schultz (*laughs*)   My 'mixing?' I'm just trying to avoid your having to open up your kitchen.

Kathleen   How very considerate of you.

Schultz   Listen, I can easily check into some other place.

Kathleen   I don't think that will be necessary. Do you?

Schultz (*laughs*)   Well, I don't know. It feels like you've got some issues with me.

Kathleen   While I'm not what might be described as a modern woman, I am aware of the world and its ways. (*She laughs*.) But this 'mixing'. It is rather trying.

Pause. They look at each other.

Schultz   I guess I'd better get my head down.

Kathleen   Indeed you must. A siesta will do you good.

Schultz   A couple of hours should do the trick.

He starts to walk off in the direction of the hotel.

Kathleen   Sleep well, Mr Schultz. Sleep well.

She stands and watches as he disappears into the hotel. She turns on the BBC World Service. It is news time. She listens to the news from London.

Scene Three

Evening. The gallery is lit by a gas lamp. **Schultz** *is on the gallery. We hear him open and then start to drink a beer. He looks at a large cassette-player that lies next to the* *wireless. He presses 'play' and the cassette-player starts to play calypso. He listens for a while then presses 'stop'. He takes out the cassette, turns it over and presses 'play'. The cassette-player starts to play reggae.*

John *appears with a bottle of rum and a shot glass. He is dressed in overalls and has a hammer and screwdriver in his pocket. He stands and watches* **Schultz**. *Then he ambles across to a chair. He starts to pour a drink.* **Schultz** *notices him and turns off the music.*

Schultz   Excuse me, but I couldn't resist checking out some of your local vibes. I didn't mean to be rude or anything.

John   I don't mind. I was fixing the banister on the front gallery and I heard the music. Everything in the hotel is blasted well falling to pieces.

Schultz   A lot of Black people in the States used to carry these things around.

John   You mean they don't carry them around no more?

Schultz   Not really.

John   No man, some of the fellars up there must still be swinging the boxes.

Schultz   Well, some, but I guess noise pollution became a dominant factor. Then Walkmans came in. And now everyone has a Discman, or an MP3.

John   Noise pollution? I don't know nothing about that, I just know that I prefer the box to the Walkman, or the Discman or whatever. The box has in more power. (*Pointing to the bottle of rum.*) Man, this is nice rum. You want me to fire one for you?

Schultz   No thanks. I'll just grab another beer.

He goes to the ice-box and takes out a beer.

Say, do you need a beer to go with that?

John   Beer and rum?

Schultz   Guess not. I thought it might be like beer and a shot.

John   A beer and a shot?

Schultz   Like Budweiser or Michelob. And a shot of whiskey. In a small glass.

John   I just take the rum by itself. Plain and simple. No messing about.

Schultz *sits.*

Schultz   The lady of the house around?

John   She's gone for her evening stroll along the beach. She likes to look at the water with the moon playing upon it.

Schultz   Is that right?

John   So what kind of business you in then? If you don't mind me asking you, that is.

Schultz   Hell, no. I don't mind. Real estate. Newman Incorporated. In New York. We deal mainly with business properties. That kind of thing.

John   Sounds like a good job to me.

Schultz (*laughs*)   It's not a bad life, but I've got other interests.

John   Like what?

Schultz   Like maybe one day writing a book. A history book.

John   I don't know much about history. I was never one for school books and things.

Schultz (*laughs*)   Come on, you know plenty, you just don't realize that you do. For instance, your family history, that's history. What your parents did, your grandparents, where they came from – it's all as valid as the stuff they teach you in school. Look at this hotel, for example. How long have you been here?

John   Twelve years.

Schultz   Then you've got twelve years' worth of history under your belt right here. You know plenty of history. It's just that people want to make you feel that your history doesn't count.

John   What people?

Schultz   Well, you know, just people. Some people like to make others feel like losers.

John   I never knew my father.

Schultz   Excuse me?

John   You asked about my parents. Where they came from, and I'm telling you I never knew my father. My mother once told me that he took off to another island. He didn't even wait to see me born.

Schultz   He went looking for work.

John   How do you know that?

Schultz   No, I'm asking. Did he go looking for work?

John   Maybe, but I don't know for sure. My mother never tell me anything about that, but if he's like the rest of the men around here then it's woman he went looking for, not work.

Schultz   But the key thing is he went. He migrated. You see, you're a part of the most important of all historical movements: migration, in your case for economic reasons. This pattern of importing and exporting labour has been a dominant feature of American life since the time of slavery.

John   You know about slavery?

Schultz   I've read quite extensively on the subject, but I wouldn't call myself an expert.

John   So you can tell me which part of Africa I come from then? I believe a man like me must have come from a warrior people.

Schultz   Well, that's possible, because only the strongest of you survived the middle passage.

John   The middle what?

Schultz   The journey on the slave ship. Naturally, the weaker ones, the holy men and peasants, they would have been the first to die in the miserable conditions.

John   Truly a man of warrior stock. (*Pours a drink.*) Man, I like this history business. It's pumping up my chest well nice.

Schultz *stands and points.*

Schultz   Was that a fish out there? Something leapt clear out of the water, it was amazing.

John   Flying fish. You get plenty on a night like this – the moon bright, the air soft and hugging you tight like a woman squeezing you up.

Schultz   That's good. Pretty poetic.

John   At school I used to like poetry. Shelley and Wordsworth and all those fellars.

Schultz   Really? You still read poetry?

John   No, man, not for a long time. But I do a bit of singing. You didn't hear me singing when I brought in your tea?

Schultz   I was dead to the world. I didn't even know that you'd brought in the tea until I woke up. Not that I don't appreciate the gesture.

John   Well, I tried to keep quiet so as I wouldn't wake you up.

Schultz   But you just said you were singing.

John   Well, I was singing quietly, to myself.

Schultz   One of your own?

John   One of my own what?

Schultz   One of your own songs – was it something you put together yourself?

John   Charmer. The big calypso man around here. The Mighty Charmer. It was one of his. It goes like this.

> Ten years ago, thing were not so
> It's clean beach and sunshine we used to know
> But now these people come
> And they treating us like scum
> So where the hell it is we supposed to go
> I say, where the hell it is we supposed to go.

He stops and looks across at **Schultz**.

John   Listen, I don't mean to insult you, but it's how it does go. I can't change the man's lines.

Schultz   Hey, I'm not offended. I understand.

John   You see, we're a young country. Tourism is important. Big money-spinner and everything, but we need to think about our own people too, you know. Tourists ain't the only people who need facilities.

Schultz   I hear what you're saying.

John   Mr Schultz, I'd appreciate any advice that you felt you could offer me.

Schultz   Advice?

John   Hold on a minute, Mrs K coming up the beach.

Kathleen *steps up from the beach onto the gallery. She is completely soaked through up to her knees. She notices how 'close'* **John** *and* **Schultz** *have become.*

Kathleen   Good evening, Mr Schultz. I trust John is treating you well.

Schultz   Just fine, but you look wet, ma'am.

Kathleen   Just an odd wave that chose not to announce its dastardly intent until the last possible moment.

John   Mrs K takes a walk by the sea every evening.

Kathleen   Thank you, John. That's enough. These shoes are ruined, look at them.

She sits and peels off her shoes.

Perhaps I might offer you a small pre-retirement brandy, Mr Schultz?

Schultz   No, thank you, ma'am. Maybe I'll take you up on your generous offer another time, but for now I'm quite happy with this beer.

Kathleen   I see. (*She gets to her feet.*) Well, enjoy the remainder of your evening. I'm afraid I shall have to retire early and change out of these wet clothes. I shall see you tomorrow. (*To* **John**.) John, after you have locked up, will you come and see to my shutters before you leave for the village.

John   I'll be with you in a minute.

Kathleen   There is no need to rush. I shall probably read by candlelight for a while. (*To* **Schultz**.) Some of my husband's old manuscripts. You see, Mr Schultz, he considered himself something of a minor poet.

Schultz   That's fascinating.

Kathleen   I'm glad you think so. Goodnight, Mr Schultz.

Schultz   Goodnight, ma'am.

Schultz *and* **John** *watch as* **Kathleen** *goes off.*

John   You need a next beer, Mr Schultz?

Schultz   Okay, but relax. I'll get it.

He goes across to the ice-box and takes another beer.

John (*laughs*)   Man, I didn't know the husband was a poet until she just say so. In fact, I never met him, although I remember seeing him when I was a youth. Tall fellar, real English-looking. Like if something drop on the floor he can't unstiffen himself and bend over to pick it up.

Schultz   She must have been a widow for quite some time then.

John   Maybe fifteen years or so. I can't say exactly.

Schultz   She seems kind of isolated.

John   She's isolated alright. Isolated and damn stubborn. (*Pours another shot of rum.*) Mr Schultz, like I was saying before Mrs K came up with her mermaid act, I'd appreciate your advice. (*Pause.*) You know, all of a sudden I don't know how I should phrase this so that it don't sound too forward.

Schultz   You don't have to be diplomatic with me, John.

John   Alright, then. I want to turn this place into a disco-dine night spot for local people.

Schultz   This place? Hotel Cristobel?

John   Yes, man, Hotel Cristobel. Where we're standing. This very spot, man.

Schultz   Well, with all due respect, it really isn't your decision, is it?

John   How do you mean?

Schultz   Well, surely, it's up to the owner of the hotel. (*Laughs.*) And that's not you, John. You might be talking to the wrong guy here.

John   Mr Schultz, I have to put you fully in the picture.

He puts down his drink and stands up.

Just wait a minute, okay? I have to get the briefcase with my papers.

Schultz   Briefcase? Papers? I'm not following you.

John *races inside. He leaves* **Schultz**, *who takes a swig of beer.* **John** *emerges again with a briefcase in his hand. He sets it down and takes out a file, which he hands to* **Schultz**.

John   Take a look at this. Plans for the new-style Hotel Cristobel.

Schultz *opens the file.*

John   Drawings done by a draftsman who owes me a few favours. I got estimates for lighting, for building work, and even for advertising in the local paper and on the radio. I've thought of everything.

He pours another drink. **Schultz** *continues to look at the papers.*

Schultz   Well, it's an impressive package, but I don't know how I can help. Unless you're figuring me for a millionaire or something.

John   No, man, it's not the money. I've already got an agreement from the national bank for a small business loan to buy the hotel. The manager says he's right behind me. All I have to do now is to convince Mrs K that she must let me take over the controls.

He sits.

Mr Schultz, Mrs K won't face up to business reality.

Schultz   Well, John, like I said, it's her place. Maybe you've just got to be patient.

John   Mr Schultz, can't you see she's wilfully letting the place fall apart. We local people need a facility like this. You've been into town, Mr Schultz. You've seen what it's like.

Schultz   Well, I've seen worse. Looked to me like there were a couple of nice places to sit down and eat.

John   Mr Schultz, those places aren't for us. We don't drink banana daiquiri and piña colada.

Schultz   Well, I guess not.

John   And even if we did we can't afford the prices in those fancy restaurants.

Schultz   Don't you local people have anywhere to go? In one of the villages, maybe?

John   Rum shops, Mr Schultz. Nasty little wooden huts full of drunken, sweating men. We got one in my village, we got one in every village, but we got nothing like this hotel. (*He gestures.*) Nothing right down next to town with beach and everything. I'm talking about making this place into something respectable for local people.

Schultz   I see.

John   Yesterday I try to raise the topic with her, but she don't want to study me.

Schultz   Did you show her your plans?

John   No, I put it to her like I would just take over in a partnership kind of thing, instead of talking about buying her out and showing her all these business details. (*Pause.*) I didn't want to sound too aggressive.

Schultz   But why would she agree to just hand over the hotel to you? Being nice isn't going to work. You've got to give her the facts.

John   But like I said Mr Schultz, yesterday I didn't want to come on too strong with her.

He mimics a 'business' voice.

'Mrs K, things are not going well so I want to buy the place, and I want you out.'

Schultz   But being aggressive is part of good business, John. You've got to get in there and pitch.

John   Mr Schultz, you're right. Maybe I should have been more straightforward. After all she probably knows I had plans made up and that I've been to the bank and got a loan agreed. This island is so small that you sneeze on the south coast, somebody on the north coast is going to say 'Bless you'.

Schultz   Pitch the honest fastball, John. Tell her you want to buy the place.

John   Maybe you can talk to her for me.

Schultz   Talk to her about what?

John   About letting me buy the place.

Schultz   John, I'm only a guest here. And I'm pretty sure she doesn't even like me. Why would she take any notice of me?

John   Why do you think?

Schultz   Because I'm white?

John   No, because you're not Black. (*Pause.* **John** *looks at* **Schultz**.) Mr Schultz, I can make this place great again. I know it. I can feel it. You've got to make her sell me the place.

Schultz   John, I can't make her do anything. It's her hotel. She doesn't have to listen to you, or to me, or to the bank.

John   Mr Schultz, I'm desperate. I've got a wife and nearly five children. I can't wait no longer, and if you don't make her see sense then things is going to be real bad for her.

Schultz   What exactly do you mean?

John   When her husband went back to England she took out a second mortgage. Mr Schultz, for the last couple of years she's not made a single repayment. When I went to see the manager with my proposal and everything, he told me that if she don't agree to let me buy the place, then he'll have no choice but to seize the hotel. The man's begged her, but she likes to carry on like there's nothing the matter. Mr Schultz, they seize the hotel then it all going just be embarrassing for her. Me, I truly don't want that to pass.

Schultz   And she won't listen to the bank manager?

John   Do you think she listens to anything Black people say? It will be easier if you can persuade her to give up with some dignity. I'll buy the place from her, then she can pay off her debts and put up her feet. Man, I'll look after her. I don't have a single bad feeling about this woman, Mr Schultz. Believe me, I just want her to go with her chin held high and her chest sticking out. It's only right and fair, don't you think?

Schultz   I guess so.

John   Mr Schultz, I don't want to see her begging for food and so on. I'm offering her a bit of charity.

Schultz   Charity?

John   Between charity and eviction is not much choice, but she going to have to make up her mind.

Pause. **Schultz** *thinks hard.* **John** *looks anxiously at him.* **John** *reaches into his briefcase and produces a letter which he hands to* **Schultz**.

John   Read this. The bank manager's letter to me. It's all down there. Mr Schultz, she don't have much time.

Schultz *begins to read the letter. He finishes and then turns to* **John**.

Schultz   How many rooms do you have here, John?

John   Twenty-two guest rooms. And a suite that can take a family.

Schultz   And staff? Besides you, that is.

John (*laughs*)   Staff? You looking at the staff. Me, I cook, I clean, I do the maintenance, the garden, everything.

Schultz   A lot of work for one guy.

John   In the old days she had maybe twenty people here. Maids, gardeners, cooks, the whole works. And staff quarters off on the land over there.

He points. Then he gestures expansively to the hotel.

But you see what happen to the place. She's ruined it.

Schultz   Twenty-two rooms. Land. Staff quarters. The property's even bigger than I thought.

John   You like the property, Mr Schultz?

Schultz   I think my company would like the property.

John   That's why you're down here, right?

Schultz   Maybe.

John   Mr Schultz, you play me for a fool.

Schultz   John, I'm going to talk to her.

John   You going to talk to her for me, or you going talk to her for you?

Schultz   Newman Incorporated expect me to do a job for them, which is to acquire property that they can redevelop.

John   So you're going to talk to her for you.

Schultz   John, I can't just pretend that I don't have responsibilities. But . . . well, I'll think about what you've said.

John   You'll think about it?

Schultz   You've got needs, John. Newman Incorporated, they've got needs. But they pay me. However . . . however, I'll think about it.

John   Mr Schultz, is there something I can do for you in return?

Schultz   Something you can do for me?

John   You need a friend? Anything you want, I can get it for you.

Schultz (*laughs nervously*)   Maybe I should just think about it.

John   You take your time, Mr Schultz. I'm not putting any pressure on you. But when you're ready, you know who to ask.

Schultz   Well, I guess so. (*Pause.*) Thanks. (*Pause.*) Say, John, is Castle Hill far from here?

John   No, not far at all, Mr Schultz. You sure you not looking for somebody?

Schultz   No. It's just that the place sounds like it's got some history to it. I thought I might take a look.

John   I see. (*Pause.*) Mr Schultz, Mrs K give you anything?

Schultz   Like what? (*Pause.*)

John   Sometimes she gets strange and gives things to the guests.

Schultz (*laughs*)   Well, if she's giving things away, a bit of civility might help.

John (*laughs*)   Yes, man. I agree with you on that. Mr Schultz, I gotta go now. Sleep good, you hear.

John *starts to walk off.*

Schultz   Aren't you going to see to her shutters?

John *stops walking.*

John   Mr Schultz, I look like her slave?

Schultz   No, of course not. But she did ask if you'd see to them. I'm just reminding you.

John   Mr Schultz, she's got two hands. It's not that difficult. I got a pregnant wife and four children at home. You think my wife has anybody to come close in her shutters at night? Four children running about the place, and a next one in her belly. No, man, tonight Mrs K can shut her own damn shutters.

Schultz   I see.

John   Goodnight, man. (*Pause.*) And this company thing. It's just between me and you. You have to be careful these days, but I can get you something safe and decent.

He starts to walk off. He turns and stresses the point as he walks.

Safe and decent.

Schultz *watches as* **John** *goes off. He goes for another beer. We hear him open it. Then* **Schultz** *hears* **Kathleen.**

Kathleen   John? John?

Schultz *scrambles back into the shadow behind the door. We hear* **Kathleen** *come out onto the gallery.*

Kathleen   John? Are you there, John?

Schultz *looks on unseen.* **Kathleen** *sighs, then goes over and turns down the gas lamp. We hear the waves breaking and the wind blowing through the palm trees.*

Act Two

Scene One

Afternoon. **Schultz** *is on the gallery looking at a photograph album.* **Kathleen** *comes out carrying a bottle of gin, some ice, a bottle of tonic and two glasses on a tray. She pours two drinks.*

Kathleen   Aren't they delightful photographs? I'm afraid the album is a little tattered, but the photographs are rather surprisingly well preserved.

Schultz   They're amazing. A real window on the past. And this island is so beautiful. All these bays and coves. And what beaches.

Kathleen   Gin and tonic?

Schultz   Thanks. It's a while since I had one of these. (*He points at a photograph.*) My God, is this Hotel Cristobel? This place was really something – look at all these people.

Kathleen (*comes to peer over his shoulder*)   The Governor's twenty-fifth wedding anniversary ball. We gave a dinner. People came from all the islands, right down to Trinidad, and from as far north as the Bahamas. In those days it was a real expedition to reach us, so you can imagine what a hoo-ha and to-do the whole thing was. (*Points.*) And that man there, with the purple waistband – although of course you can't see that it's purple in these photographs – he was a Junior Minister in the British National Government. Before the war. He was out here taking the waters with his family. Dodging some political scandal or something, but it didn't do him much good. He died about four weeks after the ball. Heart attack. It was his wife I felt sorry for, though. Sweet, mousy little thing. Went back to England where I expect she married a salesman. (*Points.*) Look, there she is.

Schultz (*points*)   And is that your husband?

Kathleen   That's me, but that's not my husband. (*Pause.*) I'm afraid I have no idea who he is. Looks pretty scrumptious though.

Schultz (*points*)   What about this guy in the corner. He looks seriously miserable.

Kathleen   Yes, well, that's Alfred actually.

Schultz   I see. I'm sorry.

Kathleen (*points*)   There's Arthur Leamington Mills. Disgraced himself by running off with a sea-captain's wife. Well, that kind of thing was unheard of. A mild flirtation, even a little romance, but to abscond with an officer's wife. Still, Mr Leamington Mills was a northerner. Bradford, I believe. I sometimes imagine that if one were to look closely enough one might see his grubby cloth cap beneath that smug little panama. (*Laughs.*) Set at such a vulgar angle.

Schultz   What happened to all these people?

Kathleen   Either back in England or dead. Which amounts to the same thing. (*Points.*) This ratbag, Henrietta Tomkins-Rye, she stayed on until last year, running an art gallery in Turtle Cove. Art, my foot. Bits of pottery with infantile crayon scratched on both sides, and canvases that I wouldn't clean my trowel with. Then she died.

Schultz   Do you miss her?

Kathleen   She was somebody to talk with. But she always returned to the same tedious topic. The time Picasso squeezed her left bosom in a Paris restaurant. I used to tell her, more likely a Paris bordello. (*She moves to sit down.*) My God, now there's a rare bird indeed. Somebody to talk with.

Schultz   Then why stay? I mean if it's that bad and there's nobody to talk to. No reason to stick around here if it's not working for you.

Kathleen   And pray, where am I to remove myself to?

Schultz   Is England so bad?

Kathleen   I'm afraid I've lost my appetite for England. These days the BBC announcers frequently drop their 'aitches'. Can you believe such a thing?

Schultz   But when were you last there?

Kathleen   Since my departure I have never ventured to return.

Schultz   Not even for a vacation?

Kathleen   I am led to believe that England now considers herself to be a European country. (*Laughs.*) I barely amounted to much in the old England, which is why I chose to leave. I shudder to think what this new England would make of one such as I.

Schultz   Well, retire then. Stay here and write your memoirs. Let John take over the place.

Kathleen   I beg your pardon.

Schultz   I said you might want to stay here and write your memoirs.

Kathleen   That much I heard and understood.

Schultz   Well, I suggested you might retire and let John take over the hotel. He seems kind of keen on the idea.

Kathleen   I see, so am I to understand that John has attempted to convince you that he should succeed me as owner and proprietor of Hotel Cristobel?

Schultz   Well, he ran a few ideas past me.

Kathleen   He ran a few ideas past you? What else did he tell you about me?

Schultz   He just shared his plans, that's all.

Kathleen   When you've lived among them as long as I have, you'll soon discover that there's no such thing as 'that's all'. (*Pause.*) Alfred was right.

Schultz   I'm afraid I'm not following you.

Kathleen   Alfred loved the life on the island, but he did not trust your beloved Negroes one jot. (*She takes a drink.*) These days the coloured people seem to display little more than aggression and envy towards us.

Schultz   Well, it's not entirely surprising, is it, ma'am. After all you don't see any poor white people around here.

Kathleen   Is this my fault?

Schultz   But comparatively speaking, you're rich. You've got it all.

Kathleen   Mr Schultz, I am not, as you may have already surmised, a wealthy woman. These days there are countless Negroes on this island whose material assets far exceed my own.

Schultz   I see. (*Pause.*) I don't mean to be out of line. I'm not trying to pry or anything.

Pause. **Kathleen** *takes a drink.*

Kathleen   I think I mentioned to you that my husband died. He actually returned to England, unable to face the increasingly depressing hostility of the Negroes. The final straw was when the bloody gardener threatened to go on strike unless Alfred bought him a lawnmower. Suddenly a machete and a scythe weren't good enough anymore. (*Pause.*) Something of a soft pear, old Alfred. He preferred to remember the island as it had once been. Tranquil and harmonious. A place where people got on.

Schultz   So your husband's not dead?

Kathleen   He might be. I have not heard from him in years. I'm afraid we parted on rather bad terms. My fault, of course. (*Pause.*) In fact, the only person I do hear from, and that curtly and very infrequently, is my brother Gerald, who constantly beggars me to return to my 'roots'. But I'm a stubborn old bat. Hotel Cristobel is all that is left of Alfred and I.

Schultz   But didn't you feel it your duty to go with him?

Kathleen   My 'duty' was to maintain my dignity in the face of unhappiness. Dignity, Mr Schultz. Without it what else do we have?

Pause. They stare at each other.

Schultz   So you'll not entertain John's offer to you?

Kathleen   Is this any of your business, Mr Schultz?

Schultz   With the bank's help, he's prepared to buy the hotel from you.

Kathleen   Mr Schultz, please. I can think of few things more demeaning than advancing a Negro's suit.

Schultz   Would you listen to an offer from me?

Kathleen (*laughs*)   Well, I have been waiting. You seem somewhat reluctant for a businessman. (*Pause.*) Well?

Schultz   My company will pay you twice the local price for the land, and a substantial sum for the property of course, plus your first-class passage back to England. Or should you choose to stay here, we can help you buy an ocean-front apartment and come to some kind of arrangement for health insurance.

Kathleen   Really?

Schultz   Well, if you don't want to sell to John, then this would seem to be a great alternative, don't you think?

Kathleen   And this is the sum total of your offer?

Schultz   I'm offering you a top-drawer deal. In fact, I may even be going a little beyond my authority.

Kathleen   And what exactly do you have in mind should your company manage to acquire my home?

Schultz   Well, a hotel, of course. But upscale. Individual villas. Exclusive, with privacy and security being the key features.

Kathleen   You intend to raze Hotel Cristobel to the ground?

Schultz   Sure. I mean, nobody does wood anymore.

Kathleen   I see.

Schultz   Ma'am, this is a fabulous offer. Trust me.

Kathleen   Trust you? Have you listened to anything that I have shared with you about what this hotel means to me?

Schultz   I listened to you, ma'am, but . . .

Kathleen   But you heard nothing.

Pause. They stare at each other.

Schultz   Ma'am, according to what John's told me, if you don't sell to him then it pretty much looks like my company could walk straight into the bank and buy your hotel from them. We could cut you out of the deal.

Pause. They continue to stare at each other. Then **Kathleen** *gets up to mix a gin and tonic.*

Kathleen   So John has informed you that the bank wishes to eject me from Cristobel? And that this lamentable course of action is liable to commence in the very near future.

Schultz   Well, sure.

Kathleen   (*sighs*)   Yet another attempt to humiliate me.

Schultz   I don't think he was trying to humiliate you. He was just trying to put me in the picture. Maybe he figured that if you wouldn't sell the hotel to him, then you might sell it to Newman Incorporated and at least there might still be a job for him.

He's frightened that you're going to let the bank foreclose and then he'll be out of work. How's he going to feed his family in these circumstances?

Kathleen   For heaven's sake, grow up, man. John was attempting to humiliate me. He wants you to think of me as little more than a stubborn old fool.

Schultz   No, ma'am, I beg to differ. He just wants the hotel.

Kathleen   He's getting the bloody hotel.

Schultz   John is getting the hotel?

Kathleen   I said he's getting the bloody hotel! What choice do I have? (*Pause.*) Mr Schultz, it is crushingly obvious to everybody concerned that my immediate need for cash is going to result in my prematurely relinquishing control of Cristobel.

Schultz   So you intend to sell to John?

Kathleen *says nothing.*

Schultz   Ma'am, my offer is still on the table.

Kathleen *sips at her drink.*

Kathleen   John enjoys humiliating me. He presents himself as the new forward-looking, easy-going, but so-horribly exploited Negro. And I am the silly old English lady who doesn't know what is good for her. To John it is simply a game to play with the guests. And bloody oafs like you only encourage his insubordination. (*Pause.*) Did John inform you that he makes love to me whenever he so desires?

Schultz   He does what?

Kathleen   He does nothing of the sort, but it suits his purpose to spread such rumours abroad.

Schultz   Now wait a minute, he never suggested anything like that to me. He'd have to be a total . . . a complete

Kathleen   A what, Mr Schultz?

Schultz   A total asshole to say that about you.

Kathleen   Hurrah. On this we agree.

Pause. **Schultz** *is shocked.*

Schultz   He says that kind of thing?

Kathleen   Your Black friends, including our Johnstone, don't give a stuff for my sort. (*Pause.*) Perhaps you ought to leave, Mr Schultz.

Schultz   Leave?

Kathleen   After all, this is a business visit. And things are hardly proceeding swimmingly.

Schultz   And my offer?

Kathleen   An offer from an American is not an offer.

Schultz   I take it the answer is 'no'.

Kathleen   We British still have our principles.

Schultz   I'll get my things together.

He begins to walk off. Then he stops.

What about you?

Kathleen   What about me?

Schultz   I'm concerned. If you're really selling the hotel to John, then . . .

Kathleen   You may keep your concern, Mr Schultz. Do you understand me?

Schultz   I guess so.

Kathleen   Did you find your Mr Denmark Smith?

Schultz   I'm not following you?

Kathleen *produces the letter.*

Kathleen   Your friend, Mr Denmark Smith, he sent a boy with this letter. It's addressed to you.

Schultz   I see.

Kathleen   You said that you did not know anybody on the island. (*Pause.*) It would appear, Mr Schultz, that I have caught you with one foot in the stirrup.

Schultz   Denmark spent last summer in New York.

Kathleen   Yes. A government-sponsored visit so that he might receive instruction in how to operate the island's new computerized airline ticket system. It is a small island, Mr Schultz.

Schultz   We became friends.

Kathleen   Did you come here to attempt to purchase my hotel, Mr Schultz, or did you come here to rekindle your 'friendship' with Mr Denmark Smith?

Schultz   When Newman Incorporated targeted this island and your property, I asked my company if they would send me.

Kathleen   And how exactly does Mr Smith feel about this fortuitous coincidence?

Schultz   Maybe I should read the letter.

Kathleen   I suspect you already know what it says.

An embarrassed **Schultz** *stares at* **Kathleen**.

Kathleen   I'll leave it here for you. On the table.

She puts the letter on the table.

Meanwhile, I shall order you a taxi.

Schultz   Thanks.

Kathleen   And I shall make your reservation with the airline.

Schultz   I wish you'd reconsider my company's offer.

Kathleen   You don't listen, Mr Schultz.

Schultz   Well, I'm sorry that things are going to end this way.

Kathleen   Are you not happy that Hotel Cristobel is about to become a den of Negro entertainment?

Schultz   I'm talking about you, ma'am. I'm sorry that things are going to end this way for you. That you're going to lose this place. (*Gestures to the hotel.*) This is your home.

Kathleen   Ah, the penny has dropped. Finally, Mr Schultz, you appear to understand. This is my home. (*Pause. They stare at each other.*)

Schultz   I'll get my things.

Kathleen   Don't forget your letter, Mr Schultz. I feel sure that Mr Denmark Smith meant for you to read it with some care.

Schultz   I guess so.

Kathleen   Take your time, Mr Schultz. I shall go and make your arrangements. Please. Take a seat.

Schultz *sits and watches as* **Kathleen** *goes off. Then we hear him begin to open the envelope and read.*

Scene Two

Afternoon. **Schultz** *is standing on the gallery, bags packed and ready to leave. He is listening to his messages on a cellphone.* **John** *saunters onto the gallery,* **Schultz** *sees* **John** *but he keeps on listening. Then* **Schultz** *closes the phone.*

John   Mr Schultz, truly you're a man who likes to keep in touch with the world. You doing a little business?

Schultz   Just seeing if I have any messages in New York.

John (*points to the bags*)   Mr Schultz, you going someplace?

Schultz   I'm waiting for the taxi to take me to the airport.

John   You going back to the States?

Schultz (*looks at his watch*)   If I can catch the plane.

John   Mr Schultz, sit down, man. Take a drink.

Schultz   No, thanks. I don't have time.

John   Something happen to upset you?

Schultz   It's best that I leave.

John   Take a drink, Mr Schultz. Let's talk a little.

Schultz   I told you, I don't have time.

John   You order a taxi from Winston's Yellow Bird Cabs then you got all the time in the world.

Schultz   I don't want to miss my flight.

John   You taking the inter-island to connect with the jet in Antigua?

Schultz   Yes.

John   Relax, you have time. A beer?

Schultz   Well, maybe a quick one.

John   One beer coming up. Winston's only have one car. An old Austin Cambridge. The thing is thirty-seven years old, man. Somebody should give it a medal.

He gets the beer. He hands it to **Schultz**.

Schultz   Thank you.

John   Did you tell her?

Schultz   Did I tell her what?

John   Mr Schultz, you forget?

Schultz   Did I forget to suggest to her that she should sell her hotel to you. No, I didn't forget.

John   I bet you she said she won't sell me the place?

Schultz *says nothing.*

John   I thought as much. Mrs K really don't have no use for Black people.

He takes a drink.

I suppose that's it then. Back to square one. Waiting for the bank to repossess the place and then throw her out.

Schultz   You asked me to talk to her so you could embarrass her, right? Make her look like a silly, poverty-stricken old lady.

John   No, man. I just wanted her to hear my plans from a proper businessman. I already tell you, the bank agree to give me a mortgage, so either I buy it from her, or just wait till they pitch her out and I buy it from the bank. You can't see that I'm trying to help the woman? I thought maybe if she hear the situation from you, then she might see some sense. You know, hear the situation from somebody she might respect.

Schultz   And you really think she respects me?

John   As a white man, maybe. As an American, no.

Schultz   You knew she would never sell to me, didn't you?

John   Mrs K is prejudiced against Americans. (*Pause.*) Mr Schultz, I beg you don't look so miserable. I can see that you're unhappy, but the woman is too damn stubborn.

John *takes a long drink. Then he gets up to get another drink.*

John   Mrs K gone for her walk?

Schultz   I don't know.

John   I shouldn't really be working tonight but I decide I might as well help her out, otherwise you getting no service. Two weeks ago, we had a little bust-up about the daily roster.

Schultz   The daily roster?

John   About who has to do what around here.

Schultz   Well, I thought you did everything.

John   That's what the argument was about.

Schultz   Well, I guess she owns the joint. She's perfectly entitled to do nothing if she wants to do nothing.

John   You're on her side?

Schultz   I'm not on anybody's side. I'm simply making an observation.

John   Easy now, man. You're acting all conceptual like you itching to slap me down or something.

Schultz *looks at* **John**. *He is momentarily stung.*

Schultz   Do you tell people that you see to her comforts for her?

John   Her comforts? What are you talking about, man? If you mean I don't want to see her out on the streets, you're right.

Schultz   No, I mean her comforts. Her sexual pleasures.

John   What the hell she been telling you? Her comforts is her own problem. Nothing to do with me! Not a damn thing!

Schultz   Don't treat me like some dumb-ass tourist! Do you, or do you not, tell people that you make out with her?

John *takes the bottle from his mouth.*

John   Maybe I better make clear a couple of things to you. First of all, I never touch her. To tell the truth, I don't think she'd let me, and I don't want to anyhow. It's innocent, man.

Schultz   Innocent?

John   Nothing going on, but you know how people talk. Everybody knows that she's gone with others, that's why the husband take off for England. Still she's sitting here telling everybody that he's dead, but the truth is he couldn't take no more of her fooling around with the guests. The last man she start messing with was her own husband's brother. Everybody know the story about how the man came out here for a holiday, then the next thing he know Mrs K all over him. Then the husband and the brother fall out and start to fight, and the next thing the husband had enough and pack up for England. Mr Schultz, her own husband's brother!

Schultz   But you haven't answered my question.

John   Mr Schultz, she's never gone with me. I mean, look closely. I'm a Black man. We just strictly mistress and servant. And if she tell you about me spreading rumours in the village about having she, it also don't be true. I just tell a few fellars, but they don't tell nobody. I tell them it's just the way she is to make them jealous and think I getting a bit of extra butter on my bread than Marva giving me. Give me a little status in the village, but it's strictly rumulation.

Schultz   So she was telling the truth?

John   Yes, but that is a long time ago. I mean look at her! You think I want anybody to think I'm checking her now? (*Laughs.*) You must be joking, brother. These days she's looking too mule-ish. You don't find so?

Schultz   You've actually told people that you make out with her?

John   Well, she does lie too, for I bet she still telling you that her husband is dead to get your sympathy.

Car horn sounds.

Listen, I can bring you fellars who actually helped the man with his luggage as he got on the boat for England.

Schultz   Hell of a thing you two got going here. And you wonder why nobody stays here anymore?

John   I keep telling you, the damn hotel is out of date.

Schultz   Hey, and you're out of line, Johnstone! Ridiculing an old lady behind her back like you've been doing.

John   Me? Ridicule her?

Schultz   I mean, how goddamn low can you get?

John   Mr Schultz, you're a real jackass. Any prejudiced thing that she wants to tell you about Black people, you listen to. That we greedy, or we don't speak English, or we can't be trained, or we breed like dogs. I'm sure she tell you all of this, and yet I bet you don't have the nerve to run off your mouth in her face like you doing to me.

Schultz   That's different, for Christ's sake.

John   Different, my backside! She's worse than me, for what I said about doing it with her is a long time ago. But Mrs K is always trying to make me look ridiculous in front of people. Tell me why you don't get upset then, for it seems to me that you're coming on like a hypocrite.

Schultz   I'm not a goddamn hypocrite. I just came down here for . . .

John   Yes, man, I know what you came down here for.

Car horn sounds.

So I take it that Denmark write to you and remind you that he's been married for ten years, and that he has a wife and three kids? (*Pause.*) Mr Schultz, Denmark don't carry on with men and that kind of palaver down here. We all know what kind of man Denmark is, but Denmark don't carry on so down here.

Schultz   You know, John, you don't strike me as a man who's ever been lonely. Always the life and soul of the party, right?

John   Something like that.

Schultz   I thought so. (*Pause.*) When my parents found out that their only child, their grown son, wasn't all that they hoped he might be, they pretty much stopped talking to me. That was twenty years ago. (*Laughs.*) Since then nobody's ever accused me of being the life and soul of the party. (*Pause.*) Did Denmark talk to you about me?

John   Mr Schultz, you have to understand this is a small island. Denmark tell me that when he was in New York, he was lonely and missing his wife and kids.

Schultz   I started talking to him in a bagel deli on St. Mark's Place. Then I explained to him what his name meant and he smiled. And then . . .

John   And then you had a friend for the summer, Mr Schultz. But just for the summer.

Schultz   I live in a one-bedroom co-op in the East Village. Denmark liked my place and eventually he moved out of his hostel and for the last six weeks of the summer he stayed with me. And then he came back here.

John   And when he reach back he don't want to know you, right?

Schultz   I wrote to him but I never heard anything. But then when I had a chance to come down . . .

John   Mr Schultz, you really think you have the right to go messing with people's lives just how you feel?

Schultz   I loved him.

John   What the hell does that have to do with anything? What was done was done and then Denmark have to come back home to his family. Don't you understand how these things work? You acting like you is some kind of dunce, like you never had a 'fling and move on' before.

Schultz   I explained to him about Denmark Vesey. He was a slave rebellion leader from Charleston in South Carolina. In 1822 he was planning to lead an uprising of slaves against the white man, but he was betrayed and they hanged him and his conspirators. He's a real hero of your people. That's where Denmark must have got his name.

John   Mr Schultz, how you know his father didn't name him after some fellar he met off a cruise ship from Denmark? You American people always feel like you must explain everything and take charge, but it doesn't always make sense.

Schultz   But you said you liked it when I talked about history.

John   I like it alright, but you must still let other people live their lives in peace. Just because you think you know about Denmark's name, and just because one summer you and he have a good time, don't mean you can come down here and mess up the man's life. I mean, you really think you're the first white man Denmark's gone off with?

Schultz   John, I can't help what I feel.

John   Mr Schultz, I understand. I'm not stupid. I understand feelings.

Car horn sounds.

Schultz   I met the local librarian this morning. A Mr Cedric Williams. He showed me some boxes full of papers that nobody has looked at in years. I talked to him for maybe three hours about local history. About the abolition of the slave trade, and how the island was at one time the most important British colonial possession. And then he showed me some pictures of the Independence Day celebrations. (*Pause.*) But it's not my history, right? Is that what you're saying? That I should leave other people's business alone and concentrate on sorting out my own life. Is that it?

John   Mr Schultz, I can see you're a lonely fellar. But Denmark ain't the answer to your problems. And this island ain't going to give you any answers either. I think maybe you should talk to your parents.

Schultz   My parents?

John   Twenty years is a hell of a long time, Mr Schultz. And it don't seem to me like you got too many friends in that big city up there. You got to talk to somebody. Me, I talk to Marva, and she talks to me. Why don't you try and make your parents understand who you are? A big man like you, I'm sure you can make them see sense.

Schultz   And what about you, John? What's to become of you?

John *looks around at the hotel.*

John   When I get my hands on this place then things will soon change. I can make this a hell of a place, man. A crucial spot for locals and visitors alike.

Schultz   And visitors?

John   The right kind of visitor, Mr Schultz. For too long we had no choice but to put up with the wrong kind. Once I'm running this place, it's only the right kind I'm dealing with. They got hotels in town for the other kind.

Schultz   The other kind?

John   The kind who look down on us.

Pause. **John** *looks across at a pensive* **Schultz**.

Schultz   I see.

Car horn sounds.

Schultz   I better go now.

John   Mr Schultz, you got a lot of knowledge. And it's true, all this history thing set me thinking. But you got to put it to better use than going looking for people in bars and restaurants in India and Africa and all those other places that you does like to travel.

Schultz   New York City can be a lonely place, John.

John   Mr Schultz, you think you're lonelier than Mrs K?

Schultz   I guess you're right.

John   Man, I beg you take the taxi.

Schultz   You'll be alright?

John   Mr Schultz, we manage just fine before you get here, and we going to manage just fine after you gone. Just go home. (*Pause.*) Back to America. And square up to yourself, man.

Schultz *gathers up his things and begins to move off. Then he stops and turns to* **John**.

Schultz   Will you speak to Denmark?

John   Mr Schultz, most of my family from Castle Hill. I speak to Denmark nearly every day.

Schultz   You speak to him every day?

John   I'll tell him he can relax now. That you gone and he ain't going to hear from you again.

Schultz   Thank you. I'm sorry to ask you to do this for me.

John   Mr Schultz, I'm happy to set Denmark's mind to rest. He don't deserve what you put him through.

Schultz   I'm sorry.

Car horn sounds.

John   Mr Schultz, I beg you now, go.

Schultz   So long, John.

John   Talk to your parents, man.

Schultz *hesitates for a moment.*

John   Mr Schultz, you can't keep the taxi waiting like this.

Schultz   Take care, John.

He turns from **John** *and walks off. We hear* **John** *take another bottle of beer. We hear the taxi door slam and the taxi begin to pull off. Then* **John** *slumps down into a chair.* **Kathleen** *steps up onto the gallery having completed her walk by the sea.*

Kathleen   And where is our Mr Schultz? Has he taken his leave?

John   So it seems.

Kathleen   I see. (*She looks up.*) Such a beautiful sky. (*Pause.*) A hand of rummy often provided a pleasant conclusion to the day.

John *ignores her. We hear* **Kathleen** *making herself a drink. Then she looks hard at* **John***.*

Kathleen   John?

John   Yes, Mrs K, what do you want?

Kathleen   You had better go home to your wife and children. (*Pause.*) I am sure our Mr Schultz wouldn't even know the rules of rummy. I would have to teach him. Poor man.

She sits and begins to rub her feet.

I suppose poker's still all the rage in America. Gamblers. That's what Alfred used to call them. Life's gamblers. No discernible past, therefore no rules. No tradition. Like your own people, John. (*Laughs.*) Alfred would have said, 'Rummy's an old game, Schultz. No doubt you're not familiar with the rules.' (*Laughs.*) John?

John   Yes, Mrs K.

Kathleen   I have been thinking.

John   Yes, Mrs. K.

Kathleen   You will have your 'bar and bistro'.

John   Mrs K, I got to have the place this week. End of next week at the latest.

Kathleen   It will be arranged.

John   Mrs K?

Kathleen   It would appear that I have somewhat mishandled my affairs. (*Pause.*) It will be arranged so that you may purchase my hotel from me. This week.

John   Mrs K, you sure?

Kathleen *is too overcome to say anything.* **John** *goes to get another beer.*

John   Drink?

Kathleen   No thank you. (*Pause.*) John.

John   Mrs K.

Kathleen   Might I broach the subject of a partnership?

John   A partnership?

Kathleen (*laughs*)   Well, I'm not entirely without experience. A manageress of some sort.

John   You want to work for me?

Kathleen   With you, for you, it is a little late in the day to be splitting hairs.

John   To be my manageress?

Kathleen   You seem shocked. Well?

John   Mrs K, the place needs a clean break with the past

Kathleen   But is this wise? Surely there is a case to be made for a transitionary period. A period in which Marva and I might work together.

John   Marva and you?

Kathleen   I am not aware of a history of any animosity between Marva and myself.

John   It's not that.

Kathleen   The piano will need tuning, but I can still keep a song. Sing-a-long evenings, now these always proved very popular. You remember, don't you?

John   I remember the piano.

Kathleen   And you are blessed with a decent enough voice, John. You might be our resident cabaret star. You'll need a tuxedo, of course.

John   A disco-dine, Mrs K.

Kathleen   No cabaret?

John   Mrs K, I'm talking a kind of upmarket 'Roots Cabin'. Shirt-jacks and sandals, not tuxedo. Steel pan and rhythm. Winding up and working up. Saltfish, johnnie cakes, souse. Goat water, fried plantains, black-eyed peas.

Kathleen   I entirely understand. (*Pause.*) Might there be a little garret in this 'Roots Cabin' for a relic of the past?

John   Mrs K, you won't like it. It won't suit your purposes.

Kathleen   I seem to remember that only the day before yesterday my retirement quarters were being advertised as an extremely agreeable abode for one such as I.

John   Mrs K, you want me to remind you of what you called me?

Kathleen   I don't think that will be necessary. (*Pause.*) The heat of the moment, John.

Pause. She points.

What a marvellous sunset.

They both look. Then **John** *turns back to look at her.*

John   Mrs K, I'm sorry but . . .

Kathleen   Stop! (*Pause. Collects herself.*) No more. I won't hear another word. Now tomorrow we might try another letter to Gerald. This time, I fear, of a more reconciliatory tone. (*Pause.*) I shall announce my impending arrival.

John   I understand.

Silence. **John** *is embarrassed.*

Kathleen   John, could you please go home now. (*He stares at her.*) Do you hear me?

John *stands.*

John   I hear you, Mrs K.

Kathleen   Tomorrow I shall dictate my final dispatch.

John   I'll be ready, Mrs K.

Kathleen   'John's Hideaway Bar and Bistro'.

John   Mrs K?

Kathleen   I said, 'John's Hideaway Bar and Bistro'. It sounds so ugly.

John   You prefer me to still call it Hotel Cristobel?

Kathleen   You will do no such thing! Really, how dare you! I shall take the name with me and drop it into the middle of the Atlantic Ocean.

John   Whatever you want, Mrs K. Whatever makes you feel happy.

Kathleen   Goodnight, John.

John   Goodnight.

He starts to walk off. Then he stops.

Mrs K, I'm sorry for telling the American man about the bank and the hotel and everything. But I really wanted to find a way in which we can avoid the bank just taking the place from you. I thought maybe he could talk to you, but I was wrong.

Kathleen   Thank you. For your apology. (*Pause.*) I have my dignity, John. The Mr Schultzes of this world, they simply won't do. It's just the way I am.

John   Mrs K, Mr Schultz ain't no problem.

Kathleen   I didn't say he was a problem. I said he simply won't do.

John   I hear you, Mrs K. (*Pause.*) Mrs K, I'm proud that I worked here. What I said before, about being a small boy and growing up to work here, I meant it. It was really something else for me.

Kathleen   I'm glad. But I suppose all things must come to an end.

John   Hotel Cristobel was really a great place. Nobody will ever forget it, Mrs. K. Nobody.

Kathleen   I hope not, or my life should have been wasted.

John   The brightest, the swankiest, the most enviablest place on the island. Boy, this place really carried some style.

Kathleen   We tried our best. And yes, we had our minor successes.

John   Mrs K, this place is in the history of this island. You can take away the name, but Hotel Cristobel is always going to be a part of us.

Kathleen   Yes, I suppose it will, won't it. (*Long pause.*) Goodnight, John.

John   Goodnight, Mrs K. And I'm sorry.

Kathleen   I don't need your pity, John. I won't have it. Now go.

John   Mrs K.

Kathleen (*begins to weep*)   For God's sake, go! Go home!

She clasps a handkerchief to her mouth. She sobs into it. **John** *stand and stares at her. Then he turns and walks away and leaves her alone, weeping.*

A Long Way from Home

Broadcast Details

BBC Radio 3, 30 March 2008. Directed by Ned Chaillet.

Characters (in order of appearance)

Woman
Mother
Marvin Gaye
Announcer
Jimmy
Stu
Gaby
Radio Announcer
Father
Sam
Patti
Shop Owner
Jean-Claude
Louise
Beatrice
Hotel Manager
House Agent
Karen
Judge
Musician
Journalist
Mitchell
Voice
Interviewer

Notes on the Play

Most of this radio play zooms in on Marvin Gaye's final years, especially the time that he spent in Ostend (Belgium) in the 1980s, at a difficult moment in his career. Dealing again with a displaced artist figure tormented by celebrity, this drama also explores the theme of Black masculinity and fatherhood, which are important underlying concerns in Caryl Phillips's writing, for example his 2009 novel *In the Falling Snow*. A sexually ambiguous creative individual who has a social message to deliver, Marvin Gaye is an emblematic figure in Phillips's imaginary, as is also made clear by the long, well-researched essay that he devoted to the singer's career and which was published in the 2001 collection of essays *A New World Order*.

Scene One

Sound of seagulls, waves, hooting trawlers passing in the distance. A peaceful coastal North Sea town at sunset. Mix through to a Black American gospel choir and the congregation singing in a DC church. Mix through to the sound of a young **Marvin Gaye** *singing the Lord's Prayer by himself. He finishes. Silence.*

Woman (*quietly, to* **Marvin**'s *mother*)   Mrs Gaye, young Marvin's got a beautiful voice. Just beautiful.

Mother   That's right. He does.

Cross-fade to **Marvin** *and* **Mother** *after service.*

Mother   Marvin, everybody is saying how beautiful you sing.

Marvin   But why doesn't Father ever say so? Doesn't he like me?

Mother   He likes you and he likes your singing, Marvin.

Marvin   You don't have to lie, Momma.

Mother   Your father's an unhappy man. I guess God made him that way.

Marvin   But that doesn't mean that he has to be mean to me, does it?

Mother   No, son, it doesn't. I've tried to protect you and I always will. I'll always look out for you, Marvin.

Scene Two

We hear the restless noises of a large audience in an arena auditorium. They are waiting for the artist to appear onstage. One senses that they are becoming impatient and restless. Over the PA system we hear 'I Heard it Through the Grapevine' playing. A voice shouts out 'Come on! Get on with it!'

Announcer   Where is he?

Jimmy   They say he's on his way. Just keep playing the music.

Announcer (*laughs*)   Keep playing the music? I've played 'Greatest Hits' twice now.

Jimmy   Well, play it again. (*Phone rings.*) That'll be Stu now.

Announcer   Do me a favour, Jimmy. Princess Margaret is in the audience. You'd better tell Stu to get the loser here now. He's a bloody junkie. And he doesn't listen to anyone and he always has to be right. Oh yeah, and there's also the other problem of him thinking that he's God's gift to women.

Jimmy   Shut it, alright? (*Answers the phone.*) Yeah, Stu, it's me, Jimmy. Where's Marvin now?

Cross-fade to:

Scene Three

We are in a London hotel room. In the background we hear the sound of a television blaring and glasses clinking. We hear people talking and partying.

Stu   Hey, Jimmy. Can you hear me?

Jimmy   Stu, I can hear you. I said, where the hell is Marvin now?

Stu   You hearing me? (*To the people in the room.*) Hey, keep it down a bit will you. I've got Jimmy on the phone.

Gaby (*drunk. She laughs*)   He's got Jimmy on the phone. Jimmy Cagney. 'You dirty rat.'

Stu   Marvin, keep her quiet will you.

Marvin   Gaby, the man's trying to do some business for me.

Jimmy   Stu, don't tell me you're still at the hotel?

Stu   Marvin's waiting for a delivery. And not from the postman, if you know what I mean.

Jimmy   For God's sake it's going to take you half an hour to get here, even with a police escort.

Stu   Do me a favour and keep the police out of it, man. Give me a minute and let me talk to him. Hang on.

Marvin   Everything cool, Stu?

Stu   Marvin, no everything's not cool. We can't wait for the stuff, we've got to go now.

Gaby   You can't tell Marvin what to do. He's not your slave.

Stu   And you can shut it, Gaby, I've just about heard enough from you. Marvin, where's Beatrice? Come on, man, you don't need to be hanging out with slappers from Tonbridge Wells.

Gaby   I'm from Faversham, mate.

Marvin   Hey, man, give her a break.

Stu   Look, Jimmy will fix you up in the dressing room, but we've got to go now. Marvin, Princess bloody Margaret is waiting to hear you sing.

Marvin   Let me tell you something, Stu, you limeys don't know shit about me or where I come from or what I've been through or what it takes to be me. I'm a Black man from America trying to make a living in a white man's world, and I figure I'm doing okay, don't you? I'm not a performing clown or a fool; I don't dance to nobody's tune. When Marvin Gaye says he'll perform, he'll perform. When he says 'no, I need this' or 'no, I require that' then I expect somebody to listen and help me get what I need. What I don't want to hear is a man telling me that he hasn't done his job and got the shit to my hotel room on time, and that I better go anyhow because some princess is sitting waiting to see my Black ass entertain her. You do your job, Stu, then talk to me about me doing mine. But you do yours first. Now you get back on the damn phone and tell Jimmy whatever the hell you want to tell him, but I ain't moving out of this brokeass hotel till the man arrives. Go on and tell that to Jimmy!

Gaby   'You dirty rat.' (*Giggles.*)

Marvin   Bitch, shut your goddamn mouth.

Scene Four

We hear a BBC news broadcast on the radio. In a London hotel room.

Radio Announcer   . . . in this morning's papers describing it as a 'snub' by the American singer Mr Marvin Gaye. Kensington Palace has declined to comment on the circumstances surrounding last night's non-appearance of Mr Gaye, at a performance in the presence of Her Royal Highness Princess Margaret and her guests. Mr Gaye's representatives cite an unspecified illness, but an audience of over four thousand people waited for nearly two hours before the announcement of Mr Gaye's illness was made, leading to speculation about the real reason for his absence . . .

Over the radio.

Marvin   Gaby, pull the goddamn drapes back.

Gaby   But it's the afternoon already.

Marvin   I don't give a damn what time of day it is, how many times do I need to tell you that you always keep the drapes closed, okay?

Gaby   I don't know why you're so angry with me. I'm only trying to help.

Marvin   You can help by turning that shit off.

Gaby (*turns off the radio*)   People feel you've snubbed them.

Marvin   Done what?

Gaby   Snubbed them.

Marvin   They can bend down and kiss my ass.

Gaby   Yeah, you'd like that wouldn't you.

Marvin   What did you say?

Gaby   Nothing.

Marvin   Bitch, what did you say?

Gaby   I said you'd like that wouldn't you. Everything's always got to be about you, hasn't it. She's our princess, you know. You could have just turned up for her, it wouldn't have killed you.

Marvin   Get your shit and get out of here! Now!

Gaby   So me as well? I'm also not allowed to say what I think, is that it? Marvin, I'm your only friend. Stu is a waste of time, and I don't know who the other hangers-on are, and neither do you. They just come round and drink your booze and snort your coke and smoke your weed . . . They're a waste of time, but *I* actually care for you.

Marvin   Gaby, get the hell out of here before I beat your pasty whore ass.

Gaby   You called me a whore?

Marvin   Well, you sure as hell don't look like a nun to me.

Gaby   A whore? How dare you?

Marvin   Just get your skinny ass out of here.

Gaby   Don't worry I'm going. I don't want to be anywhere near a bastard like you.

The door slams shut.

Marvin   And don't come back either. I don't need to be around tramps and hookers. I got me a real family. A momma and a father who care for me. Real family values.

Scene Five

In a church. We hear **Marvin** *playing the piano and changing the words of 'Precious Lord' to secular lyrics. He is practising and replacing 'God' with 'Baby' and 'Dear Lord' with 'Honey', etc.*

Father   Boy, you think that's anyway for a Christian young man to be carrying on in the house of the Lord?

Marvin   Father, I don't mean no disrespect.

Father   Something wrong with the words of the gospel? Something the matter with singing for good old-fashioned church people?

Marvin   No, sir. Nothing wrong with that, but it ain't what I intend to do with my life.

Father (*laughs*)   With your life? Boy, you don't know a damn thing about anything.

Marvin   I'm old enough to know that I'm gonna be a singer. Rhythm and blues and sweet soul music. That's what I'm gonna do. Sing the kind of music that makes people feel good.

Father   Boy, you know I'm a preacher of the Lord, don't you?

Marvin   Yes, sir.

Father   And how do you think it's going to look if I allow you to go running about and carrying on in these sinful ways?

Marvin   Father, you got your life and I've got mine.

Father   Boy, you disappoint me.

Marvin   I want to do right by you, but I can't be whatever it is you want me to be. I have to be what I want to be.

Father   You been talking with your mother?

Marvin   Only thing Momma ever says to me is, 'Marvin, I want you to be happy and do what pleases you.'

Father   So it's about what pleases you?

Marvin   Yes, sir, it's my life.

Father   Let me ask you, boy. You ashamed of me, is that it?

Marvin   I don't believe so.

Father   You don't believe so?

Marvin   People say things. About how you dress in womanish clothes.

Father   You don't think I'm a man? I'm man enough to be your father.

Marvin   I know that.

Father   Let me ask you again. You ashamed of me?

Marvin   I'm not ashamed of you.

Father   Then why do you not show respect for me?

Marvin   Father, I'm going to Detroit to try to get a contract and make some recordings. Like I said, I'm going to sing music that will make people happy. Some people might even want to get up and dance, but the main thing is I'm going to make them happy. That's what I'm going to do, Father, and I don't see how that is disrespecting you. This sound evil to you?

He begins to sing at the piano.

Well, that sound evil to you?

Father   That's not the word of the Lord. I hear the devil in your music.

Marvin   Then you better listen more closely. I hear the Lord wherever people are happy and are not hurting one another.

Father   This kind of music will lead to temptation, and then to ugliness, and then it will take your life. Only other thing that will kill you is me, if you ever disrespect me. You understand, boy?

Marvin   I hear you. I respect you, but I figure everything would be just fine if you would respect me back.

Father   I ain't making no deals with you, boy. You and your damn devil music.

Marvin   Father, listen. How can this music do harm to anybody? It's soulful music.

Father   If it isn't sacred, then it will corrupt your soul.

Marvin   Love *is* sacred.

Cross-fade choral 'Precious Love' to 'I Want a Witness'.

Scene Six

We are in a Detroit studio. **Marvin** *finishes playing a recording tape of 'How Sweet It Is'.*

Marvin   Well, Sam. What do you think?

Sam   I think, Marvin, that you want to marry the man's sister. At least that's the word on the street. (*Pause.*) Well, it's the first time I've heard you lost for words.

Marvin   I'm asking you what you think about my new songs.

Sam   Why do you want to mess with the man? He's made you a star.

Marvin   I'm already a star. I'm not looking for favours from anybody.

Sam   Boy, I just hope that the man's sister knows who she's messing with.

Marvin   I love Patti. She's like a big sister to me.

Sam   Or a mother?

Marvin   I already got a mother.

Sam   And a father?

Marvin   Yeah, I got one of them too.

Scene Seven

Announcer *trying to speak over the sound of excited people cheering in the streets. We are outside in Washington, DC on 'Marvin Gaye Day'.*

Announcer   And here he is, all the way from Detroit, back in his home city of Washington, DC on 'Marvin Gaye Day' – your own, your very own, Mr Marvin Gaye.

The crowd begins to cheer wildly.

Patti   Marvin, get up and talk to the people.

Marvin   Patti, don't be telling me what to do.

Patti   Marvin, they want to hear from you.

Marvin   Why are my parents looking so damn miserable?

Patti   Your mother looks happy.

Marvin   But look at my father! It's like the man's seen a ghost.

Patti   It's got to be hard for a proud man to have a son like you, Marvin. You get all the attention and the adulation.

Marvin   You telling me the man's jealous?

Patti   No man likes to live in the shadow of his son.

Marvin   Well, what's he ever done except dress like some fool.

Patti   It's 'Marvin Gaye Day'. Say something to the people.

Marvin *stands and crosses to the microphone.*

Marvin   Thank you, thank you. It's great to be back home in wonderful DC. (*The crowd cheers*). Ain't nothing like playing to your own folks, and I'm especially blessed to have my mother and my father here today to share this homecoming. If it wasn't for them I wouldn't be here in front of you today. Hey, Momma, Father, stand up and take a bow.

The crowd begin to applaud.

Father, you ain't going to stand up? (*Pause.*) I guess my father's shy, but you can all see him good in that neat purple crushed velvet jacket. These are the people that made me, right here in Washington, DC. I've come home to them, and I've come home to you all. I know that right now we got some problems in this country. Serious problems. The civil rights struggle ain't done with yet. Discrimination, unemployment staring us down every day. We got problems with the ecology and we still got a war going on in Vietnam. Damn, we got problems alright, but this is what I'm singing about for all of you. Our problems. America's problems.

The crowd continues to cheer wildly as 'Inner City Blues' begins to play over the PA system.

Scene Eight

Mix through to a record shop in London. 'Inner City Blues' is playing. It comes to an end.

Shop Owner   How many times do you want to listen to the album, mate?

Jean-Claude (*Belgian accent*)   But surely this is the greatest album ever made.

Shop Owner   Maybe it is, maybe it ain't. Either way, you wanna buy it or not?

Jean-Claude   Of course I want to buy it. Whenever I come to London I always buy a new copy. For the past ten years this album has been like my Bible.

Shop Owner   You know he's living in London at the moment.

Jean-Claude   Marvin Gaye is living here in London?

Shop Owner   It ain't so bad here is it? Where are you from then? Paris?

Jean-Claude   No, no, no. Belgium. Ostend, by the sea.

Shop Owner   Oh yeah. That's where the ferries go, right?

Jean-Claude   Yes, the ferries go there. I have a nightclub. At the weekends, on a Friday, Saturday and Sunday we have rhythm and blues music. You sell the best music in London. I have the best jukebox in Belgium. I want to turn the Belgian people on to R and B.

Shop Owner   Well, do you want his autograph, then? Give me a day or so and I can try and find out where he's staying.

Scene Nine

We are in a phone box on a London street. There is traffic going by.

Jean-Claude   Louise, I know that I said I would be back this evening, but I have the possibility of something special.

Louise   Is she in London with you?

Jean-Claude   I swear that nothing like this is going on. That episode is finished, I am here on business, that is all.

Louise   You cannot keep cutting us out of your life like this, just when it suits you.

Jean-Claude   Louise, I will see you tomorrow, alright?

She hangs up the phone.

Louise? Louise, are you there?

Scene Ten

In the corridor of a London hotel.

Beatrice   I have already told you, I am Mr Gaye's girlfriend and I have just arrived from Holland. You must open up the door. He's not answering the phone.

Manager   Do you have any identification?

Beatrice   My passport. I am Dutch. (*Shows it to him.*) See. Please, it may be serious.

We hear the sound of the door opening.

Beatrice   Marvin? Oh, my God! (*To the hotel manager.*) Get a doctor, he's unconscious.

Marvin   Beatrice, baby, I ain't unconscious. I'm sleeping. Or rather, I was sleeping.

Manager   Mr Gaye, forgive the intrusion, but the young lady claimed to know you.

Beatrice   You scared me.

Manager   Well, unless there's some other way that I can be of assistance, I'll leave the two of you alone for the evening.

We hear the door to the hotel room close.

Marvin   What time is it?

Beatrice   Late. Or early, depending on which way you look at it.

Marvin   You playing games with me?

Beatrice   Look at the state of this place. I was worried out of my mind when you did not pick up the phone. You cannot live like this.

Marvin   You come back to just run your mouth?

Beatrice   This place is no good for you, Marvin. There's nothing here for you in London. Let's go to America. That's your home.

Marvin   America? I got problems with the tax man, my ex-wife's lawyers are chasing me down, and as usual my parents are hardly speaking to each other. What the hell do I need to go back to America for?

Beatrice   To sing, Marvin. And to make hit records again.

Marvin   Baby, I need to get strong first. I need to heal myself and then I'll be ready to face that place.

Beatrice   Then maybe you need to get rid of the bloody drugs.

There is a knock at the door.

Marvin, you expecting somebody?

Marvin   Sure, the IRS or my wife's lawyers. Whoever gets here first.

Beatrice *crosses to the door and opens up.*

Beatrice   Can I help you?

Jean-Claude   I am looking for Mr Marvin Gaye.

Beatrice   And who are you?

Jean-Claude   My name is Jean-Claude Levalle. I am sorry, but I do not have an appointment.

Beatrice   And your business?

Jean-Claude   I am a fan. But maybe I could talk to Mr Gaye. I have a proposal.

Marvin   If the man has a proposal then we better listen to him, baby.

Beatrice   Come in.

She closes the door as **Jean-Claude** *enters.*

Jean-Claude   Mr Gaye. It is an honour.

Marvin   Take a seat, Mr Jean-Claude. It's a little before my getting dressed time.

Jean-Claude   I am sorry to disturb you, but I didn't have a phone number or anything.

Marvin   You want an autograph, Mr Jean-Claude, is that it?

Jean-Claude   That would be nice, but I also have an idea.

Marvin   An idea? Haven't heard one of those in a long while now. What's the idea?

Jean-Claude   I have a club in Belgium. I am from Ostend. Ostend is quiet, but my club is the only place that plays rhythm and blues.

Beatrice   You want Marvin to visit your club?

Jean-Claude   It would be an honour.

Marvin (*laughs*)   Let me ask you, Mr Jean-Claude, how many people does your club seat?

Jean-Claude   Two hundred. Maybe two hundred and fifty.

Marvin   Man, I was playing bigger places than that as a teenager in DC.

Jean-Claude   Ostend is a nice clean city. Beaches, fresh air. I have read that you like to exercise.

Marvin   Basketball. Boxing. I like all sports, man.

Beatrice   Jean-Claude, Marvin is a big star. What can he do in a small town like this Ostend?

Jean-Claude   Perhaps change his lifestyle. Go back to how he used to be.

Marvin   How do you know how I used to be?

Jean-Claude   Please, Mr Gaye, it is obvious that you weren't always like this or how would you have made that magnificent music? Perhaps you simply need a change of venue?

Marvin   I need a hit record, man, that's what I need.

Jean-Claude   Then you have to write one. But if you are to write one you need the right ambience. I will find musicians to work with you. Good Belgian session musicians who will be honoured to work with the great Marvin Gaye. And I can try and get you a new record contract.

Marvin   You want to manage me?

Jean-Claude   I just want to help.

Beatrice   Do you have a card, Mr Jean-Claude Levalle?

Jean-Claude   Yes, I have a card.

Beatrice   Then we'll call you, okay.

Jean-Claude   Alright, yes. I understand.

Marvin   I like your style, Mr Jean-Claude. But you say you want to negotiate for me. You gotta be tough to do that, that's all I'm telling you. No friends in the music business, man. No friends at all.

Beatrice *shows him out and closes the door.*

Scene Eleven

Marvin's *parents are being shown around a house by a real estate agent.*

House Agent   Either of you good folks ever lived in California before?

Mother   We're from Washington, DC. It's our son who wants us to relocate out here. He's a singer and he's also relocating here to Los Angeles.

House Agent (*laughs*)   I think everybody knows who Marvin Gaye is. You must be so proud.

Mother   Well, yes, of course we are, aren't we? (*Silence.*)

House Agent   The house is a modern ranch-style property, and one of the features is that each bedroom has its own bathroom.

Father   I don't see why we have to come and live in no goddamn California.

Mother   Well, you don't have a church anymore since they decided to vote in a new pastor . . .

Father   Why the hell the boy want us out here? Buying us a house like he's doing us a favour.

House Agent   Perhaps I'll leave the two of you alone for a few minutes to talk things over.

The **Agent** *leaves the room.*

Mother   I thought that we agreed that we would try to live in Los Angeles.

Father   So, the boy's the leader of this family now, is he?

Mother   Marvin's just trying to do something nice for us.

Father   A father isn't supposed to ask for, or receive, favours from his son. The good book makes it clear that the son must respect the father in all things and in all ways.

Mother   In all things? (*Pause.*) Well? In all ways?

Scene Twelve

We are in a London pub. **Stu** *places the drinks on the table.*

Stu   Vodka tonic for you, Marvin, and an orange juice for Beatrice. You can always rely on Stu. Cheers everyone.

We hear the glasses clink.

Good to have you back here, Beatrice. How was Holland?

Beatrice   Nothing special. Just 'home', that's all.

Stu Hey, don't underestimate 'home', you know. We spend half our lives trying to get away from there, then the rest of our lives trying to get back there so we can work out why we left in the first place.

Marvin I figure that you didn't ask us here so that you could talk shit about 'home'.

Stu Hey, come on, Marvin. Let's all be cool.

Marvin Stu, you wouldn't know how to be cool if you found yourself in an igloo.

Stu Jimmy's suing you.

Marvin Suing me?

Beatrice Jimmy told you he was going to sue Marvin and you decided to buy us drinks, is that it?

Stu Well, what do you want me to do? Marvin came to this country and I offered to help him. But Marvin chooses not to show up half the time, and he's always high on drugs, and that's just unprofessional, man. I don't care what problems he has in the States with taxes, or alimony, but you can't come to England and behave like this.

Marvin You talking about me?

Stu Yeah, Marvin, I'm talking about you.

Marvin Well, talk to me then, not to my woman. As long as your little faggot ass has got two eyes in your head to see me with, then you talk to me.

Stu (*puts glass down on the table*)   Okay, I've had enough of this. I'm leaving.

Marvin Get your punk ass out of here, Stu. You figure you were doing Marvin Gaye a favour?

Stu Best of luck, Beatrice.

Beatrice Get lost, Stu, I don't need your luck.

Stu Actually, I think you need it more than you realize.

Scene Thirteen

We are in the living room of a Belgian house. We hear an excited young girl running and screaming and happy.

Louise Okay, Catherine. You go upstairs to play while I talk to your daddy. Go on!

A reluctant **Catherine** *leaves.*

Jean-Claude (*excited*)   Louise, this is going to work.

Louise You want to bring this Black man here and then do what? Have him stay in our house?

Jean-Claude We run a guesthouse. We have spare rooms.

Louise If he is as big a star as you say he is, then he's not going to stay here. Look at the place. It's for people on a budget. This is not the Palace Hotel.

Jean-Claude Then I'll get him a flat in town.

Louise With what? We don't have any money. The club is closed because you can't afford to pay the bills.

Jean-Claude I can promote this man, help him to get his career back on track and then . . .

Louise And then what? Come on, tell me, and then what?

Jean-Claude Manage him and promote him. Look after him. He is a great artist.

Louise You are a dreamer, Jean-Claude. You always were. A Black American singer coming to live with us in Ostend. I don't think so.

Jean-Claude I'm going back to London to get him.

Louise Jean-Claude, Jean-Claude. Please. Concentrate on the hotel, for the sake of us all. Let's just sell the club and make a go of it at the hotel.

Jean-Claude In the morning I'm seeing the bank manager and finalizing a loan so that we can improve the hotel. When the money comes through from selling the club, then I will pay back the bank.

Louise So we will be able to renovate the hotel?

Jean-Claude It's what you want, isn't it?

Louise And the Black man?

Jean-Claude He will come for a while and we can see if it is working. But you are right. He may not stay. But this is too good an opportunity. I can promote him. Put his career back on track.

Louise Here, in Belgium?

Jean-Claude Why not here in Belgium? Why not?

Scene Fourteen

Flashback. We are in the living room of a house in Los Angeles.

Mother Here's your coffee, Karen.

Karen Thank you.

Mother Marvin's father is resting upstairs, but I can go and wake him if you would like to talk with him too.

Karen No, it's alright.

Mother Karen, I know my son has left his wife, but is he being good to you?

Karen   Marvin says he's going to England. That there's too many pressures on him here and he can't concentrate.

Mother   Is he beating you?

Karen   No.

Mother   Karen?

Karen   He doesn't mean to. (*Pause.*) Has a man never raised his hand to you?

Mother   Karen, that isn't the point that I'm making.

Father (*enters*)   What the hell's going on down here with all this noise?

Karen   Mr Gaye. I'm sorry for waking you up.

Father   Can't the two of you conduct a civil conversation without raising hell?

Mother   Karen says Marvin's planning on taking off to England.

Father   And that's why you're all shouting?

Karen   I'm sorry.

Mother   Nobody's shouting. (*Pause.*) I don't see why Marvin's got to go so far from us.

Father   That boy will do whatever the hell comes into his damn head. Ain't no point in you worrying why he does this or why he does that.

Karen   I better be going now.

Mother   Karen, you've only just got here. You just sit yourself back down, girl.

Father   You carrying my grandchild?

Karen   I'm pregnant.

Father   Then my son ain't got no right talking about taking off for no London and leaving you behind.

Karen   He won't be going for too long, he says.

Father   One day is too long with you in this condition.

Mother   She's not ill.

Father   I know she's not ill. I'm not stupid.

Karen   I can manage by myself.

Father   Somebody ought to give that boy a good ass-whupping carrying on like he does.

Mother   Maybe we can all go to London to see him.

Father   I ain't going to no goddamn London. The boy asks us out here to California claiming we're going to be a family. The next thing I know he's turned around and he's planning to clear off for London. Are we going to spend our whole lives chasing after him because he fancies himself some kind of big shot? Is that what you want to do? The boy should take his girl with him to London, or else keep his backside here.

Karen   I'm sorry, I didn't mean to cause any trouble by telling you all of this. I really didn't.

Scene Fifteen

We are in a London hotel room and there is a knock on the door. **Beatrice** *and* **Marvin** *are asleep.*

Marvin   Who the hell is banging on the door at this time of the morning?

Beatrice *gets out of bed and crosses to the door.*

Beatrice   Who is it?

Jean-Claude   Jean-Claude Levalle. From Belgium.

Beatrice   Who?

Jean-Claude   Jean-Claude. From Ostend. Belgium.

Marvin   Jesus, it's the promoter guy.

Beatrice (*quietly, to* **Marvin**)   We need money, Marvin. Maybe the man has money.

Cross-fade to:

Scene Sixteen

We are in the hotel room a few minutes later.

Jean-Claude   I am sorry that I did not call before, but I thought that I would just come up and surprise you.

Marvin   Well, you got that right, man.

Jean-Claude   Well, everything is ready.

Marvin   Everything is ready?

Jean-Claude   For you to come to Ostend. I went back to Belgium and we are all good to go now.

Beatrice   You want us to come to Belgium. You're serious?

Jean-Claude   Of course I am serious. Did you think I was making a joke?

Marvin   Hey, man, what am I going to do in Belgium? I don't even know where Belgium is.

Jean-Claude   Well, for a start you will stop with the drugs. It is no good for you.

Marvin   Baby, I already got one father. I don't need another, you dig?

Jean-Claude   If you come to my town, to my family, then you cannot behave like this. I am sorry, but I have a small daughter.

Marvin   Beatrice, show this man the door.

Beatrice   Mr Jean-Claude said they have fresh air and beaches there. You will be able to get your strength back and start to live healthily again.

Marvin   Something wrong with how I'm living now?

Jean-Claude   I think maybe you are trying to kill yourself.

Marvin   And I think you've lost your damn mind. Why don't you take your ass back to this Belgium or whatever you call the place and leave us in peace.

Jean-Claude   I am sorry but I have no desire to tell you what to do, I am just being honest with you. This is not good for the great Marvin Gaye. You should not be living like this. If London is no good, and if the United States is no good, then what do you have to lose by trying my country? You can have some peace and quiet and I will look after you.

Marvin   And what's in it for you?

Jean-Claude   I can manage and promote you. Ten per cent, normal contract. We can talk about what you want and I will try to get it for you. This morning I have written to your record label.

Marvin (*laughs*)   You *wrote* to America?

Jean-Claude   You told me you wanted to get out of the contract.

Marvin   Writing to my label ain't none of your goddamn business.

Beatrice   When are you going?

Jean-Claude   'Taking my ass back to Belgium.' Isn't that what you want?

Marvin   Wait a minute now.

Jean-Claude   No, please. You wait a minute. I will come back here at one o'clock this afternoon with a car. If you want to come to Belgium then please be packed and ready. If this seems like a bad idea to you, and you want to die here like Jimi Hendrix or Jim Morrison, then I will understand. Perhaps you think it is romantic? Either way it has been an honour to meet Marvin Gaye. I have no desire to pressure you into anything.

Marvin   That's it? You're leaving?

Jean-Claude   I will come back in a few hours.

Beatrice   And you want us to be ready to go with you?

Jean-Claude   No. I want you to do what you want to do. If you want to come to Belgium then you will be ready. If not, then we can shake hands and wish each other good luck.

Beatrice   You always do business like this?

Jean-Claude   People tell me I am not much of a businessman.

Marvin   Seem pretty damn good to me.

Jean-Claude   I will be back.

We hear **Jean-Claude** *leave the room.*

Marvin   Man, that's one strange French brother.

Beatrice   Belgian.

Marvin   Whatever the hell he is, he's a strange cat. We have to pack.

Beatrice   Pack?

Marvin   Sure. Don't you want to go?

Beatrice   Are you serious?

Marvin   Baby, it ain't so much where I want to go, it's where else I got to go? I don't have nothing else going on. And like you said, maybe the man has money.

Scene Seventeen

We are in a house in Ostend. February 1981.

Jean-Claude   Please, come in. You must meet my wife Louise. This is Marvin Gaye, and Beatrice.

Louise   I am pleased to meet you. Jean-Claude has talked a lot about you. Please sit down. I will make some coffee for everybody.

Jean-Claude   Or maybe something stronger. A brandy perhaps? Or a glass of wine. We have to celebrate.

Beatrice   Coffee is fine for me.

Jean-Claude   Marvin, a brandy?

Marvin   Sure, if that's what you are having.

Louise   How long will you both be staying?

Jean-Claude   Louise, you can't ask our guests that. They've only just got here.

Marvin   Hey, Louise, we're staying as long as Jean-Claude will have us. Time to regroup.

Louise   But maybe for you Ostend is boring. What will you do?

Marvin   What I always do. Make music.

Scene Eighteen

In a seafront flat. We hear the sound of the North Sea pounding in and gulls wheeling overhead.

Beatrice   Check it out, Marvin. It is a nice view from the window.

Marvin   I can't see a damn thing except that nasty brown water. Man, I thought the sea was supposed to be blue.

Beatrice   But it's peaceful. People are walking by below us, and ships are passing in the distance. It's nice and quiet.

Marvin   What the hell does he expect us to do here? Close the window, it stinks of fish out there.

Beatrice *closes the window.*

Beatrice   Do you want me to cook something?

Marvin   You can cook?

Beatrice   Well, we can go out if you prefer. There's got to be a restaurant or a bar someplace. What do you want to do?

Marvin   What the hell is this thing?

Beatrice   It's a video tape recorder. We can watch tapes of TV shows or movies.

Marvin   I've never used one of these before.

Beatrice   Well, it's not that difficult. Would you like to watch a movie?

Marvin   Jesus, I got to get out of here. I feel like I'm in prison.

Beatrice   Give it a chance, Marvin. We've only been here for an hour or so. I know it's not a big apartment, but it's good of Jean-Claude to find it for us.

Marvin   You got some money?

Beatrice   Jean-Claude gave me some.

Marvin   He gave *you* the money?

Beatrice   I don't think he imagined you doing any grocery shopping.

Marvin   Let me have it. I'll be back soon enough.

Beatrice   Do you know where to go?

Marvin   Woman, I look stupid to you?

We hear the door slam and **Marvin** *going out*

Scene Nineteen

Mix through. Late at night. There are a couple of attempts to get the key in the door, and eventually it works. We hear **Marvin** *fall clumsily through the door.*

Marvin   Where's the goddamn light switch?

Beatrice   Marvin, where have you been? I've been worried sick about you? I even went round to see if I could find Jean-Claude.

Marvin   You went to Jean-Claude's place to tell on me?

Beatrice   I didn't know where you were. I thought something might have happened to you.

Marvin   I'm a grown-ass man from the streets of DC. What the hell can happen to me in a little town like this? You think I can't handle these streets, is that it?

Beatrice   Please, Marvin. Let me help you up.

Marvin   Don't put your hands on me!

Beatrice   I thought you came here to get better and make a new start? Why are you doing this to yourself?

Marvin   I said don't touch me!

He slaps her.

What's the matter, you don't understand English now?

Beatrice   It makes you feel good hitting a woman, is that it? Makes you feel like a man.

He hits her again.

Yes, you keep hitting me, Marvin, if it's the only way you can feel like a man. Not much else about you that's a man, is there?

He punches her and she falls over furniture and to the ground.

You're a coward, Marvin. A coward and a drunk. Go on, hit me again if it makes you feel like a man. Go on, hit me, you pig.

Scene Twenty

We hear the sound of two men running on the beach.

Jean-Claude (*out of breath*)   Marvin, you have to slow down a little bit. This is not a race.

Marvin   You're out of shape, Jean-Claude.

Jean-Claude   When I was younger I used to box. You ever try boxing?

Marvin   Marvin Gaye tried all sports, man. However, music is my love. Don't have no time to be messing with sports.

Jean-Claude   But you want to get fit again?

Marvin   I got to get fit again if I'm going to get back into the studio and record.

Jean-Claude   I have some good news for you.

Marvin   What kind of news?

Jean-Claude   From Detroit.

Marvin *stops running.*

Marvin   From Detroit?

Jean-Claude   Everything is agreed. You're released from your contract and you are now free to negotiate with whoever you wish.

Marvin   Jean-Claude, you serious?

Jean-Claude   But that isn't everything. I have a studio booked for rehearsal, and you play at my club a week on Saturday. Your debut in Belgium.

Marvin   I thought your club was closed down.

Jean-Claude   Well, you will be reopening it.

Marvin   And who are the musicians?

Jean-Claude   Local guys. They can't believe that they're going to have the chance to play with Marvin Gaye. On the night of the gig I will invite some executives from the States and begin negotiating a new deal for you.

Marvin   Guys coming over from the States to hear me play in Belgium?

Jean-Claude   We have to get your career back on track again.

Marvin   Then I don't have no time for running on no beach, Jean-Claude. We have to start rehearsing.

Jean-Claude   I told you that everything could work for you in Belgium. I'll get some journalists to come over too. Maybe *The New Yorker*. Or *Rolling Stone*.

Marvin   Man, it looks like I'm making a comeback.

Jean-Claude   You were never really away, Marvin. But this is your future now. It's here in Belgium.

Scene Twenty-one

We are in a Los Angeles courtroom. We hear the knock of the judicial hammer.

Judge   I have listened to the case prepared by the attorneys for Karen Williams, and I am convinced that she should be awarded sole custody of her son. The court notes that the father has neither acknowledged the child, nor paid any money towards the child's upbringing. In this situation I order that whatever assets he has be seized and held until restitution is made to the mother and child. It's truly pitiful that a man held in such esteem by so many throughout the length and breadth of this country should deem it appropriate to behave with such indifference towards his responsibilities. Court adjourned.

Again we hear the knock of the hammer.

Scene Twenty-two

We are in a rehearsal room in Belgium. The band are playing 'Let's Get It On' badly. **Marvin** *starts to sing, then he stops.*

Marvin No! (*The band stops.*) What's the matter with you people. You never heard my music before?

Jean-Claude Marvin, they're trying. But it's difficult for them to get into the soul groove straight away.

Marvin What do you mean straight away. We've been here for three days trying to get this right. For Christ's sake just let me get one song right, that's all. Is that too much to ask?

Musician Jean-Claude, the guys are tired. Maybe we take a short break now?

Jean-Claude Take an hour. Have lunch or something. I will talk to Marvin.

We hear a group of disgruntled musicians begin to troop out.

Jean-Claude What is it, Marvin? Is there something on your mind?

Marvin You need to get me some Black American musicians, I don't want any Africans or West Indians. I had enough of that shit in London.

Jean-Claude But how am I going to find Black American musicians? We have no time.

Marvin You said it yourself, these people don't have any soul or rhythm. It's like they're playing for an orchestra.

Jean-Claude They are trying to be faithful to your sound.

Marvin It sounds like supermarket music. Marvin Gaye can't go out in front of people sounding like this. I need some Black people here.

Jean-Claude Is everything alright with you and Beatrice?

Marvin What the hell you calling Beatrice's name for?

Jean-Claude She came to see Louise.

Marvin Jean-Claude, you listen to me, and you listen to me good, okay. I don't want you ever messing about in my personal business. Beatrice is like all women; she wants to play me, and she'll use whatever it takes to get her own way. I know this and I know how to deal with her.

Jean-Claude Are you going to send her back to Holland?

Marvin And what business is it of yours?

Jean-Claude I just want you to be able to concentrate on your music, Marvin. Look at you, you're fit and exercising on the beach every day. You sound good. You've just got to help my boys to get in the groove. Show them a little patience. I want Saturday to be a big success for you.

Marvin For me or for you?

Jean-Claude For us, Marvin. And I know 'us' doesn't include Beatrice or any women. I'm hip, so give me some credit. I want you to know that if you want her to disappear I can help.

Marvin Disappear? You sound like some damn Mafia don.

Jean-Claude I mean go back to Holland. I can give her some money and put her on the train.

Scene Twenty-three

We are in the Levalles' living room.

Louise You are drunk, Jean-Claude.

Jean-Claude I had some beers with the musicians. They are worried.

Louise Worried about what?

Jean-Claude Marvin's attitude. He doesn't like the flat. He doesn't like the weather. He doesn't like the way they play. Everything is a problem with Marvin.

Louise No, Jean-Claude. Everything is not a problem with Marvin. Everything is a problem with you. You take the money we were supposed to put into the hotel and you give it to Marvin.

Jean-Claude We have money coming from America. I'm just waiting for the new record company to send the cheque.

Louise And then you borrow even more money to reopen the club that you are supposed to be selling.

Jean-Claude We can afford it. When Marvin makes his new album we are going to be doing just fine. In fact, better than just fine.

Louise And so Mr Marvin is going to make a new album. In the meantime, what about us?

Jean-Claude I have given you all the money that I have. Are you short of money?

Louise You're making a fool of yourself, Jean-Claude. People in the town are laughing at you. You're like the butler for this Black man. When you're not around they call you the white slave of Ostend. It's as though you've fallen in love with this man and you will do whatever he asks of you. You used to be a proud man, Jean-Claude. A dignified man, but what has become of you? I said 'yes' bring the Black American to Ostend, and let's see if this can work. I said 'yes' to make you happy, but I'm losing my husband to this situation.

Jean-Claude   You're not losing me. I'm not going anywhere.

Louise   You want to be like him and live without rules? Without any sense of responsibility?

Jean-Claude   What do you mean?

Louise   That girl is pregnant.

Jean-Claude   Beatrice?

Louise   She's too frightened to tell him in case he hits her again.

Jean-Claude   What do you mean hits her.

Louise   Oh Jean-Claude, Jean-Claude. What has happened to you that you're now pretending. You know what is going on. Don't make yourself any more foolish, please. Not for . . .

Jean-Claude   Not for what? A Black man, is that what you want to say?

Louise   I've got nothing more to say to you.

Jean-Claude   Louise, please.

Louise   I'm going to bed.

We hear a door slam.

Scene Twenty-four

Mix through to the concert on Saturday night. The band is playing the intro. to 'What's Going On'.

Jean-Claude   Ladies and gentlemen, welcome to the Ostend Lounge where tonight I have the great pleasure and honour of presenting one of the great stars of American music. For the first time ever in Belgium, live and direct from Los Angeles, California, I give you, the great Mr Marvin Gaye.

There is a burst of applause and **Marvin** *starts to sing 'What's Going On'.*

Scene Twenty-five

Mix through to a hotel room late at night.

Marvin   You say your name's Keisha? And you're with *Rolling Stone*?

Journalist   Kimona. Kimona Jackson from Pittsburgh, Pennsylvania.

Marvin   Well, Kimona Jackson from Pittsburgh, Pennsylvania you sure are a foxy-looking lady.

We hear sniffing of coke.

Journalist   You know I got to file my story when I get home.

Marvin   Baby, you write what you gotta write. That band ain't worth shit, anybody can hear that, but nothing wrong with my voice.

Journalist   That's for sure, but it ain't your voice that I'm looking to sample right now.

Marvin   Baby, you sound like you got a train to catch. You in a rush?

Journalist   Only for some sweet loving.

Marvin   All good things eventually come to those who wait.

Journalist   So what's a fine, broad, coloured American man like you doing in some washed-up place like this. I guess that's what my readers want to know.

Marvin   You can tell them that Marvin Gaye is resting and recovering and getting himself back together.

Journalist   But why not Paris or Barcelona or London?

Marvin   And maybe your little chocolate ass should mind her own business.

Journalist   And maybe your fine manly ass should put a little less of Peru up your nose and start putting some loving on a sister. Don't worry, this part of the evening ain't going to make it into my piece.

Marvin (*laughs*)   You come all this way to see me perform at the Ostend Lounge?

Journalist   Let's just say I came all this way to see you perform.

Marvin   People back home haven't forgotten me?

Journalist   Forgotten Marvin Gaye? You crazy? People don't forget that easy. You just need to put out a decent record and they'll be begging you to come home and do your thing again.

Marvin   They waiting for me?

Journalist   Like I'm waiting for you. Can I help you with anything down there, Mr Gaye?

Marvin   Hey, back off. I told you, ain't no rush.

Journalist   Well, if you don't hurry up, baby, your dinner's liable to get cold.

We hear a loud knocking on the door.

Marvin   You expecting company?

The knocking continues.

Journalist   Who is it?

The knocking continues.

Journalist   Baby, cover up that powder and let me see who it is trying to raise the devil at this time of the night.

We hear the door open.

Journalist   Little white lady, can I help you?

Beatrice   Marvin, is this all you think you're worth? Sneaking off to screw groupies in hotel rooms.

Journalist   Baby, maybe that's all he thinks your sad flat ass is worth.

Marvin   Hey, don't talk to her that way.

Journalist   You're siding with Miss Ann over this brown sugar?

Marvin   Beatrice, wait.

Beatrice   I think I've done enough waiting, Marvin. I just came to tell you that enough is enough.

Marvin   No, baby, we're going to make this work out just fine.

He starts to follow her out of the room.

Journalist   You seriously prefer Miss Ann over this?

Marvin   Beatrice, wait!

Beatrice   Marvin, stay away from me!

Scene Twenty-six

We are in the living room of a Los Angeles house.

Karen   I meant to come round before, but . . .

Mother   I know, Karen. It's not been easy for you, but you doing any better now?

Karen   I'm fine, but what about *you*? When I heard about Mr Gaye, I didn't know what to do.

Mother   The man has been dressing in that way for years. It's not as if he's the first minister to have problems in that department.

Karen   I know, but . . .

Mother   But nothing, Karen. I've been living with Mr Gaye's confusion for a long time, and for a long time now this marriage has been over.

Karen   But you're still in the same house.

Mother   Yes, we are, and Marvin's father has his part of the house and I have my part. I want him to keep his distance and I'll keep mine.

Karen   I'm sorry.

Mother   My husband has spent his whole life trying to get into Marvin's head. Why has he got to be jealous of the boy and drive him away from me?

Karen   I sometimes think that it's me who drove him away from you.

Mother   Child, Marvin was running long before you met him. But all it would take is for his father to just reach out a hand of friendship to the boy and treat him like a son instead of being so mean to him. Marvin just needs to feel wanted.

Karen   I wanted him, Mrs Gaye.

Mother   You and me both, Karen. But I don't think it's a woman's love that he's craving. Now don't you get me wrong. Marvin ain't no cissy or anything, but he just takes women's love for granted. It's some other kind of approval he's looking for, and he's not looking for it from us.

Karen   From his father?

Mother   I learned a long time ago to steer clear of whatever it is that's going on between my husband and my son. People say that mothers and daughters have a complicated relationship, but I do believe it's nothing compared to how fathers and sons act around each other.

Scene Twenty-seven

We are in a bar in Ostend. In the background we hear a pinball machine and the sound of quiet conversations. The door opens and then closes.

Jean-Claude   Beatrice. Over here.

Beatrice *crosses towards him.*

Jean-Claude   Please take a seat. Thank you for coming.

Beatrice   I don't think I can stay long. Marvin has gone to rehearse and . . .

Jean-Claude   Don't worry. He doesn't know that I am meeting you. And he won't know. Can I get you a drink?

Beatrice   No thanks. I'm fine.

Jean-Claude   I am sorry to hear that you lost the baby.

Beatrice   Thanks. It was probably for the best anyhow. I'm not ready to be a mother.

Jean-Claude   Beatrice, I need your help. I have done everything for Marvin that I said I would do. We have a new record contract. I have found him somewhere to rehearse, organized a major gig in Switzerland. I have even brought over his friend, Sam Wilson.

Beatrice   Sam from LA?

Jean-Claude   He said he wanted Black musicians so I have got him Sam Wilson. I surprised him earlier today with his friend.

Beatrice   Then I don't see what the problem is.

Jean-Claude   Remember how I met him in London? The drugs? It was pathetic. I don't want to see Marvin like that again. It is not . . . dignified. I have kept my end of the deal, why can't he keep his?

Beatrice   You are asking me things I can't answer.

Jean-Claude   Are you going home?

Beatrice   Yes, I'm going home. But I just have to find the right moment. I don't want to run away and leave him feeling abandoned. (*Pause.*) I'm sorry, Jean-Claude, but Marvin is Marvin. You knew what you were dealing with when you brought him back here.

Jean-Claude   So now maybe I lose everything? My wife. Marvin. Money.

Beatrice   I thought you made a deal for a new album?

Jean-Claude   Sure, but I am only Mr ten per cent. The money belongs to Marvin, and I have already spent more than my share on the flat and the studio and paying musicians and reopening the club. I have lost money.

Scene Twenty-eight

We are in the Ostend flat late at night. There is the noise of a guitar playing and a tape machine playing backing tracks.

Sam   Marvin, hit that line again.

Marvin   Ooh baby, what I need is sexual healing.

They laugh out loud.

Sam   Okay, I'll put in a little drum this time. Marvin, you mind if I use the coffee table?

Marvin   Sam, my brother, you just use whatever you want, let's just hit it again.

Beatrice   Anybody want another beer?

Sam   Marvin, where you get such a sweet-looking chick. (*To* **Beatrice**.) Honey, you got a sister?

He bursts out laughing.

Marvin   Hey, Sam, don't you be talking about my woman like that.

Sam   Damn, I wouldn't need any sexual healing if I had a fine piece like that on tap.

Marvin   Sam, show some damn respect. Coke got you talking some disrespectful shit, so you better knock it off if you know what's good for you.

Sam   Man, I don't mean nothing by it. (*To* **Beatrice**.) Baby, you ain't offended by a little jive talking are you?

Beatrice   I asked you boys if you wanted another beer.

Sam   Boys? Bitch, who the hell you calling boys?

Beatrice   What did you call me?

Sam   White girl, you better remember to never call a brother a boy. You maybe get away with that shit in Europe, but not with an American brother. Marvin, you let her talk to you that way? You turned faggot or something?

Marvin   Get the fuck out of here!

Sam   Damn, looks like I hit a nerve. No wonder you talking about needing some sexual healing. Marvin, I hear things about your pop, but I didn't know you got those issues too.

Marvin   I said you better get the hell out of here before I take this baseball bat to your nigger ass.

Beatrice   You heard what he said. Take your nigger ass out of here.

Sam (*to* **Marvin**)   Man, you let a white woman use that word in front of you? I believe you turned faggot for real.

We hear a door slam.

Marvin   You hush your mouth, woman!

Beatrice   I ain't your woman. I haven't been your woman for a long time, Marvin. You can look at me however you want to. If you want to hurt me go ahead, but I'm not your woman anymore.

We hear another door slam.

Scene Twenty-nine

Out of the darkness we hear the strains of the recording of the song 'Sexual Healing' begin to rise.

Jean-Claude   That's it, that's the groove. Marvin, this is a hit. I can feel it. Sam sounds tight doesn't he?

Marvin   Sam, you like it?

Sam   Man, we sound cool. Marvin, this is a million seller. You're going right back to the top with this one.

Jean-Claude   I sent the demo to Los Angeles and they want to put it out in a month, six weeks maximum.

Marvin   But what about promotion? You can't just put a single out without promotion.

Sam   This track don't need no promotion. Pretty soon everybody's going to be talking about how much 'sexual healing' they need.

Jean-Claude   I don't think it's a good idea for you to go back to America, Marvin. It's better for you to be here. You are making great music here. Belgium is good for you.

Sam   Shit, Jean-Claude. That sound like Belgian music to you?

Jean-Claude   No, but Marvin made the song here. And there are bound to be other songs, yes?

Marvin   What do you mean other songs?

Jean-Claude   Well, we signed a deal for a whole album, not just for a single. You can't go anywhere until the album is complete.

Sam   Come on, man. You're not telling Marvin what to do, are you?

Jean-Claude   Of course not. (*Laughs nervously.*) But Marvin, you are not going to leave Belgium?

Marvin   Jean-Claude, right now I'm going to get a drink and get away from you bitching in my ear. Can't you hear the sweet music playing?

Scene Thirty

Mix through to a Los Angeles kitchen where 'Sexual Healing' is playing on the radio.

Father   Turn that devil music off.

Mother   But it's Marvin. His new song.

Father   I know who it is. You think I'm stupid? You think I don't know the sound of my own son's voice?

Mother   Every time I turn on the radio they're playing his song. Just like the old days.

Father   Just like the old days with the boy singing his songs of vulgarity about matters that ought to be left for adults to deal with behind closed doors.

She turns down the radio so that the song is now only barely audible.

Mother   I got a letter from Marvin.

Father   You don't need to tell me nothing about your own business. Remember, the two of us are not studying each other anymore.

Mother   I know that. I didn't forget. But he is still your son.

Father   The boy is *your* son. He wrote to you, not me.

Mother   He says he might be coming back soon.

Father   And what is that to do with me? He sure as hell isn't coming back to see me.

Mother   I imagine if he comes back he'll want to come and stay here.

Father   In our house?

Mother   Well, it's really Marvin's house.

Father   He gave us the damn house; I don't see why he can't go and stay someplace else. You know he's only coming back to cause trouble.

Scene Thirty-one

We hear the sound of a doorbell. There is no answer. We hear anxious knocking on a door and then we hear the door open.

Louise   What do you want, Jean-Claude?

Jean-Claude   Are you not going to invite me in?

Louise   This is my mother's house. If we are going to argue I'd prefer it if we didn't do so here.

Jean-Claude   Louise, please. Everything is fine now. Marvin is recording his album. We have a gig lined up for him in Switzerland. I'm managing him and he has a Black musician friend living in Ostend.

Louise   Go back, Jean-Claude. He needs you. You need him too.

Jean-Claude   That is all you have to say?

Louise   Why are you always trying to have everything like those greedy Americans that you love so much? Life isn't like this, Jean-Claude. You have to make choices.

Scene Thirty-two

We are in a noisy bar in Ostend. There is R and B music playing on the jukebox.

Marvin   Hey, Jean-Claude. Sam brought these records from the States and these cats said they'll put them on the jukebox. Sure as hell livens up this place.

Jean-Claude   It is good music.

Marvin   That's all you have to say? 'It is good music.'

Jean-Claude   You are supposed to be recording the album.

Marvin   You're beginning to sound like a slave driver or something. Ain't that so, Sam?

Sam   Give the brother a break, Jean-Claude.

Jean-Claude   The company are asking when they're going to get the album to go with the single.

Marvin   Man, I'm just relaxing. This is how we go about making music. It's not like I'm on the factory line or some bullshit.

Jean-Claude   I know, I know, I'm just a little worried.

Marvin   Well, you have to stop being so worried. And I need some money.

Jean-Claude   You need money for what?

Marvin   Hell, you my father now? I don't have to tell you what I need my own money for.

Jean-Claude   But I have given you the advance on the album.

Marvin   You didn't give me all the money, man. Don't mess with me, I'm not stupid.

Jean-Claude   No, I kept back ten thousand dollars which you owed me.

Marvin   I owed you ten thousand dollars? You crazy?

Jean-Claude   Of course, the money that I loaned to you after you arrived here.

Marvin   Man, you've got some imagination, Mr Jean-Claude.

Jean-Claude   Marvin, you are joking, right?

Marvin   Jean-Claude, I want my money.

Jean-Claude (*laughs nervously*)   Ask Beatrice, she was there when I gave you the cash.

Marvin   You gave me ten thousand dollars in cash?

Jean-Claude   Please, Marvin, this is no time for games. Saturday we go to Switzerland to play at the jazz festival.

Marvin   Switzerland?

Jean-Claude   Yes, with Sam, and we have three of the best Swiss session men who know all your music.

Marvin   Jean-Claude, baby, I need my money.

Jean-Claude   I know you are joking, Marvin. If you need more money I can give you another advance, but . . .

Marvin   You know, you sound like my pimp, Jean-Claude. In fact, you're sounding real confused at the moment. I think you better go and chill out. Do some real thinking.

Sam   Yeah, you better split, Jean-Claude. Clear your head then come back with Marvin's money.

Scene Thirty-three

We hear the sound of a door buzzer. There is no answer. It sounds again.

Beatrice (*answers through the intercom*)   Hello?

Jean-Claude   Beatrice, it's me. Jean-Claude. I need to talk with you.

Door opens.

Beatrice   I'm going back to Holland. I'd invite you in but . . .

Jean-Claude   Does Marvin know?

Beatrice   I don't know if Marvin knows, but the real question is does he care. I don't think so, Jean-Claude, do you?

Jean-Claude   You remember I lent Marvin some money just after you got here.

Beatrice   Yes, ten thousand dollars. What about it?

Jean-Claude   Now he is saying that I didn't lend him the money.

Beatrice *starts to laugh.*

Jean-Claude   So, what is so funny? I do not understand.

Beatrice   Marvin doesn't remember a lot of what goes on around him. It goes up his nose, Jean-Claude. Or he gets high on weed. And he also likes to play games. You know all of this so what are you saying?

Jean-Claude   But you remember I gave him the money?

Beatrice   Of course I remember, but why are you doing all of this for Marvin? You give him money, you find him a place to live, find him a studio, fly musicians in. You lose your wife and child, and still you're trying to do more for this man? Why are you doing all of this, Jean-Claude? Do you think Marvin likes or respects you because of this?

Jean-Claude   Maybe you can tell him that you remember about the money and then everything will be fine.

Beatrice   Go home, Jean-Claude. Pour yourself a drink and think about what you're doing with your life. This is the second time I have asked you to do this. Please. Just go home.

Scene Thirty-four

We are in the same Ostend bar with the music playing. It is later and it sounds as though there are more people there now.

Sam   Marvin, this is the cat I was telling you about. Mr Mitchell Richards. He's flown here all the way from the States to see you.

Mitchell   Mr Gaye, an honour to meet you. Sam's told me a lot about you, but you're one of those guys who needs no introduction.

Marvin   Hey, man, sit down. Take the weight off your suit.

Mitchell (*laughs*)   Guess I am a little overdressed for this bar.

Marvin   You're a little overdressed for this country.

Sam   Hey, what are you guys drinking? Let me go get something.

Marvin   I'll take another beer.

Mitchell   I guess a Martini with a twist is out of the question?

Sam (*laughs*)   What do you think?

Mitchell   Whiskey. Whatever's local.

Sam   Okay, leave it to me.

He gets up and leaves them.

Mitchell   Mr Gaye, it's a little more basic than I was expecting.

Marvin   Sometimes a brother needs to go to a place far away to figure things out. To re-group and re-think.

Mitchell   Well, I guess this would qualify as far away. I feel like I've been travelling for days to get here.

Marvin   And now you're here.

Mitchell   And honoured to meet you. Sam tells me that things are about to hit again.

Marvin   Now you didn't use the word 'comeback' did you, because I ain't never been away.

Mitchell   No comeback, man. Just a return, with a new hit single, and a new album.

Marvin   That's how I see it.

Mitchell   But I hear you got some business matters need sorting out over there.

Marvin   Ain't that the truth.

Mitchell   Well, as you know, your label's not a problem anymore. And I've taken the liberty of straightening things out with the women.

Marvin   They okay?

Mitchell   You care?

Marvin   I guess.

Mitchell   Fine.

Marvin   What about Uncle Sam?

Mitchell   Actually, Uncle Sam is the easiest of them all. So long as you agree on some kind of schedule of payments there will be no problem.

Sam *returns with the drinks.*

Sam   One beer and one whiskey straight up. Only got Scotch whiskey.

Mitchell   That's fine. Looks like we might have a reason to make a toast.

Sam   Marvin, I told you this was a good brother. You need to have your own people looking out for you. This Jean-Claude, he's no good, man. Mitchell knows which way's up, and he can fix everything for us.

Marvin   'Us'?

Sam   Well, aren't we all going back to start touring with the new album.

Marvin   What new album?

Sam   The one we're recording.

Mitchell   I already got the venues booked on the back of the single. But it doesn't make much sense hitting the road till you get the album finished. Man, the media interest is already hot as hell.

Sam   Marvin hasn't done no TV or radio in a long time. People really want to know where he's been, how he's been doing, and all about this sexual healing.

Mitchell   That's a hell of a groove, man. Let's drink to 'Sexual Healing'.

Sam   Yeah, to 'Sexual Healing'.

They clink glasses.

Mitchell   You ready to hit the circuit again? And I mean the American circuit, not this European bullshit.

Marvin   I need an advance.

Mitchell (*laughs*)   Baby, I know that. Everybody knows that the artist needs something to make him feel loved.

Marvin   Thirty thousand dollars.

Mitchell   How soon you need it?

Marvin   How soon you can get it?

Mitchell   I guess they got banks in this place.

Marvin   I wouldn't know.

Mitchell   Well, is Monday morning at 9 o'clock good enough?

Marvin   My man.

Sam   Marvin, don't you love the way this brother does business?

Scene Thirty-five

We are in a recording studio. There is light music playing back over the system.

Jean-Claude   But Sam, we have to leave for Switzerland now. Marvin knows that he's supposed to meet me here at the studio.

Sam   I thought I heard that he and a friend were planning on taking off to Paris or someplace. Maybe this weekend?

Jean-Claude   Paris? But we're supposed to be playing in Switzerland.

Sam   Hey, baby. Take it easy. Can't you see that I'm here and good to go. Don't be blaming me for nothing, man.

Scene Thirty-six

We are in **Marvin**'s *flat in Ostend. We hear a light knock on an open door.*

Marvin   Jean-Claude, come on in, man. What you waiting by the door for like you're some kind of stranger.

Jean-Claude   Are you going somewhere?

Marvin   Mitchell here is just helping me to pack my stuff up.

Jean-Claude   We're supposed to be meeting at the studio and then going to Switzerland.

Mitchell (*to* **Jean-Claude**)   I don't believe we've met. I'm Mitchell Richards. From the United States of America.

Jean-Claude   Who are you?

Mitchell   Man, now I know you people are a bit slow, but I do believe that I just told you who I am! You dig?

Jean-Claude   Marvin, what is going on here?

Marvin   Jean-Claude, take it easy man. Mitchell is helping me sort out my shit before I go back.

Jean-Claude   Go back where?

Marvin   Come on, man, you didn't expect me to stay here forever did you?

Jean-Claude   Marvin, we have to go to Switzerland to play the gig. I told you, it's a big gig. The jazz festival. A lot of people are going to be there.

Marvin   People like who, Jean-Claude?

Mitchell   Marvin, he means white people, man.

Marvin   Mercy, mercy, me.

Jean-Claude   All sorts of people. Important people.

Mitchell   Hey, hey, Mr Jean-Claude. The important people in my man's life are back in the States, which is where this brother is heading.

Jean-Claude   Marvin, you cannot go back to America now.

Mitchell   And when does Massa think it's okay for Marvin to go back to America?

Jean-Claude   Please, I am talking to Marvin. Who are you?

Mitchell   Damn, we have to go over this again? I represent Marvin Gaye in the United States, in this country, globally. This is my client.

Jean-Claude   Marvin, is this true?

Marvin   Jean-Claude, you owe me money. You know you do.

Jean-Claude   I don't owe you a penny, Marvin. I spent money on you. If anyone owes anybody anything, you owe me money.

Marvin   I owe you money?

Jean-Claude   You owe me more than money, Marvin. I came and got you and took you in at a time when you needed help.

Marvin   I needed help?

Jean-Claude   At least you can work here.

Marvin   Jean-Claude, I'm going home. I got a big US tour and I got a hit record again. Mitchell's sorted out the problems that I had with Uncle Sam. There's nothing to stop me now. Keep the money, Jean-Claude. If you need it that bad, you just hold on to it, okay.

Jean-Claude   I don't have any of your bloody money, don't you understand me?

Marvin   I told you, you keep the money, Jean-Claude, if it means that much to you. I gotta go home and take care of business. I got some good memories of here.

Jean-Claude   Memories of here? That's all it means to you now? Marvin, you changed your life here. We ran together on the beach. You came back to yourself.

Marvin   Jean-Claude, you deserve a little happiness in this world, so take care of yourself.

Mitchell   I got everything packed, Marvin. We gotta get the hell out of this place and back to LA.

We hear the sound of a car horn.

Jean-Claude   You're leaving now?

Mitchell   You want to drive us to the airport? (*Pause.*) Hey, I'm only joking, man. We got a driver.

Marvin   Take care, Jean-Claude.

Jean-Claude   Take care?

Marvin   Look after yourself, man.

We hear the sound of a car horn again.

Scene Thirty-seven

Mix through to a bedroom. Late at night. We hear somebody dialling the phone. It rings out then it is answered.

Louise   Jean-Claude? (*Pause.*) Is that you, Jean-Claude?

Jean-Claude   Yes. How are you?

Louise   What's the matter?

Jean-Claude   Is everything alright?

Louise   Yes, of course everything is alright. Jean-Claude, what is it?

Jean-Claude   And how is Catherine?

Louise   Stop playing games with me, please. What is going on? You sound strange.

Jean-Claude   I'm tired, Louise, that is all. I'm tired.

He puts down the phone.

Louise   Jean-Claude? Jean-Claude, are you still there?

Scene Thirty-eight

We hear the sound of the North Sea and gulls wheeling overhead. Mix through to the sound of a jet plane landing. Then the music of a TV chat show and the studio audience beginning to applaud. We are in the green room where **Marvin** *is being made up for his appearance.*

Mitchell   Man, I don't know anybody who's done eleven shows in five days before. Breakfast TV, late night TV, there's nothing that you haven't done.

Marvin   When does it end? In Ostend nobody knew who I was. I could walk down the street and people wouldn't even break stride.

Mitchell   Well, now you're here and you're getting some respect.

The music begins to swell onstage.

Voice   Okay, we're ready for you now, Mr Gaye.

Mitchell   Give 'em hell out there, Marvin.

Marvin   I'm not sure who is giving who hell.

Scene Thirty-nine

Mix through to the sound of a TV interview.

Interviewer   But you spent all this time in Europe. Now, you're a little old to be dodging the draft, if you don't mind me saying.

The studio audience begin to laugh.

Marvin   Well, that's right, Vietnam's over, unless Mr President started a new war while I was gone.

The audience laugh again.

Interviewer   Well, if they did they didn't tell me anything about it. But seriously, Marvin, I guess what everyone wants to know is just what were you doing over there? Some people say you were running from the mob; others that you were hiding from your wife, or the IRS. Lots of rumours out there floating about, and then when you come back you do so with this super super hit about sexual healing. Now what's been going on? Anything you want to talk to us about? You been having a little fun over there with those European girls?

The audience laugh again.

Marvin   Marvin Gaye likes to have a little fun everywhere he goes.

Interviewer   And have you come back to anybody special, Marvin? A little somebody who's been keeping the nest warm for you.

Marvin   Ain't nobody special. As they say, situation vacant if anybody's interested.

There is whooping and hollering from the girls in the audience.

Interviewer   Situation vacant, eh? Sounds enticing.

Marvin   Hell, you better not apply.

The audience laugh again and applaud.

Interviewer   You don't need to worry about that, Marvin. There'll be no application from me.

Scene Forty

Mix through to a restaurant in Los Angeles. **Marvin** *is having dinner with his parents.*

Mother   And how long will you be staying with us, Marvin?

Marvin   Momma, I ain't planning on going anywhere again.

Father   You mean you're going to be staying up in the house with us?

Marvin   I have to go out on tour, but then I'm coming home. That's where I'll be coming back to.

Mother   It'll be good for us to be all under one roof again.

Father   Woman, remember we ain't together anymore. You're speaking like it's some kind of family reunion you're planning.

Marvin   No need to take that tone with her. You know she is only trying to say what's right. Father, I have something I want to show you.

Father   Something you want to show me?

Marvin   After we finish dinner.

Mother   You have a surprise for your father?

Father   Well, you could surprise me with a little respect. Now that would be some kind of a surprise.

Scene Forty-one

Mix through to a street corner. We hear a car pull up and stop.

Marvin   Well, there it is.

Father   There what is? What is it that I'm supposed to be looking at?

Marvin   The church.

Mother   On the corner, over there. The small church.

Marvin   It's yours.

Father   Mine? What do you mean it's mine?

Marvin   I bought it for you so you can start to preach again.

Father   How do you know I want to go back to the church?

Mother   Marvin's only trying to help. He doesn't mean anything bad by it. It looks beautiful.

Marvin   You don't want the church?

Father   I already had a church in DC.

Marvin   And they took it away from you.

Father   Who told you that?

Marvin   Well, didn't they?

Father   I'm ready to go home.

Marvin   Father, I bought you a church. What do I have to do to make you happy?

Father   I didn't ask for a damn church, can't you get that into your head? I'm not interested in a church.

The car engine starts.

Marvin   Then you don't have to have the church.

Mother   Marvin, have you paid for it already?

Marvin   I said I'd bought it. That means I've paid for it.

Mother (*to* **Father**)   Maybe we can at least take a look inside and see if it's a nice place.

Father   I want to go home. Let's go!

An angry **Marvin** *starts to rev the engine of the car. The car moves away at speed.*

Scene Forty-two

Mix through to the night of the Grammys. The audience are happy and loud.

Announcer   And the Grammy for the best rhythm and blues single of the year goes to Marvin Gaye for 'Sexual Healing'.

The crowd begin to applaud as the song starts up; a band is playing the song live onstage and **Marvin** *starts to sing. Mix through to a dressing room.*

Scene Forty-three

Mitchell   Marvin, you can't just walk offstage in the middle of the damn concert, man. People here in Chicago don't play. Can't you hear them out there screaming and hollering. They're mad as hell.

Marvin   Mitchell, where's the stuff?

Mitchell   Hey, I told you we'd have it before the end of the gig.

Marvin   Well, I need it now.

Mitchell   Hey, brother, just finish the concert okay and you'll have it. The people of Chicago paid good money to see you, man. You can't just leave the band out there jamming by themselves.

Marvin   I don't give a damn about the people of Chicago. We had an understanding, right?

Mitchell   I ever let you down before?

Marvin   Tonight's gig is over. I ain't going back out there. But I'll finish the tour, Mitchell. I'll finish it, then you and I are through.

Mitchell   What do you mean 'through'? You firing me?

Marvin   Well, you want to manage me you have to deliver.

Mitchell   I delivered everything I said I would. One little jive ass supplier screws up and that's it. We're finished?

Marvin   If you don't stop running your mouth, man, I'll head right back to LA now.

Scene Forty-four

Late at night. We hear a phone being dialled. An international tone.

Jean-Claude (*he was clearly asleep*)   Yes, who is it? (*Pause.*) I said, who is it?

Marvin   Jean-Claude?

Jean-Claude   Marvin? Where are you?

Marvin   I'm in Chicago. On tour.

Jean-Claude   How is everything, man?

Marvin   You heard we won the Grammy.

Jean-Claude   No, Marvin, you won the Grammy.

Marvin   *We* won it. Without you, Jean-Claude, no Grammy.

Jean-Claude   How is the tour?

Marvin   Another week on the road, then back to LA. I'm tired, man.

Jean-Claude   You sound tired. You're not . . .

Marvin   No, Jean-Claude, I'm not. I'm finished with that stuff.

Jean-Claude (*laughs*)   Marvin, you don't fool me anymore like you used to.

Marvin   Show me some respect, man. I'm done with it.

Jean-Claude   And what now? You seen the girl? Karen. And the child?

Marvin   No, but I guess I should.

Jean-Claude   Maybe that would be a good idea.

Marvin   I will, when I get back to LA. (*Pause.*) Jean-Claude, you've never been to LA, right?

Jean-Claude   You know I've never been to America. The land of the free and the home of the brave.

Marvin   So why don't you come visit?

Jean-Claude   What are you saying?

Marvin   I'm saying that you should come to LA. It's nice weather, man, not like that Belgian bullshit. Sunshine and palm trees. What d'you say?

Jean-Claude   Marvin, I don't have any money for you. I didn't cheat you.

Marvin   Forget all that shit, man. That was just the coke talking. I'm good now. Come on out to LA. Let's take the country by storm, man, me and you.

Jean-Claude   The two of us?

Marvin   Coast to coast. I got ideas for a new album.

Jean-Claude   Where do you want to record it?

Marvin   LA, man. Ain't no place else. After this tour I'll go back there and straighten everything out with Karen. I'll wait to hear from you. You gonna call me?

Jean-Claude   Call you in LA.?

Marvin   Just let me know when you'll be arriving.

Jean-Claude   The tour is over in a week?

Marvin   Then I'll be back in LA. Call me, Jean-Claude. I'll be waiting.

Scene Forty-five

Mix through to bedroom in LA. We hear the sound of knocking on a door.

Mother   Marvin, you ready to get up, baby?

Marvin   I'm up, Momma.

Mother   What you doing in there all by yourself?

Marvin   Reading the Bible.

Mother   Since you came back from your tour, Marvin, you've hardly been out of this room. I'm worried about you.

Marvin (*laughs*)   Nothing to worry about. Momma, I'm meditating. Thinking on higher things.

Mother   But you got to go to court this morning.

Marvin   I know I got to go to court. Hold on. (*He opens the door.*) You and Father ready to come with me?

Mother   Marvin, you look so good in that suit. So handsome and . . .

Marvin   . . . and just like I used to be, is that what you want to say?

Mother   No, I'm worried that's all. I didn't know what you was doing locked up in here for all this time.

Marvin   All this time?

Mother   Three days, Marvin.

Marvin (*laughs*)   I told you I was meditating and reading the Bible.

Mother   Your father and I were worried.

Marvin   He been bullying you again?

Mother   I don't want no trouble, Marvin.

Marvin   I said, he been causing you any aggravation, Momma?

Mother   We both living our separate lives under this one roof without any problems. Let's not make any now, Marvin, please.

Marvin   He coming to court this morning?

Mother   So he says.

Marvin   Well, then, he better be ready. I'll go and see.

Mother   Marvin, if he doesn't want to come then the two of us can go alone.

Marvin   You wait here, I'll speak to him.

We hear a knock on a door.

Marvin   Father, you ready? (*There is no answer.*) I said, Father, you ready. I have to go. Now.

Mother   Leave it, Marvin. Let's go or we'll be late for the hearing.

We hear the door open.

Marvin   Father, you were asleep?

Father   What do you want?

Marvin   What the hell you doing dressed up in those faggot clothes?

Father   Boy, you questioning the way I like to dress in the privacy of my own bedroom?

Marvin   Momma, you wait by the car.

Mother   Marvin, please let's go. Leave him.

Father   Boy, you don't ever question anything I choose to do, or how I choose to dress, or anything about me, you hear? As long as I'm on the face of this earth and breathing I'm always going to be your father, you understand me? Woman, get away from here.

Marvin   That woman is my mother and you better keep a clean tongue in your head when you talk to her.

Father   I said woman get out of here. And you too, boy. Go on, get out!

Mother   Marvin, let's go, we're going to be late. (*Pause.*) Please, Marvin, let's go.

Marvin   I haven't finished with you yet.

Father   Boy, you better leave before I put you in your place. The son is below the father, or have you forgotten that? Read your Bible, boy. It's all in there.

Scene Forty-six

*We are in **Jean-Claude**'s house in Ostend.*

Louise   Is Catherine asleep?

Jean-Claude   Yes, it was just a cough. She didn't wake up.

Louise   She's probably still getting used to being back here in Ostend.

Jean-Claude   We're all getting used to it, I suppose.

Louise   What's the matter, Jean-Claude? I thought you might be happy to have us back. I thought that is what you wanted?

Jean-Claude   It is what I want.

Louise   Then what's on your mind? I know you, Jean-Claude. I can tell when something is bothering you. Is it Marvin?

Jean-Claude   I spoke to him.

Louise   When?

Jean-Claude   Not so long ago. (*Pause.*) He wants me to come to Los Angeles.

Louise   What are you going to do?

Jean-Claude   I don't know. He sounded bad, but . . .

Louise   But?

Jean-Claude   But I cannot lose you and Catherine.

Louise   Do you want to go?

Jean-Claude   No.

Louise   I'm sorry, I can't hear you.

Jean-Claude   No, I don't want to go.

Louise   Are you sure?

Jean-Claude   I'm sure. (*Pause.*) What did they call me? The white slave of Ostend. (*Pause.*) I don't want to go.

Scene Forty-seven

Mix through to late night in Los Angeles. We hear somebody stumble, then the door to a bedroom is thrown wide open.

Father   Boy, what the hell are you doing in here? Are you drunk?

Marvin   I've come to tell you to get out of the house.

Father   Get the hell out of my bedroom before I throw you out. You damn drunk fool.

Mother   Marvin, what are you doing? Please, leave your father alone.

Marvin   Go back to your own room, Momma.

Mother   Marvin, please, stay away from your father.

Father   Boy, you don't take another step toward me or I swear I'll take care of your Black ass myself.

Marvin   Yeah, you'd like that wouldn't you. Everything I tried to do for you you end up throwing it back in my face. You jealous, Father, is that it? Is that all it comes down to? Is that what this is about? Come on, tell me what it is?

Mother   Please, Marvin.

Father   Boy, you too stupid to see that I've got a gun in my hand.

Marvin   Nothing about you is a man is it, Father? People laughing in my face and behind my back all my life because of you. And you think that just because you've got a gun in your hand now that I'm going to think of you as a man. (*Laughs.*) Father, you ain't a man. You were never a man, but you were too stupid to see that at least I tried to treat you as one.

Father   A man takes his responsibilities seriously. A man doesn't run away or hide behind drugs or alcohol or beat women. You tell me who the real man is!

Marvin   A man stands up for his kids and loves them no matter what.

Father (*laughs*)   Boy, now I know you're crazy. What the hell happened to you? I'm looking at you now, boy, and I can see that you're suffering. You're in pain. You think drinking and doping is going to help? You can save yourself by first of all learning some respect.

Mother   Leave your father alone, Marvin. Just go to your room.

Marvin   Momma, I know you tried, but nothing I could have done would have been good enough.

Father   Boy, you disappoint me. Just back off and get out of here.

Marvin   I don't want to hear anymore from you.

Father   I said back off.

Mother   Marvin!

*We hear **Marvin** strike his father, and then a gunshot is heard. A brief pause. Then another gunshot. **Marvin**'s **Mother** begins to scream.*

Scene Forty-eight

*Mix through to **Marvin** singing 'Save the Children'. Mix through to church music. Conclusion of a church service. People are filing out of a church and greeting **Marvin**'s **Mother**.*

Jean-Claude   Mrs Gaye, I am Jean-Claude. From Belgium. I am so sorry.

Mother   Thank you.

Jean-Claude   I knew Marvin over there. In Europe. He was my guest.

Mother   Yes, Jean-Claude. I know who you are. Thank you for looking after my son.

Jean-Claude   Is there anything I can do to help? Anything.

Mother   I have lost my son. My husband may go to prison. No, Jean-Claude, I don't think there is anything you can do, but thank you.

Jean-Claude   This is my first time in Los Angeles. In America. Marvin asked me to come.

Mother   Do you have a family, Jean-Claude?

Jean-Claude   Yes, a wife and a daughter. They are here with me.

Mother   Then, Jean-Claude, go and be with them. Show them Los Angeles. The nice things. The things that Marvin liked. The beach. The trees.

Jean-Claude   I will do this.

Mother   And Jean-Claude, thank you again.

Jean-Claude   For what?

Mother   For looking after my son. For looking after Marvin.

Jean-Claude   I think . . . I think everything would have been alright if he had stayed with us. In Belgium.

Mother   Marvin never let himself acknowledge that people cared. I never understood why. I'll never understand.

Scene Forty-nine

We hear the sound of two men running on the beach. Gulls crying overhead.

Jean-Claude (*out of breath*)   Marvin, you have to slow down a little bit. This is not a race.

Marvin   You're out of shape, Jean-Claude.

Jean-Claude   When I was younger I used to box. You ever try boxing?

Marvin   Marvin Gaye tried all sports, man. However, music is my love. Don't have no time to be messing with sports.

Jean-Claude   But you want to get fit again?

Marvin   I got to get fit again if I'm going to get back into the studio and record.

Scene Fifty

We mix through to outside of the church.

Jean-Claude   I have brought some of his clothes and other things that Marvin left behind.

Mother   Thank you. But you keep them.

Jean-Claude   No. Thank you, but I cannot.

Mother   They are part of his life there with you, in your country. Please, Jean-Claude, keep them. Marvin is now back in his country. With us.

Dinner in the Village

Broadcast Details

BBC Radio 4, 4 October 2011. Directed by Judith Kampfner.

Characters (in order of appearance)

Constance
Interviewer
Richard Wright (Dick)
C. L. R. James (Nello)
Norman
Stranger
Gloria
Ellen
FBI Man
Pearl
Waitress
Barman
Judge
Guard

Notes on the Play

This text concentrates on two other artists admired by Caryl Phillips, Richard Wright and C. L. R. James, whose works have been decisive in shaping his ambition to become a writer. The play deals with a series of strained relationships: between the two authors; between the authors and their respective wives, Ellen and Constance; and between these two white women, who met when they lived in Greenwich Village in the 1940s. While this text offers another glimpse into the difficulties that face writers from ethnic minorities and threaten their endeavours to define themselves, it also touches upon the difficulties encountered by mixed-race couples in their attempts to hold their marriage together, a theme that is at the heart of several stage plays and fictions by Caryl Phillips, notably *In the Falling Snow* (2009) and *The Lost Child* (2015).

Scene One

Int. Apartment. Day.

A little 'yappy' dog barks.

Constance Be quiet, Felix. I take it you don't mind dogs. He's harmless.

Interviewer I assume he'll be quiet while we're recording.

Constance Assume away, young man, but I think you'll find that Felix is quite independently minded. Much like his owner. Sugar? Milk? I've put everything there on the tray.

Interviewer Thank you. You're very kind.

Constance You don't look like either of them. (*Pause.*) Mr Wright or Mr James. My former husband was a tall and elegant man. Mr Wright was shorter, and a little rotund. But certainly not fat. One might say, plump.

Scene Two

Flashback. Lively New York restaurant. Day.

Dick (*laughing*) Come on, James man. You West Indians are so secretive. Or should I say, you reds are so secretive. How old is the girl?

Nello Twenty years younger than me.

Dick And white, like Ellen?

Nello She's white, but she's not like Ellen. Constance can be a handful. She needs a lot of attention.

Dick And you say she has green eyes and high cheekbones. Well, when am I going to meet this beauty?

Nello Tonight, Dick. I'll bring her to dinner here. At Pearl's restaurant. You said it's the only place that bi-racial couples can eat in peace in New York City.

Dick (*laughs*) That's true. So, are you looking for the young lady to devote her life to you?

Nello Well, Ellen's made a commitment to you and your work. I've been trying to give Constance some instruction.

Dick Damn, it must be love if you're prepared to take on a challenge that might distract you from your work. (*Laughs.*) Man, I never thought I'd see it. Nello's in love. You wait till I tell Ellen. Nello's fallen in love.

Scene Three

Back to present. Int. Apartment. Day.

Interviewer   But you don't think I look like either of them? Mr Wright or Mr James. (*Laughs nervously.*) We don't all look the same, you know.

Constance   Young man, there's no need to be sassy with me. I married a very distinguished coloured political theorist, Mr C. L. R. James. And I was the biographer of the most famous coloured writer of his generation, Mr Richard Wright. I'm very well aware of the fact that you don't all look alike.

Interviewer   I'm sorry. I didn't mean to cause offence.

Constance   None taken. Now come along, drink your tea. I've always found so-called English humour slightly puzzling. As for the French, heaven knows what goes on in their minds.

Interviewer   I telephoned Mrs Ellen Wright. In Paris. I told her I was making a programme about the friendship between Mr Wright and Mr James.

Constance   I see. Did she ask after me?

Interviewer   Not really.

Constance   What exactly am I supposed to make of 'not really'?

Interviewer   It's none of my business, but was there some tension between the two of you?

Constance   I see. Apparently you've done your research. (*Pause.*) We were friends. All four of us. (*Dog barks.*) For heaven's sake, Felix. Apartment dwelling isn't very conducive to keeping one's pet happy. Is this your first time in San Francisco?

Interviewer   Yes it is. It's a beautiful city.

Constance   Too many hills for an old crock like me. These days I have to pay the doorman to take Felix for his walks.

Interviewer   You were born in California. Do you mind if we record? (*He switches on the tape recorder.*)

Constance   I take it we've begun.

Interviewer   If that's alright with you. You were born shortly after the end of the First World War.

Constance   Indeed, I was. However, you claim that *I* am not the focus of your story. The friendship between the aforementioned coloured gentlemen, Mr Wright and Mr James, deserves your full attention. So let us begin properly. I was a teenager, perhaps nineteen, when I first met Mr James, or Nello as his friends called him. A childhood nickname which he was clearly quite fond of. At the time I was already married to a boy not much older than myself. I was a student and, yes, something of a communist sympathizer without ever being a real believer. However, my circle were all, as you might say, reds. One day we were all terribly excited because our guest speaker was a man from the Caribbean, by way of England, called Mr C. L. R. James. That evening my husband and I clambered into our rickety old automobile and made our way over to the hall to hear Nello speak.

Mix through to . . .

Scene Four

Int. Hall. Evening.

Fade up on speech.

Nello   But the plantation-based economies of the West Indian islands are very similar to those of the American South, and produced a radicalized Negro who would inevitably find himself at odds with authority. In a little over a week, I will have the opportunity to sit with Mr Trotsky in Mexico and discuss with him these critical questions of race. But not only this. I will talk with Mr Trotsky more specifically about the party's position on the Negro question as it pertains to the struggle for the liberation of all colonized peoples, but with particular relevance to inequality in the present-day United States of America. Thank you.

A thunderous burst of applause.

I believe I have time to take perhaps two or three questions.

Scene Five

Int. Car. Night.

Norman   But, Constance, he asked to meet with us – just the two of us – over coffee and a sandwich. What's your problem?

Constance   My problem is tomorrow morning I have to go to college.

Norman   But Mr James is one of the rising stars of the party. Good God, a coffee and a sandwich with the comrade who's going to meet Trotsky. That wouldn't have killed you, would it?

Constance   Well, maybe *you* should have stayed and offered him *your* expert opinion on the Negro question. I'm not ready to be a college drop-out.

Norman   And if I'd stayed, how exactly would you have gotten home?

Constance   Somebody else would have given me a ride.

Norman   Constance, you're my wife. I'm not going to leave you in the hands of some stranger. I know my responsibilities.

Constance   I'm your wife, Norman, not your child.

Norman   I'm sorry but I find your behaviour unacceptable.

Constance (*laughs*)   Unacceptable?

Norman   You're hysterical. Get a hold of yourself.

Constance   My behaviour is 'unacceptable'?

Norman   Either you stop this right now, or . . .

Constance   Or what, Norman? Or you'll report me to Joe Stalin? (*She starts to laugh.*) If only you could hear yourself. (*He turns on the car radio. Big band music is playing.*) Are you listening to me, Norman? (*Pause. She raises her voice.*) I said, are you listening to me?

Scene Six

Back to present. Int. Apartment. Day.

Constance   Well, as you might imagine, our squabbling went on for much of the night, with the aid of a little whiskey, if I remember rightly. The truth is we married for sex. Now, now, don't look so surprised. That's what people did back then. We tried to put a respectable face on youthful urges. However, Norman and I were very ill-matched and, as I later discovered, the sex wasn't up to much either. But, at that stage, I wasn't to know. The following morning my young husband stormed off to his office job and left me alone in the apartment with something of a teeny hangover and precious little desire to go to college that day. It was then that the phone rang out.

Scene Seven

Int. California apartment. Morning.

Phone rings out.

Constance (*bleary voice*)   Hello.

Nello   Ah, good morning. My name is James. C. L. R. James. I believe you were present at last night's talk.

Constance   Excuse me?

Nello   I took the liberty of acquiring your number from a fellow comrade.

Constance   I'm sorry, Mr James, but my husband is out at the moment. Might I have him return your call?

Nello   Ah, but it is you with whom I wish to speak.

Constance   Me?

Nello   On matters to do with the party.

Constance   Mr James, I'm flattered, but my husband is better informed about such things.

Nello   You're very modest. Might I arrange for a comrade to collect you in one hour? Perhaps a stroll by your Pacific Ocean?

Constance   Mr James, I'm a married woman. It's simply not possible for me to meet you without an escort.

Nello (*laughs*)   Then bring an escort. Bring an army. My dear Constance . . .

Constance   You know my name?

Nello   Is it a secret?

Constance   No, of course not, but . . .

Nello   May I call you Constance? Or would you be more comfortable were I to address you formally?

Constance   You can call me Constance.

Nello   And you must call me Nello. A childhood nickname meaning . . . well, nobody really seems to know. Anyhow, it's what my friends have always called me. And we *are* going to be friends, aren't we?

Constance   I really don't know you, Mr James.

Nello   Nello.

Constance   Nello.

Nello   Then the matter is settled.

Scene Eight

Ext. Beach. Day.

Nello   Now, do you know where Trinidad is?

Constance   Among the Caribbean islands. You explained yesterday evening at your talk.

Nello   We refer to them as the West Indian islands. Trinidad is the most southerly of the chain. It is located near to South America. I miss the bright sunlight. The cooling sea breezes. The noisy, bustling street markets, and most of all the food. My food. On a clear day one can sit on a beach like this one and see Venezuela in the distance.

Constance   It must be very beautiful.

Nello   But this country is also beautiful. I have travelled over mountains and across deserts from New York City to your California.

Constance   And do you give talks every day?

Nello   Almost every day. I lecture in exchange for accommodation and the opportunity to learn more about the race question here in the United States.

Constance   And this is what you'll talk about with Mr Trotsky?

Nello   One must always be well prepared.

Constance   One day I'd like to visit New York City. It must be exciting.

Nello   If this is what you desire then there is no reason why this should not take place.

Constance   It's not that simple. I'm a married woman and I'm studying.

Nello   But these are details, not impediments to your travelling to New York City.

Constance   I see. (*Pause.*) Mr James, I believe some of my husband's comrades are over-friendly with coloureds. It makes me uncomfortable. (*Pause.*) Maybe I shouldn't be speaking in this fashion?

Nello   I'm grateful to you, Constance. Truly I am. Please, take a chance.

Constance   They speak with such authority about coloured lives, but they don't know any coloureds. And when they come across them it quickly becomes a performance. None of them wishes to cause any offence.

Nello   And do you include your young husband among the transgressors?

Constance   I don't like injustice, Mr James. Sorry, Nello. That's why I started going to meetings, and it's where I met Norman. But I'm more interested in fair play and decency than I am in politics. But my husband is a good party member.

Nello   I admire your loyalty, Constance. (*Pause.*) May I write to you? From Mexico.

Constance   Write to me?

Nello   Please, you must trust me a little, Constance. After all, you came without an escort.

Constance   How can I trust you? I don't know you.

Nello (*laughs*)   A leap of faith, Constance. A leap of faith.

Constance   You want to write to me?

Nello   A correspondence. You should feel under no obligation to respond. I am enjoying our conversation and I have no desire for it to end. There are many things that I feel I can say to you.

Scene Nine

Int. California apartment. Day.

We hear the sound of an envelope being opened.

Nello   My dearest Constance, my exchanges with Trotsky continue to prove difficult as we seem to differ on so many issues of basic party policy. However, even in disagreement we manage to maintain the most cordial of relations . . . In my last letter I asked about your studies and was somewhat surprised to learn that you are considering abandoning college in favour of a career in the fashion industry. I can certainly understand how your friends and your family might feel some anxiety about your decision, but I am delighted to learn that you intend to pursue your dreams and move to New York City. You don't say what this might mean for your marriage and, of course, it is no business of mine to pry. However, I hope you understand that I will support you in whatever it is that you decide to do . . . (*Fade up.*) . . . One subject I wish to raise with you is that of the role of a wife when married to a leader. Trotsky is blessed with a supportive wife, but I feel that in some respects he needs more help than he is being presently offered. A man in a leadership position must carefully choose his female companionship otherwise the distraction of unsuitable domestic arrangements might begin to overshadow the vital importance of his more public role. Clearly this is a subject that is somewhat awkward to raise directly with Trotsky but perhaps, before I leave Mexico, there will be the opportunity to discuss this matter with him.

Scene Ten

Back to present. Int. Apartment. Day.

Interviewer   Were all the letters so . . . well, formal.

Constance   You have to understand that Nello came out of the colonial world. I suspect that your modern England has forgotten the good manners of the old world. More tea?

Interviewer   No, thanks. I'm fine.

Constance   His early letters were lengthy affairs. One ran to fifty pages. Can you imagine how long it took him to write such letters? I generally wrote back, but Nello always made it clear that he wasn't expecting a response.

Interviewer   But he was pleased if you did write back?

Constance   Well, of course. But it soon became clear that Nello's interest in me was not as innocent as I first thought. You have to remember that I was young. And, admittedly, a trifle naïve.

Interviewer   And you were married.

Constance   Well, soon after Nello and I began our correspondence, I divorced Norman. I mean we were babies. I'm not even sure what we were thinking of, besides the obvious.

Thereafter I moved to New York City and started to model. I began to pursue my dreams.

Scene Eleven

Ext. Manhattan streets. Day.

Footsteps on a busy, Manhattan street. Car horns are honking and traffic rushes by.

Constance   Dear Nello, I have taken your advice and started to walk all about Manhattan looking at the faces of the wealthy as well as the poor, trying to imagine the diversity of their many stories. Every day I find it easier to enter the minds of others and simply dream, so much so that I'm hopeful that one day I might achieve my ultimate ambition of becoming an actress. I think I am slowly coming to love New York City, as you predicted I would. I like the hustle-bustle of the streets – the newspaper boys shouting above the roar of the traffic, the smell of hot dogs, and the roar of the El overhead. Even the constant blare of the car horns enchants me, and everybody is always rushing to or from somewhere. I believe I'm beginning to think of Manhattan as home.

Mix through to quieter, indoor, space. Her room.

You asked about the possibility of our meeting again after nearly five years of written communication, but I have to be honest with you, Nello. Your affection for me cannot be reciprocated as I am once again a married woman. It is not my intention to cause you hurt or offence, but would you be able to respect the boundaries that come with my new situation? I am not entirely sure that you would. My new husband would find it difficult to tolerate my being wooed by another man, as I am sure you would find it equally difficult were you in his position. Forgive me, but will you be able to control your ardour? If you are absolutely sure that the answer is in the affirmative, then it might yet be possible for us to meet in a public place.

Scene Twelve

Ext. Bryant Park. Day.

We can hear the noise of Manhattan traffic. In the foreground birds are singing and it is clear that we are in an urban park. Suddenly we hear the clattering of stiletto heels.

Constance (*breathless*)   I'm so sorry.

Nello   Five years and you haven't changed a bit, Constance.

Constance   Thank you.

Nello   Your hair is longer, and I see you now wear it tied back from your face. But Constance, your beauty remains radiant. I take it you were busy with a work engagement?

Constance   Looking for work.

Nello   Please take a seat.

Constance (*sits*)   Thank you.

Nello   Surely a young woman with your features can pick and choose her assignments?

Constance   I can't afford to be too particular. Things are slow. I'm sitting for artists two days a week. (*Pause.*) Posing.

Nello   Oh, I see. (*Pause.*) And how does your new husband feel about your 'posing'?

Constance   My soon-to-be former husband, if that answers your question. Apparently I have a stubborn streak that some might not appreciate.

Nello   Are you making fun of me?

Constance   They're your words. In one of your first letters. What I can't figure out is how you knew.

Nello   I knew you, dear Constance from the moment I first set eyes upon you. A beautiful young student who wanted to be involved in the fight against American injustice.

Constance   I attended a few meetings, Nello. That's all. And now I'm a model. And I'm rooming with a friend, Gloria, on the East River in the forties. She's also a model.

Nello   And your newly disposed-with husband?

Constance   Must we talk about him? It's so long since I've seen you. Surely we can just enjoy our time together?

Nello   I have a meeting in forty minutes.

Constance   It's my fault for being late.

Nello   Please don't look like that. I can't bear it if you're unhappy.

Constance   I'm sorry.

Nello   Constance, party members look to me to discuss and formulate theoretical positions on a variety of issues. My time is not my own. You surely understand that my primary responsibility is to the party. But perhaps we could meet later? At Times Square and visit the cinema. It is my only avenue of entertainment.

Constance   So you're dismissing me?

Nello   I could never dismiss you. Have I not been writing to you, and paying you all the attention that a beautiful woman could ever wish for?

Constance   I don't want to be thought of as a pretty face and not much else. I want to do something with my life.

Nello   And have I not encouraged you?

Constance   I don't want to be told what to do. Gloria says men don't feel like men unless you let them put a leash on you and walk you around like a dog. Twice I've been fooled by men who pretended that they valued what I had to say when, in fact, all they wanted was . . . you know.

Scene Thirteen

Ext. Times Square. Night.

Nello *and* **Constance** *are emerging from a movie theatre. Over the noise of the busy night traffic.*

Constance   I love Bette Davis. And I liked the picture, Nello. I had so much fun.

Nello   Let's walk a little.

Constance   Yes. It's a beautiful evening, and the streets are so busy. Even at this late hour, it's incredible. And so many taxi cabs. Really, Nello, where is everybody going?

Nello   They're all rushing to meet their futures, Constance. Aren't you?

Constance   Should I be rushing? Am I doing something wrong?

Nello   My dear Constance, you're a young woman making her way in the world. And you appear to be doing so admirably. Now then, Miss Davis is the most extraordinary of all your actresses. Have you noticed the way she looks side on into the camera? She possesses the most powerful gaze. A rare gift.

Constance   It's as though she's always thinking about something else. Something beyond what's actually going on.

Nello   And she only offers the best side of her face. Have you discovered yet which is your best side, Constance?

Constance (*excited*)   This is my best side. It's the one all the photographers prefer.

Nello   Then I must quickly kiss it. (*He kisses her.*) I hope I haven't offended you.

Constance   Perhaps I ought to be going back now.

Nello   But why? You said your friend Gloria was occupied for the evening.

Constance   I must leave early in the morning to begin looking for more work.

Nello   Will you not marry me, Constance? Do you doubt that I love you?

Constance   Please, Nello. We have had a wonderful evening.

Nello   I have never before said this to any woman, but I need your support, Constance. I have difficulty balancing everything in my life. Everything is work, work, work. I want to open another window on . . . happiness. Don't ask me how, but from the moment I saw you in that lecture hall I knew it was you and you have never left my heart or my mind. Take a chance on me, sweet angel.

Constance   I think I should walk back from here.

Stranger   Hey, lady. Everything okay?

Constance (*snaps*)   Why shouldn't it be? Kindly mind your own business.

Stranger   If this Negro is . . .

Constance   Go away!

Stranger   Sorry. I thought you were a lady, but I see now what you are.

Constance (*to* **Nello**)   Please, Nello. I want to go.

Nello   Constance, come and live with me in the Bronx. I understand that marriage may be out of the question at the moment, but let us explore a trial period together. Give me a chance to show you what you are worth.

Constance   Why are you doing this? We had such a wonderful evening. Nello, why are you spoiling everything?

We hear her stiletto heels quickly clicking against the sidewalk as she moves off.

Nello   Constance!

Scene Fourteen

Ext. Balcony. Night.

We are on a balcony of an apartment overlooking the East River. The sound of traffic below mixes with the hooter of a ship passing in the distance. A sliding glass door opens.

Gloria   Constance, what on earth are you doing sitting out here staring at the East River?

Constance   Did you have a nice time with Brad?

Gloria   He's a swell guy. But, Navy boys. You never know with them, honey. They can always disappear on you. But child, your face looks like a slapped fish. Pour me some of that whiskey, will you? (*She pours.*) Bottoms up. (*They clink glasses and drink.*) Ah, that's better.

Constance   Gloria, Nello asked me to marry him.

Gloria   What did I tell you? Letter. Letter. Letter. The guy's obsessed with you. So what did you say?

Constance   Nothing. Then he said that we didn't have to get married. We could just live together.

Gloria   He's fast, isn't he? But I kind of like the sound of him. Direct and to the point.

Constance   But he doesn't really know me.

Gloria   Listen, sister, if you don't want him somebody else will. You better make up your mind.

Constance   He's coloured.

Gloria   Yeah, what colour?

Constance   Gloria, don't be a wiseguy. You know what I mean.

Gloria   You're telling me you don't want him because he's coloured? I thought you commies were all for equality no matter what race or creed. Isn't that right?

Constance   I told you, I've got nothing to do with the party.

Gloria   But he does. And you know how obsessive lefties can be. They can bore you to death with their commitment. So how's that going to work?

Constance   And he's older. Nearly twenty years older.

Gloria   Ah, so what? (*Pours more whiskey.*) Listen to me, honey. Do you love him?

Constance   I don't know. He takes me seriously.

Gloria (*laughs*)   Listen to you. For five years the guy has been single-handedly keeping the post office in business. Sure he takes you seriously. And if you think you could love him then maybe you should give the guy a break. Come on, hit me again with that whiskey.

Scene Fifteen

Int. **Wrights**' *apartment. Village. Day.*

A radio is playing light jazz.

Dick   Ellen for God sake, turn down the music. I'm trying to write.

Ellen   We need a bigger apartment, Dick.

Dick   I know, I know. Truth is we need a house.

Ellen   So what do you know about Nello's girl?

Dick   He says she's called Constance, and he's going to introduce us to her at Pearl's.

Ellen   Is that all?

Dick   She's young. And beautiful, he says. Green eyes. Face of a Greek beauty, whatever that means.

Ellen   And stupid if she thinks she'll get him to talk to her, rather than at her. All that man does is work and lecture. Nello doesn't know how to relax.

Dick   Come on, you know Nello loves the movies.

Ellen   Dick, Nello loves to analyse movies, not watch them.

Dick (*laughs*)   Well, maybe this Constance knows how to relax him.

Ellen   There's no need to be vulgar.

Dick   So the crazy West Indian's got himself a plaything. Why not? He works hard. A man who works that hard should have a little bit of loving at the end of the day.

Ellen   You think that's a woman's role in the world? To just provide a little bit of loving for a man at the end of the day?

Dick   Knock it off, Ellen, okay. I've got work to do. And for Christssakes turn down that music.

Scene Sixteen

Int. Bronx apartment. Day.

A door shuts.

Nello   Please sit, Constance. Make yourself at home.

Constance   Thank you.

Nello   Is everything you own contained in this one suitcase?

Constance   I left some clothes at Gloria's. I can collect them later but . . . but will they fit in this small apartment? Nello, this place is like a doll's house.

Nello   It's not much, but there's a bedroom, a bathroom, and this kitchen-living area. I can't afford to live in Manhattan, Constance. But the apartment is clean, and the Bronx is full of good, honest working people of all backgrounds.

Constance   Do you write at this kitchen table?

Nello   The party keeps a small office nearby where I go from eleven in the morning until my day is done. You may use the kitchen as your office and maybe do some writing of your own.

Constance   But I'm a model, Nello, not a writer. And up here in the Bronx, it's such a long way from Manhattan.

There is a knock on the door.

Are you expecting guests?

Nello (*crossing to the door*)   Always, my dear. Always. (*Opens the door.*)

FBI Man   Ah, Mr James.

Nello   And what business do the FBI have with me today?

FBI Man   A neighbour complained that he heard a woman in distress in this apartment. May I come in and look around?

Nello   There is no woman in distress in this apartment.

FBI Man (*shouts*)   Ma'am, are you alright?

Nello   Please leave.

FBI Man   Ma'am, do you have some form of ID?

Constance (*stands and crosses to the door*)   We're under no obligation to answer your questions. Please step away from the door. (*She slams the door.*)

Nello   Constance?

Constance   This is America, not Stalin's Russia. We have the right to not be harassed by state officials.

Nello   You've got real fire in that belly of yours.

Constance   Enough to drive off two husbands. Is that what you mean?

Nello (*laughs*)   Of course that's not what I mean. (*Pause.*) I'm sorry but the FBI have been following me for the past year or two. And it's getting worse. Perhaps I should have told you.

Constance   You did tell me. In your letters.

Nello   And still you came here to be with me?

Constance   I only know Manhattan, Nello. The Bronx frightens me a little. And, I have no friends up here.

Nello   Then we must find you some friends so that you are not lonely. Tonight we shall go down to Greenwich Village. I have already thought of everything. Tonight we are expected. We shall have dinner with friends.

Scene Seventeen

Int. Village restaurant. Evening.

It's a noisy Village restaurant with the sound of clattering plates, orders being shouted in the background and raised voices over very low jazz.

Dick (*laughs*)   Nello, Nello. You make us eat this Caribbean food, but you don't explain what it is. Callaloo? Surely it has an American name?

Nello   Well, you'd better ask Pearl. She's the owner and chef.

Dick   But listen, man, you ordered it. (*To* **Constance**.) Constance, whatever you do up there in the Bronx, don't let this man cook his exotic voodoo food for you.

Constance   Do you cook, Mr Wright?

Dick   Please, call me Dick. Mind you, it took Ellen about a year to stop calling me Mr Wright.

Ellen   Well, I *was* working for you. (*To* **Constance**.) He used me as unpaid labour – a secretary of sorts.

Dick   When I met you were the daughter of Polish immigrants working as a librarian. And you were a devoted fan of my books and happy to work for me. And look at you now, you're my wife. (*Laughs.*) Is it still unpaid labour or are you getting some benefits?

Ellen   Richard, please.

Dick   Nello, are you planning on making an honest woman of Constance?

Nello   She's auditioning me. Testing me out. Unlike some people, I'm not a world-famous writer so I might have some difficulty persuading her to stay with me.

Dick   Well, if she doesn't hurry you may be gone.

Constance   Gone where exactly?

Ellen   Nello, you haven't told her?

Nello   The US government seem determined to deport me for so-called visa irregularities.

Constance   I thought the FBI were harassing you because of your politics.

Nello   There's also a practical element to their intimidation.

Dick   Nello, you should write a piece about it for our magazine. (*To* **Constance**.) Constance, has Nello told you that we're hoping to start a magazine dedicated to political and literary matters that affect the Negro.

Nello   Dick, you know we have to wait for the party to give us funding.

Dick   These damn commies regard me as one that got away from them. But there's such a powerful need for a magazine of this kind.

Nello   Well, it's just an idea at the moment.

Dick   Did I really hear you say 'just an idea'? Since when has an idea been 'just' anything? (*Laughs.*) Especially to a callaloo-chomper such as yourself?

Ellen (*to* **Constance**)   Constance, you imagine that you're going out for dinner with intelligent, famous men, then suddenly you realize that you're dealing with a pair of little boys. I believe you were married before?

Constance   Yes, twice. I'm not sure that I'm cut out for marriage.

Ellen   Always remember the difference between serving your man and servitude. If you let men like these two forget the difference, they will.

Constance   Thank you, Mrs Wright.

Ellen   Ellen. No need to be so formal.

Constance   Thank you, Ellen.

Ellen   You know, coloured and white isn't the divide we should be worrying about. The real battleground is men and women.

Dick   Hey, what are you two shooting off about?

Ellen   Well, wouldn't you like to know.

Dick   Did you tell Constance that this is the only restaurant, except the Chinese ones, that don't appear to have a problem serving bi-racial couples such as ourselves?

Constance   Can't we file a complaint with somebody? The city, perhaps?

Dick   Nello, have you bothered to explain *anything* to Constance? Nello? (*Pause.*) Damn, not again. Wake up, old man. You look like you're falling asleep at the table.

Nello   What?

Dick   Nello, Nello. Man, you've got to stop working so hard.

Scene Eighteen

Int. Apartment in Bronx. Night.

We hear noises from the street. Breaking glass. Shouting. The sound of people running.

Nello   The Bronx isn't always this noisy at night. (*Pause.*) Constance, are you listening? You seem to have a lot on your mind? Did you not enjoy the dinner with our new friends?

Constance   I like them both, but there are things about yourself, Nello, that you are not telling me. I mean, I didn't know the government wants to deport you. You found it easy enough to write to me. Do you find it difficult to talk to me?

Nello   I have no secrets from you, Constance.

Constance   Is it because I'm younger?

Nello   Constance, please.

Constance   And I didn't know that you were such good friends with Richard Wright. For heaven's sake, that's Richard Wright. And you just sit down to dinner with him like he's just anybody.

Nello   My dear Constance, I believe you might be a little star struck.

Constance   Do you know how much I admire his writing? He really understands human suffering. Reading his stories of Negro life made me interested in going to party meetings. I just didn't know what to say to him.

Nello   And Ellen? Do you think you might form a friendship with her?

Constance   I don't know. There's something about her that's . . . distant.

Nello   Ellen's a devoted and loyal wife. I'd like it if the two of you were able to form a friendship. Will you try?

Constance   Yes, I'll try.

Scene Nineteen

Int. **Gloria**'s *apartment. Day.*

Furious knocking on door.

Constance   Gloria! It's me, Constance.

Door opens.

Gloria   Keep it down a little.

Constance   I'm sorry, Gloria. Did I wake you?

Gloria   Ssh. Brad's sleeping. (*Pause.*) The Navy hasn't shipped out yet.

Constance   Shall I come back later?

Gloria   Hell, no. Come in, come in.

Constance   I'm sorry, Gloria but I've been meaning to pick up my clothes for the past week or two, but it's been difficult.

Gloria   Sit down, honey. It's my fault. I forgot you were coming round this morning. Smoke?

Constance   No, thanks.

Gloria *lights up.*

Gloria   So what on earth do you do up there in the Bronx? Your phone calls are so hurried. I feel I'm losing sight of you.

Constance   Well, I've been cleaning the place. He's a bachelor. Need I say more? And going for walks and trying to get used to the neighbourhood.

Gloria   And this writer's wife you told me about? Ellen. Do you see her?

Constance   Sometimes. I think she's one of those women who doesn't much care for other women.

Gloria   Sure, because her man's running around on her and she trusts nobody.

Constance   You think so?

Gloria   Just a guess. That kind of thing can make a gal sour.

Constance   I miss work, Gloria.

Gloria   What work are you talking about, doll?

Constance   You know, modelling. Our work. I'm ready to come back to the agency and see if there's anything doing. What do you think?

Gloria   Has nobody from the agency been in touch with you?

Constance   About what?

Gloria   Honey, they don't want you back there. They had the FBI in the office asking all kinds of questions and talking about you running around with coloured men. They said some pretty nasty things about you, but I spoke up on your behalf. Told them they were lying jackasses. But . . . but they don't want you back in the agency, doll.

Scene Twenty

Int. **Wrights***' apartment. Village. Day.*

Ellen   I don't want to see tears. You've got to pull yourself together.

Constance   I'm sorry, Mrs Wright.

Ellen   Ellen. And stop saying you're sorry.

Constance   I'm ready to help Nello in whatever way I can, but he's always out working, and now I don't have a job to go back to.

Ellen   For heaven's sake, it's only been a few weeks. But you *are* stuck up there in the Bronx in the middle of nowhere.

Constance   He leaves at eleven in the morning, and sometimes I don't see him again until eleven at night. At least Dick works in your apartment.

Ellen   Well, not always. He often complains about the noise and storms off to the library. Sometimes I feel like I don't see him for days.

Constance   Don't you get lonely? I'm not used to having nothing to do.

Ellen   Can I talk frankly with you, Constance?

Constance   Of course.

Ellen   Well, some people might expect a woman who has already had two husbands to be better informed about the behaviour of men. I don't mean this in a mean-spirited manner.

Constance   I see.

Ellen   Men like Dick and Nello are quite demanding on themselves and they therefore expect a lot of others. What you need is your own project.

Constance   I want to continue modelling, and eventually try acting.

Ellen   No, my dear. Acting will take you away from him. You need to stay in their world. I read everything that Dick writes. I attend to his correspondence. Organize his travel schedule.

Constance   Nello has people to do all of this. Party activists. And they don't trust me. And even if they did, I'm not interested in dialectical materialism or Marxist theory. How does this high talk help the common man in the street?

Ellen (*laughs*)   Now you sound like Dick.

Constance   I prefer more straightforward writing. Stories.

Ellen   Like Dick's?

Constance   Exactly. Nello suggested that *I* write something, but I've never written anything

Ellen   Well, perhaps it's time you tried?

Constance   Maybe your husband could make some suggestions?

Ellen   Well, that's an idea.

Constance   I know he's terribly busy, but . . .

Ellen   Dick's out at present finalizing something. He's ready to make an announcement at dinner tonight.

Constance   An announcement?

Ellen   It's supposed to be a surprise.

Scene Twenty-one

Int. Village restaurant. Evening.

Noisy and lively. People are talking. Light jazz in the background.

Dick   The goddamn lawyer suggested that I put the house in your name.

Ellen   But Dick, you knew there was a chance that this would happen. (*To* **Constance**.) You see, Constance, we've been trying to buy a house on Charles Street so that Dick can have a proper study at home. Today Dick was supposed to sign the contract.

Dick   They want my wife to come down and sign the papers. Apparently I'm not white enough to be the owner of a house in this part of New York City. They may as well have said, 'Boy take your black ass on up to Harlem if you want to own some property.'

Ellen   Dick, please. Keep your voice down.

Constance   What are you going to do?

Ellen   What can we do? I'll go down and sign tomorrow.

Dick   They want us to fight and die for this damn country. Put our lives on the line for so-called liberty abroad, but here in America we're asked to tolerate humiliation and abuse.

Nello *comes into the restaurant.*

Nello   I apologize for being late. The comrades needed my help on the question of a divided Europe.

Ellen   Constance also needs your help, Nello. You haven't forgotten that, have you?

Nello   How could I?

Constance   Nello, Dick has some awful news.

Nello   What is it?

Dick   The damn house. They want Ellen to sign for it.

Nello   But you will still purchase it?

Dick   I'm not going to let them win.

Nello   Dick, don't let this anxiety take you too far from your desk. You know that's what they really want. Richard Wright fuming and shouting rather than writing.

Ellen   Nello's right, Dick.

Dick   You just want me to turn the other cheek?

Ellen   No, Dick, but channel this rage into your work. You've always done this so well.

Nello   I'm afraid I have some other bad news. Apparently the party feel that they can't support our magazine.

Dick (*laughs*)   Because I left the party? Man, that was years ago.

Nello   Some people feel you betrayed the cause.

Dick   You so-called radicals are so damn predictable, sitting in your ivory towers and passing judgement with your little pamphlets.

Nello   We should perhaps look for other sources of funding for the magazine.

Ellen   Nello, why don't you let Constance help you with the fund-raising?

Nello   I have party activists ready to approach the right people.

Ellen   Well, Constance must have *something* to occupy her time now that the FBI have harassed her former employers into effectively ending her career as a model.

Constance   I'm sorry, Nello. They visited the agency.

Nello   They did what?

Dick   And told her boss that she was cavorting with Negroes. And worse.

Nello   Constance, I'm so sorry.

Dick   Constance, you should write about me. Straighten out some of this red propaganda that has me down as a sell-out. It's Ellen's idea.

Ellen   It's not my idea! I merely suggested that she write something, and Constance wondered if you might offer some advice.

Dick   What do you think, Nello? You think your Constance should write about me?

Nello   You must ask Constance.

Dick   Well, you don't seem to be giving her any work. (*To* **Constance**.) Hey, Constance, I propose we begin by your conducting an interview with me. Tomorrow afternoon. Just bring a notepad and pen and we'll begin.

Nello   I asked Pearl to bake a special cake for Constance's birthday.

Constance   But, Nello, my birthday's not for a few days.

Nello   But surely we can celebrate it tonight. With friends.

Constance   What kind of cake?

Nello   A Caribbean rum cake.

Dick   Nello, you're in America now. When are you going to settle down and eat good American food?

Nello   When your authorities stop harassing me then I'll settle down. But in the meantime Pearl will bring the Caribbean rum cake and you shall like it, you hear me. You will respect the Caribbean rum cake.

They all laugh. **Pearl** *brings in the rum cake.*

Pearl   Move the plates out of the way. I've only got one candle for the cake.

She puts down the cake.

Nello   Thank you, Pearl. You treat us like royalty.

Pearl   You people coming in here and making so much noise that you're driving away all my customers with your arguing and carrying on. It seems like I better keep treating you right for soon you'll be my only customers.

Constance   Thank you, Pearl.

Pearl   You're welcome, my dear. Just you remember. Whatever worries you have out there in the world, just leave them at the door when you come to dinner at Pearl's. I want to see a smile on everybody's face, you hear me?

They all laugh. 'Thank you, Pearl', etc.

Pearl   Happy birthday, Constance, my dear.

Dick   Come on, Constance. Blow out the candle.

Constance *blows out the candle. They laugh and applaud.*

Scene Twenty-two

Int. **Wrights***' apartment. Village. Day.*

Fade up on **Dick**.

Dick   No, Constance, I've never really felt the need to go back to Mississippi. It's where I was born and raised, but I soon exchanged the rural life for the anxieties of the city and I wouldn't have it any other way. But you were born in California. Isn't that right?

Constance (*laughs*)   But, Dick, shouldn't I be asking the questions?

Dick   You've already asked plenty, Constance. Now it's my turn. Are you happy up there in the Bronx?

Constance   Nello gives his work to the party activists, so I don't have much to do. But . . .

Dick   But what? (*Pause.*) But what, Constance?

Constance   But he should have thought of this before he asked me to move in with him. I didn't have much of a modelling career, but I least I had work.

Dick   Well, the crazy West Indian should fix the problem now that he realizes you're unhappy.

Constance   I suppose so.

Dick   Our friend from the islands is married to his work, and I don't believe that even in Nello's native West Indies is it possible for a man to have two wives. There. That might be your problem.

Constance   Neatly summed up like a writer.

Dick (*laughs*)   Let's go for a walk and talk about life and literature.

Constance   And Ellen? Shall we ask her to join us?

Dick   No, no. Ellen is packing for France.

Constance   You're going to France?

Dick   A short publicity tour to promote the French editions of my books.

Constance   That's exciting. (*Stands.*) Shouldn't we tell her we're leaving?

Dick   And disturb her? She'll figure it out. Come on, it's a glorious day. We can stop for coffee.

Scene Twenty-three

Int. Coffee shop. Day.

The coffee shop is busy. We hear the sound of the till and people chattering.

Dick   Man, that Caribbean rum cake the other night was more rum than cake. First time I ever got drunk on dessert.

Constance   Nello also eats something called salted cod. He loves it, but I can't stand the smell and so he prepares it himself.

Dick   What does it smell like?

Constance   Feet.

They both laugh.

Dick   That Nello is one strange Negro. But I find that most of the Africans and West Indians have a high sense of themselves. Have you noticed?

Constance   Nello says that some American Negroes don't trust him.

Dick   Well, West Indians come here and they do nothing but work and keep their heads down.

A **Waitress** *sets down the coffee.*

Waitress   Two coffees.

Dick   Thank you.

Constance   That was rude. She spilt them.

Dick   Well, we don't have to stay for a second cup.

Constance   Shall I mail whatever I write about you to France?

Dick   Good Lord, no. We won't be gone for that long. You know, maybe we can do this again when I come back? Would you like that, Constance?

Constance *drinks her coffee and then violently spits it out.*

Constance   This tastes of salt. It's horrible!

Dick   Here, let me taste that. (*Takes a sip then puts the cup down.*) Waitress!

The **Waitress** *comes over.*

Waitress   Something the matter?

Dick   This coffee has in salt, not sugar.

Waitress   Really? I believe that's how we serve it here. You have a problem with that?

Scene Twenty-four

Int. Bronx Apartment. Evening.

Sound of bath water as **Nello** *moves about in the bathtub.*

Constance   Nello, would you like me to scrub your back?

Nello   Why are you asking? You know it's the favourite part of my day.

Constance   Nello, I feel bad about something that happened today.

Nello   I'm listening.

Constance   I made fun of West Indians. With Dick. We both made fun of West Indians.

Nello   I see. You made fun of West Indians or you made fun of me?

Constance   Both, I think.

Nello   I understand. (*Pause.*) My age. Was this a factor?

Constance   Nello, I'm sorry. It won't happen again.

Nello It's forgotten. Let's not speak of it.

Constance The FBI were waiting by the front of the building again tonight.

Nello Did they question you?

Constance They didn't say anything this time. You know. About . . .

Nello About your being a whore for living with a coloured man. (*Pause.*) We're moving, Constance.

Constance Moving where?

Nello To the Village. To be closer to our friends. Away from here. The Bronx is too isolated for you.

Constance Thank you, Nello. (*She kisses him.*)

Nello A new beginning for us both, my dear. Downtown where I hope you'll feel happier.

Scene Twenty-five

Back to present. Int. Apartment. Day.

Constance And so we moved to Greenwich Village where, at least to begin with, I did feel happier. The streets were livelier than the Bronx. And there were more young people, and of course there are no skyscrapers in that part of Manhattan so I could see the sky. But I saw even less of Nello as he seemed to feel that he'd made an effort and it was now my responsibility to entertain myself.

Interviewer And did you look for work with another modelling agency?

Constance I tried, but even Gloria, with her perfect figure, was struggling to find work. However, I filled in my time by writing an article about Dick's work. 'What next for Richard Wright?' It was only a short piece, but I poured everything I had into it and, I have to say, Nello was very supportive. He read it, and he made suggestions, but once it was done I was once again left with long, sprawling days and nothing to do. And then, one autumn day, there was a knock on the door of our village apartment.

Scene Twenty-six

Int. Downtown apartment. Day.

We hear a knock on a front door, then footsteps crossing. The door opens.

Constance Dick! You're back from France. But why didn't you let us know?

Dick Well, we've only been back a couple of days and things are so confusing.

Constance Confusing?

Dick   I just wanted to give this back to you. It's your piece about me. 'What next for Richard Wright?' I've only just got around to opening the mail, Constance, and it's wonderful. Thank you so much.

Constance   Well, you must make any changes you see fit. I'll only submit it for publication when you think it's ready.

Dick (*laughs*)   Hell, it's ready. What are you waiting for?

Constance   Won't you come in and see the apartment. We've been here for two months now.

Dick   Look, I'll see the apartment at some other time. Let's just go. Let's go for a walk. I need to clear my head.

Constance   A walk?

Dick   Or maybe the cinema. Come on, Constance. Let's go to the movies.

Scene Twenty-seven

Int. Cinema. Day.

We hear the sound of a cowboy movie playing.

Dick   At least it's dark in here and they can't see us. Maybe that's why Nello likes the movies so much. In here a coloured man is just like any other man.

Constance   Dick, you mustn't talk like this. Is coming back to America so bad?

Dick   Over there in France they treated me like a man. No, like a king. But Ellen couldn't wait to come home.

Constance   Nello says there's a rumour that they want to make a movie of your novel *Native Son*. That's exciting, isn't it?

Dick   Constance, I feel like America's a huge weight on my shoulders keeping me down.

Constance   I think it will take time for you to adjust to being back here.

Dick   But that's just it. I don't want to adjust. I don't see why a coloured man should have to adjust. In New York we always have to eat at Pearl's. In Paris we ate wherever the hell we wanted to eat.

Constance   How does Ellen feel?

Dick   I'm not talking about Ellen.

Constance   She's your wife, Dick.

Dick   I know she is. But I think she suspects how I feel.

Constance   How you feel about what?

Dick   I tried hard not to write to you.

Constance   Dick, I think perhaps it's time for me to go.

Dick   Constance, please listen to me.

Constance   I'm sorry, but I really should be getting back to Nello.

Dick   Do you ever see anything of him, Constance? It doesn't sound to me like too much has changed since I've been gone.

Constance (*stands*)   Dick, I really must leave. I'm sorry.

Scene Twenty-eight

Int. Village apartment. Evening.

Sound of bath water running.

Nello   But we were supposed to see that movie together. Why did you go with Dick?

Constance   Because you're never here, Nello. You say we'll see this exhibition or movie, or go to this concert or that play, but you're always too busy. What am I supposed to do? Just wait like I'm waiting for a bus at Port Authority station?

Nello   Well, is waiting for me so difficult?

Constance   Yes, Nello, it *is* difficult, because that's all I seem to do.

Nello   I see. I'm sorry. (*Pause.*) Your friend Gloria came by while you were at the movies. She said she'd like you to come to her apartment. Something about a modelling job. (*Pause.*) Do you really wish to re-enter that world?

Constance   What kind of a job?

Nello   I don't know! (*Stands up in bath.*) I must hurry now or we shall be late for dinner with Dick and Ellen.

Constance   I don't want to go.

Nello *steps out of the bath tub.*

Nello   We are going.

Constance   Nello, you can't tell me what to do. I'm not a child.

Nello   Get ready!

Constance   I said 'no'! I am sick of waiting for you. Sick of you telling me what to do. Nello, I've given up everything for you.

Nello   Constance, get ready. We're going to dinner!

Scene Twenty-nine

Int. Village restaurant. Night.

Subdued atmosphere. Light jazz playing.

Nello   But, Dick, the French are an untrustworthy people. At every turn they will attempt to win your trust, but eventually you'll feel it. The knife in the back. I made it clear in my book on the Haitian revolution.

Dick   Nello, I spent nearly two months in Paris and not a single person called me a nigger or treated me like one. You know, if that's untrustworthy then you can count me in.

Nello   What about you, Ellen? Do you feel the same way?

Ellen   Dick and I have an announcement to make.

Dick   Not now, Ellen.

Ellen   We will be moving to France, to Paris, as soon as we can settle our affairs.

Constance   You mean forever?

Ellen   My dear Constance, Dick has decided that we are moving to France.

Nello   Dick, you're abandoning the United States?

Dick   Hell, no. Who said a damn thing about abandoning the country?

Nello   But, Dick, if you leave this country then you'll be leaving the root and inspiration of your work. I saw it with Trotsky; for some men exile can become a kind of prison.

Dick   And you don't think of America as a kind of prison?

Nello   No, Dick. No, I don't.

Dick   Look, Ellen and I are just going to where we can breathe good, clear, pure air. Maybe you and Constance might consider coming to visit.

Ellen   We're not yet sure what kind of quarters we might have.

Dick   Well, dammit they've got hotels. Constance, are you ready to see Paris?

Ellen   I imagine Constance has better things to do with her time.

Dick   Well, my agent has suggested that we try and find somebody to do a full-length biography. I think Constance would be perfect. Nello, have you read Constance's piece about me?

Nello   Indeed, I have, and it's splendid. But a full-length biography?

Dick (*laughs*)   Hey, you're not doubting your lady now, are you? (*To* **Constance**.) Constance, he doesn't think you've got what it takes.

Constance *scrapes back her chair and moves to get to her feet.*

Constance   I'm sorry but you'll have to excuse me.

Nello   Constance, please take your seat.

Dick   Hey, Constance, come on. We're just joking around.

Constance   Goodnight.

Nello   Constance!

Constance *leaves.*

Dick   Nello, I'll go and get her.

Ellen   No! Dick, sit down. She's not a dog for you to chase. (*Pause.*) Nello shall go. *We* shall finish our dinner.

Nello (*stands*)   Excuse me. I'm sorry the evening has to end like this.

Scene Thirty

Int. New York bar. Day.

Sounds of drinks being ordered. A busy bar at the end of the day.

Constance   You know, Gloria, I'd forgotten how tiring it is to model all day. I need this drink.

Gloria   Whoa, wait a minute, sister. So you're telling me that you're leaving him? But you guys have only just got together.

Constance   He's not a guy. (*Pause.*) I think that's half the problem.

Gloria   If he's not a guy, then what is he?

Constance   A man. A stubborn old man who has a tendency to fall asleep over dinner.

Gloria   You mean he's set in his ways and not much fun? You knew this already, writing you letters like he's your teacher.

Constance   I had fun today, Gloria. Just modelling for headshots again.

Gloria   The photographer was an asshole.

Constance   Yes he was, but do you know how long it's been since I've laughed? I mean *really* laughed.

Gloria   But I thought you were friends with that writer guy and his wife. Don't you have fun with them?

Constance   They're leaving for France.

Gloria   I thought they'd already gone to France.

Constance   They're going back. For good. And now that's all messed up.

Gloria   Messed up how?

Constance   You know, it's just complicated.

Gloria   Sounds like it's time for you to move on with your life. Do you still want to act, because if you do I've got a friend in Connecticut who's looking for people for his company.

Constance   Really?

Gloria   Sure, what's to lose?

Constance   I haven't told Nello yet. That I'm leaving.

Barman   Can I get you ladies another highball?

Constance (*to* **Gloria**)   It's late, Gloria. I should go.

Gloria   Go where? You said he's out. And let's be honest, you don't even know where he is. Working at his office or whatever. Come on, let's have a drink to your freedom. To Constance, the actress.

Scene Thirty-one

Int. Village apartment. Night.

Constance *stumbles against a table and then starts to giggle. She is clearly drunk. She drops her keys.*

Constance   Nello? Are you asleep?

Nello (*shouts through from bedroom*)   Please, Constance. I need my rest. And you are drunk.

Constance *crosses to the bedroom.*

Constance   Yes, I'm drunk. And I have the right to be drunk, if I want to be drunk. That's what Gloria says. (*Stumbles against a chair.*) Come on, Nello, talk to me. I'm not your student or your domestic servant. Talk to me.

Constance *throws up on the floor.*

Nello   I cannot talk to you.

Constance (*resigned*)   I know, you can only write to me. Why did you want me, Nello? To cook and clean for you like Trotsky's wife? You don't need me for your work. Why don't you just let me go, Nello? I don't do anything for your life, do I? Please tell me the truth? Am I just a nice face with green eyes? Is that it? Nello, please. Talk to me.

Scene Thirty-two

Back to present. Int. Apartment. Day.

Constance   Young man, are you listening to what I'm saying?

Interviewer   I'm sorry. I'm just wondering if I should change the tape?

Constance   Don't worry, there's not much more to the story. I'm not painting a very good picture of myself, am I? A rather selfish young girl, I fear.

Interviewer   I'm not here to judge.

Constance   Quite. Well, in the morning I heard the door slam. (*Door slams.*) It goes without saying that I slept on the sofa that night. And when I finally opened my eyes I saw the letter from Nello on top of the table.

Nello   My dear Constance. I know that you feel I have disappointed you and let you down, and perhaps I have. Perhaps I simply overestimated my ability to be a support for you, but I never meant to hurt you. But now, I have to confess, I do need your help, dear Constance. A marriage will aid me in my quest to stay in this country that I cherish so much. I will fully understand if you decide that this is not possible and will, of course, never mention it again. You owe me nothing. It is simply a request made in love. Yes, my dear Constance, love not convenience. I have always loved you, and always will. My failure is my abject inability to show you just how much I love you and for that I take full responsibility.

Scene Thirty-three

Int. **Judge***'s office. New Jersey. Day.*

Judge   I now pronounce you man and wife according to the state laws of New Jersey.

Nello   Thank you, Constance. May I kiss the bride?

Constance   Of course you may. It would be wrong not to.

They kiss.

Judge   Hey, you two! Would you mind moving to the back of the room? We do have other people to attend to.

We hear them walking to the back of the room. They lower their voices.

Nello   Dick and Ellen are expecting us. For a celebration dinner. At Pearl's.

Constance   But, Nello, I have to go back to Connecticut tonight.

Nello   Tonight? Surely it can wait?

Constance   I'm in the middle of rehearsals. In fact, they needed me there today and I had to create an awful scene just to get away for a few hours.

FBI Man   Congratulations, Mr James. From everybody at the bureau.

Nello   Please leave us alone.

FBI Man   Mr James. We'd like to take a look at your marriage certificate.

Constance   Do you think you people might permit my husband and I a few moments of peace?

FBI Man   Ma'am, this is no business of yours.

Nello   If you want a copy of this certificate then you must ask the judge who just married us. Come, Constance, let's go.

FBI Man   You think it's that easy, do you? (*Laughs.*) Mr James, marriage to a woman like this isn't going to make any difference to your situation. You're a goddamn subversive son of a bitch and you stir up trouble for ordinary Americans. Red filth like you don't belong here, Mr James. Not now. Not ever.

Scene Thirty-four

Int. Village restaurant. Night.

Noise of plates, chatter and light jazz.

Dick   But, Nello, why be such a purist. Writing for the movies is a new challenge. It may not be art, like when I'm working on a novel or some stories, but just think of the audience. And what the hell, you love the movies, you old hypocrite.

Nello   But you'll have no time to work on the magazine. We have the funding now, from a source outside of the party.

Dick   But I don't see how I can work with you on the magazine. I'm going to be based in Paris, Nello. Unless you and Constance decide to take up married life over there it just doesn't seem practical.

Ellen   I don't think Paris will suit Mrs James.

Dick   I don't see why not. It will give her the chance to work on her book about me. Shame she's not here. We could have asked her directly.

Ellen (*laughs*)   I believe she is now contemplating a career on the stage. How do you feel about this, Nello?

Nello   I feel that my Constance must do whatever is necessary to make herself happy.

Ellen (*laughs*)   *Your* Constance?

Dick   Enough, Ellen.

Ellen   Yes, Dick. Enough. That's pretty much how I feel about your behaviour. Enough.

Nello   Please, Ellen. You have to understand that whatever you think of Constance, by marrying me she has given me the chance to stay in this country. She was under no obligation to do so. She did this for me. Truly, I just want her to be happy.

Ellen   Really, Nello? A young girl like that. How can she ever be happy . . .

Nello   With me? Is that what you mean to say? How can she be happy with a man like me?

Ellen   I mean with any man. (*Pause.*) Particularly any coloured man. There, I've said it now. It's impossible, Nello, and you know it. She's too selfish. She has no understanding of the . . . the sacrifices involved. She has a very bourgeois sense of domesticity that can never be reconciled to commitment.

Nello   I see. (*Pause.*) Well, my dear Ellen, I truly hope that life will be better for yourself and Dick in Paris.

Ellen   What do you think, Dick? Do you think life will be better for us in Paris? Do you think France will solve all of our problems?

Scene thirty-five

Int. Visiting room at Ellis Island. Day.

Sound of gates opening and closing. Two sets of footsteps echoing in a corridor and coming closer. Then a door opens.

Guard   You have half an hour. Not a minute more. I'll sit over here.

Constance   Nello. (*Pause.*) You've lost weight.

Nello (*stands*)   Please. Take a seat, Constance.

Constance (*sits*)   I'm sorry to see you like this here on Ellis Island.

Nello   Well, a sojourn here certainly destroys one American myth. This is not just a place of arrival. One also departs from Ellis Island.

Constance   But it's monstrous. They can't just throw you out like a common criminal.

Nello   I hear your debut as an actress was a success.

Constance   I'm not much of an actress, Nello. But it's better than the fashion world. On stage I have to . . . what was the phrase you used? Utilize a wider set of emotions.

Nello   I was too old for you, Constance. You needed to have more fun in your life and I treated you like a bird in a gilded cage. I am so sorry that I disappointed you.

Constance   It's not just you who caused disappointment. I wanted to be with you, Nello, without being married to the party. It was wrong of me to try to come between you and your work.

Nello   Perhaps. (*Pause.*) But I loved you, Constance.

Constance   I know. Thank you. (*Pause.*) I take it that Dick and Ellen have left for Paris?

Nello   They are Americans. They can always come back. For them this can be a game of coming and going.

Constance   I too am an American.

Nello   Indeed you are. (*Pause.*) Sitting here in internment on this great island of arrival makes me feel like a foreigner. An outsider. I feel as though I have failed. Failed America and failed you.

Constance   I'm sorry, Nello.

Nello   Please don't be sorry, you did all you could, Constance. You did more than I could have reasonably expected. You tried to love me in return. I know you tried.

Scene Thirty-six

Back to present. Int. Apartment. Day.

Interviewer   Did you ever see him again?

Constance   He was deported soon after our meeting. But his fame just grew as he travelled from Britain to the Caribbean and . . . well, I suppose it was always clear that he would eventually come to be regarded as one of the great twentieth-century political theorists and activists. (*Pause.*) I did see him again as, some years later when the so-called Red Scare was over, he was eventually allowed to return to the United States. By then I was married, for a fourth time, and living here in California with my late husband. Nello would sometimes stay with us. By then we could laugh about the past. There was never any ill feeling. (*Pause.*) You know he truly did love me. That much was always clear. But it was hopeless.

Interviewer   I see.

Constance   Do you? These things are quite difficult to understand.

Interviewer   And Mr and Mrs Wright?

Constance   Well, as I'm sure you know, they never returned to the United States. France became their home, and it remained so. I did go to see Ellen after Dick died. It was sad. He was so very young, you know. Only fifty-two. Some kind of heart failure.

Interviewer   And you eventually became his first biographer.

Constance   Well, I wasn't much of an actress. And he *did* ask me to write his biography. I felt obliged to follow through and not let him down.

Interviewer   And how did Mrs Wright feel about your book? You said you visited her in Paris.

Scene Thirty-seven

Int. Paris apartment. Day.

Ellen   Sugar?

Constance   No, no thank you. You really have a beautiful apartment, Ellen. And so many books.

Ellen   I work from home these days. As a literary agent. Perhaps you've heard of my star client. Simone de Beauvoir. *The Second Sex*. That's the name of her latest. Don't worry, she means it somewhat ironically. The weaker sex. Supposedly there to serve our men. You say you're touring Europe with your current husband.

Constance   Touring might be a little exaggeration. He's here on business and I'm just tagging along. I thought it would be nice to see you again. It's good of you to make the time.

Ellen   Dick would have liked us to be friends. But I'm sorry, I just couldn't bear to share him with anyone. It was rather painful to watch.

Constance   I think I owe you an apology. I was young and perhaps I needed attention. But you do know that nothing ever occurred.

Ellen (*laughs*)   Perhaps not with you. But Dick had a wandering eye. You must have sensed this. I understand you suggest as much in your biography. (*Pause.*) I'm afraid I couldn't bear to read it all.

Constance   I'm sorry.

Ellen   It's strange, but we can learn to make a kind of peace with even the most painful of situations. I blame you for nothing.

Constance   Thank you. I feel blessed that we've remained in touch, albeit at something of a distance. We did go through a torrid time back then. All four of us with our demons.

Ellen   And Nello? Did you see much of him at the end?

Constance   A little. Whenever he visited California.

Ellen   And do you miss New York?

Constance   Well, acting never really worked, and modelling . . . (*Laughs.*) Well, time took care of that. So there was no point in staying in the city. So I went home to California. (*Pause.*) I'm sorry we couldn't be friends, Ellen. At least we tried.

Ellen   Did we try? Did we really try?

Scene Thirty-eight

Back to present. Int. Apartment. Day.

Constance   I don't know what happened to Pearl's restaurant. Or Pearl for that matter. At least we felt safe there. For a little while at least. But maybe we were not safe from each other. I have to admit, it was lonely. Who would have thought that being in a relationship could be so lonely?

Interviewer   May I take your photograph?

Constance   Nobody has asked me that for a long time.

Interviewer   It may be useful for publicity for the piece.

Constance   Ah, publicity. As you please. This is my best side.

Interviewer   I imagine a professional photographer told you that.

Constance   Oh no. Somebody far more insightful. He told me there are two sides to everything. Including a face. One has to choose. (*Dog barks.*) Now come along, let's get this over with. Felix needs to be walked.

Interviewer   I'm sorry.

Constance   If I might offer you one piece of advice, young man. Stop being so sorry. It just gets in the way of living. People understand mistakes. Friends understand. We forgive. People can be actually quite forgiving when you get down to it.

Somewhere in England

Broadcast Details

BBC Radio 4, 3 December 2016. Directed by Gaynor Macfarlane.

Characters (in order of appearance)

Joyce
Customer
Len
Mother
Officer
Travis
Emile
Sandra
Stan
Man #1
Man #2
Mr Miles
Woman #1
Woman #2
Mavis
Colonel
Vicar
Soldier
Girl
Nurse
Red Cross Man

Notes on the Play

This is the dramatic radio adaptation of the eponymous section of Caryl Phillips's 1993 novel *Crossing the River*. Readers familiar with the earlier text know about the tragic story of Joyce, the white English woman who gives up for adoption the baby fathered by Travis, a Black GI stationed in a Yorkshire village during the Second World War. Yet, while the plot may be similar, the play constitutes an intriguing addition to the novel as it describes the characters more explicitly. Even more importantly, it gives a voice to one of the sons of the African diaspora, Travis, who is 'silent' in the novel, but here comes across as assertive and angry in his dealings with the segregated American Army, making the dramatic text more visibly political than the fictional one.

Sound of woman doing washing-up at the sink. The wireless is playing a Beatles song – 'I Want to Hold Your Hand'. We hear a dog bark.

Joyce   Hey, Buster. Get yourself down off that sofa. You've got a basket in the corner now get in it.

Joyce (*voice-over*)   It was two years since we'd bought the semi on the edge of town in a nice new development. Alan had stopped driving the buses and they'd made him an inspector. The girls were both teenagers now, and a bit more independent, and so we both felt like we had a new lease on life. We'd even begun to talk about me getting a job. Don't get me wrong, I loved the semi and I was content to stop at home, but we had our dreams: a new car, maybe a holiday abroad, and Alan was right when he said that *now* would be a good time to try and put something in the bank. I was at the sink washing up and thinking about this when I heard the doorbell.

Sound of the doorbell. The dog barks.

Joyce (*voice-over*)   My first thought was it's the middle of the day so it's either the postman with a parcel, or some bugger trying to sell something. So I dried my hands on a tea towel and went to get the door.

Sound of the door opening.

Joyce   Can I help you, love?

Silence.

Joyce (*voice-over*)   And so there he was standing before me, with tears in his eyes.

Joyce   Oh my God.

Joyce (*voice-over*)   He was staring at me like he'd never been hugged in his life and I could feel my knees going.

Mix through from the Beatles on the radio to the sound of a shop doorbell. It's 1942.

Customer   Just a box of matches, Mrs Kitson. Are you settling in?

Joyce   Yes, thank you. Anything else?

Customer   And some ciggies. Enjoyable honeymoon was it?

*We hear **Joyce** ring up and hand back the change.*

Joyce   I'm afraid I'm locking up for the night now.

Customer   Well, I'll not keep you then. I expect we'll see you at the pub with Len.

Joyce   I expect you will. Maybe not this evening though.

Customer   Yes, well I imagine you've got plenty to keep you occupied. Goodnight then.

*We hear the shop doorbell and then **Joyce** drawing the bolt across.*

Joyce (*voice-over*)   That night I woke up next to Len in the pitch darkness and thought to myself, what have I done?

Len   For heaven's sake, stop wriggling around.

Joyce   I can't sleep. I'm off down to make a cuppa. Do you want one?

Len   No, you daft clot it's the middle of the night. (*Pause.*) Well, are you going or what?

Joyce (*voice-over*)   One minute I'm working in a food distribution centre and going home at night to my mother's two-up, two-down. The next minute I've fallen for some sweet-talking customer who runs a village shop and who promises me that with a war on it would be a grave mistake to dilly-dally around. If we were gonna do it, we should do it now. But after a couple of days of honeymoon in Anglesey we came back to Cawthorne and he starts up treating me like it's not a wife that he wanted, but some help running the shop. But what was I to do? I was wed now, and there was a war raging, and there I was stuck in this silly little, self-important, village with a bloke who'd been classified as disabled because of a mining accident, and so he'd not be off anywhere. The only relief I had from the place was when I travelled back down the hill to the town to see my mother, whose sole occupation in life seemed to be to make me feel guilty.

Mother   I can tell you one thing, I'll not be digging for victory or growing cabbages or onions. You mark my words, soon enough they'll all be coming home in boxes like in the last war. (*Pause.*) Well, you haven't forgotten that's how your dad came back, have you?

Joyce (*voice-over*)   Then she'd pause and start up again.

Mother   And I can't be bothered with all that blessed gas mask palaver. All that spitting on the mica window to stop it from steaming up. And it smells, of rubber and disinfectant.

Joyce (*voice-over*)   Broadly speaking, I tried not to rise to her gabbing on because whenever I did she would just snap and tell me not to use Latin in front of her.

Mother   They're trying to make us live in the dark like blessed bats. It's ridiculous. And what's a person supposed to make of this Anderson shelter thingy? Two bits of bent steel stuck in the mud, not fit for a pig to wallow in. And nobody'll be hanging out any washing on the Siegfried Line, you mark my words.

Joyce (*voice-over*)   She knew I wasn't really listening to her, but she didn't care.

Mother   And don't you think that I haven't noticed that that so-called husband of yours never shows his face around here. He should be in a uniform and off fighting.

Joyce   You know full well he's classified infirm. Anyhow, he's busy doing essential work trying to keep the shop going.

Mother   You must think I fell out of a Christmas cracker. What's so special about him that he's too busy to pop his head in and be civil to his mother-in-law? Conceited, that's what he is.

Joyce (*voice-over*)   When she finally fell asleep I would make the long, slow bus journey back up the hill to the village. It was pretty, I had to give it that. The view from the road carried all the way across the moors. Nothing but green fields and small villages for miles. But then entering our village was like coming into a tunnel. You couldn't see anything except small houses dotted on either side of the road. And then a big church. A small pub. A nob's hall. Our shop. Some more houses. And so, heaven help me, this was my home now.

We mix through to a dockside. Noise of trucks and American Troops disembarking from a ship.

Officer (*screaming*)   You boys, move it! I said, move it! You ain't in the cotton fields now, so get down the goddamn plank.

Travis   Hey, white man, who you calling 'boy'?

Emile (*urgent whisper*)   Travis, take it easy, man.

Officer   Boy, what did you say?

Emile   He didn't mean nothing by it, sir. We've had a long voyage to England and . . .

Officer   Am I talking to you, *boy*?

Travis   My *name* is Private Travis Johnson. (*Pause.*) Sir. And this other 'boy' is Private Emile Sandford. (*Pause.*) Sir.

Officer   Because your Black ass is standing on English soil you figure that you can get away with sassing an officer, is that it?

Travis   That ain't what I'm thinking. (*Pause.*) Sir.

Officer   Nigger, you ain't thinking at all. (*Pause.*) These poor Limeys been fighting this war for nearly three years and maybe they ain't familiar with how we run things back in the United States, but you sure as hell are. Am I making myself clear? (*Pause.*) I don't hear you, Private Travis Johnson.

Travis   Yes, sir.

Officer   Boy, you better believe I got both my eyes trained hard on you.

Mix through to the loud grating sound of a truck engine as it labours its way along a road. **Travis** *and* **Emile** *are in the back with the other Troops. They speak with raised voices.*

Emile   Travis, what is it that you're writing in that journal of yours?

Travis   I already told you, I promised Mavis that I'd write her every week.

Emile (*laughs*)   Seriously, man, you're riding on this truck through England and you've got your mind stuck on your fiancée back home in South Carolina?

Travis   She ain't no fiancée, she's just a girl I know. A friend. Writing to her keeps me from feeling like I'm gonna kill one of these white officers.

Emile   Hey, I told you, man. You've got to knock it off with that kind of talk. (*Pause.*) Travis, just look at this crazy little country. They got their cute little fields, with their little cows and sheep. It's like a kid's picture book.

Travis   I wonder where they keep their coloured folks?

Emile   Man, ain't no coloured folks over here. This is a white man's country.

Travis   Then we're in even deeper trouble than I thought. You think anybody told these Limeys that we're bringing two armies over here. A white one to do the fighting and a coloured one to clean up the white man's mess.

Emile   Come on, Travis, we've only been here a day. You gotta quit letting things needle you. We're caught up in this foolishness so let's just make the best of it.

Mix through to the sound of **Joyce** *walking down a cobbled street and knocking on a door.*

Joyce (*voice-over*)   Eventually I made friends with Sandra, the woman who used to help Len with the shop before I came along. She was married to a mate of Len's called Stan and they had a small baby boy called Tommy. I don't know if she and Stan thought calling him Tommy was funny or something, but when she invited me over I never mentioned it.

Sandra   I can see you're still a bit lost round here. Rich Tea? (*Pause.*) You know, biscuits. You've no doubt got plenty of these in the shop to have whenever you want them, but you have to remember that for the likes of us it's a treat.

Joyce   No thanks, I'm fine.

Sandra   I've been wondering if I should grow my hair like Veronica Lake, or if I should just stick to the normal two and sixpenny shampoo and set. What do you reckon?

Joyce   Have you heard from Stan? Isn't he due a leave or something?

We hear **Tommy** *starting to fuss and cry.*

Sandra   I've not heard a thing from Stan, but I'm sure I will. Here, can you hold Tommy for a minute while I adjust myself. I had to get married and get started 'cause women in my family go off early. But you've got plenty of time yet. Does Len want kids? He's a bit of a slippery one, isn't he? Has he said anything to you about kids?

Joyce   Not really, but . . .

Sandra   Well, like I said. You've got plenty of time. You alright with Tommy? You've got the touch, I can see that.

Joyce   He's adorable.

Sandra   You've no idea what it's like when the postman passes by the door without stopping. The day is ruined. Absolutely ruined. A lot of the girls from up here have gone. ATS, munitions work, there's always something to take them away. Mind you, there's some Land Army girls supposed to be coming our way. But it's basically just us mothers left.

Joyce   I'm not a mother.

Sandra   But working in the shop is vital work. They won't put you in the factories, will they?

Joyce   No, I've got to help Len run the shop.

Sandra   Have you had enough of Tommy now?

Joyce   No, no. He's no bother; I think he might nod off.

Sandra   Give him here. (*Pause.* **Joyce** *hands him to her.*) I'm glad you're up here in our village, Joyce. You make things more bearable.

Joyce   What's the matter, Sandra?

Sandra   I can't breastfeed him anymore because my milk's all dried up. And he won't take the bottle so I'm having to spoon feed him which can take ages.

Joyce   No, I mean with you. I can see it in your eyes.

Sandra   I think I'm pregnant. No, I know I'm pregnant. Nearly three months gone. (*Pause.*) Don't you want to know.

Joyce   Stan's been gone for six months, Sandra.

Sandra   It's Len's mate, Terry. The farmer. He gives me extra things for Tommy.

Joyce   Apparently. Like a baby brother or sister.

Sandra   Do you think that's funny?

Joyce   I'm sorry, Sandra. I was just trying to . . . I don't know. It was foolish of me.

Sandra   I'm not going backstreet. I don't want to get rid of it. I'm too frightened.

Joyce   What does he want? He does know, doesn't he?

Sandra   Terry wants what they all want. The easy way out. I expect you're wondering why I didn't just keep my legs shut, aren't you? I haven't got any real excuses, Joyce. I suppose I was a bit mixed-up. And stupid.

Joyce   I think you'd best write to Stan and let him know before he comes back.

Sandra (*starts to cry*)   And what's Tommy going to do for a father if he doesn't want to come back?

Joyce   He'll come back, and the two of you can sort things out. Listen, love, am I the only one who knows?

Sandra   You, Terry, and the doctor.

Joyce   Well, let's just keep it that way for the moment, shall we?

Sandra   I'm glad to have you to talk to, Joyce. Thank you.

Mix through to a barrack room late at night.

Travis (*voice-over*)   Dear Mavis, We've been in England for a week now and they've got us in something called a 'holding camp' while they decide where exactly we'll be sent to. I've made one good friend, Emile, the guy I told you about before. He's an upbeat fellow who tends to want to see the positive side of every situation. We haven't seen much of the English people, but they seem friendly enough and wave at us as we pass by in the trucks. However, the white officers keep warning us that we mustn't mix with the local people as they won't like it, but it doesn't seem to me like the English people are the problem. They drive these small little cars and keep themselves to themselves. Only quarrel I got with the English is their beer, which is warm and nasty. None of us guys can figure out how people can drink this stuff.

Mix through to **Joyce** *in her kitchen.*

Joyce (*clearing away the plates*)   Have you had enough? There's still some more soup in the pot.

Len   I'm fine.

Joyce   Well, pass us your plate then.

Len   I expect that fat so-and-so Churchill will be on the wireless tonight huffing and puffing and reminding us that one Englishman is worth two Germans and all the rest of it.

Joyce   The Local Defence Volunteers meeting tonight, isn't it?

Len   I've had enough of it. Sitting in the pub listening to some army instructor telling us the German for 'hands up' or how to spot different types of enemy aircraft. Last Sunday he took us in the woods and made us chuck grass sods and pretend they were grenades. Terry and me are going to run over to Withenthorpe in his car.

Joyce   What for?

Len   What business is it of yours?

Joyce   Charming, I'm sure. (*Pause.*) Where did all the eggs out back come from?

Len   Chickens, I expect.

Joyce   People are talking, Len. They're coming in the shop dropping hints and I don't know what they want.

Len   Your job is to . . .

Joyce   Get your finger out of my face, Leonard Kitson. (*Pause.*) I said move it now!

Len   You listen to me. Just look after the shop and if anyone asks about anything you know nothing, right? Nothing about eggs, milk, or anything. (*Pause.*) Well?

Joyce   I've got nothing to say to you except if you want to behave like some kind of spiv that's your lookout.

Len   You'll keep your trap closed if you know what's good for you. Me and Terry might be gone for a day or two. In the meantime, you just button it.

He leaves and slams the door. Mix through to an afternoon in the shop. **Joyce** *is serving.*

The shop bell rings out.

Joyce   I'll be with you in a minute, love. (*To the* **Customer** *she is serving.*) Is that everything then?

Customer   Yes, thanks.

We hear a shot ring out.

Customer   Bloody hell, what was that?

Joyce (*voice-over*)   A few weeks after Len and Terry went off on their little jaunt, I was serving a Land Army girl and we both heard the shot.

Sound of the shop door opening and **Joyce** *running up the street. We hear the noise of* **Tommy** *screaming and then* **Joyce** *crashes through the door.*

Joyce   Sandra! Oh my God. Sandra! Stan, what have you done?

Stan   You'd best fetch the police, Joyce. I've done in my missus.

Joyce   Oh no, what have you gone and done to her?

Tommy *continues to cry.*

Joyce (*voice-over*)   Sandra had her eyes open and was staring into mid-air as if nothing was the matter. As if she couldn't quite understand what all the fuss was about. The thing I noticed about Stan, though, was his uniform. It seemed odd that he should be standing there in his uniform. Back from the war to kill. His wife.

Stan   Please, Joyce. Fetch the police, will you? I want it over with.

Joyce   You stupid sod, she was confused. It was a mistake. Why didn't you listen to her and give her a chance?

Joyce (*voice-over*)   When the coppers came one of them put a blanket over Sandra like she was asleep. Then he offered to escort me – his words – out of the house. Somebody had already taken Tommy. That night I put on my coat and walked up the road to the pub where I saw Len with Mr Terry, the smug farmer, who was perched on a bar-stool like Lord Muck, and everybody in the pub knowing that it was him who'd put Sandra in the family way.

Mix through to the noise of the pub in the evening.

Len   You didn't tell me you were coming up to the pub for a drink?

Joyce   Am I supposed to report my movements to you? Is that what you think a wife is for?

Len   Just keep your voice down, will you? What'll you have?

Joyce   I'll be having nothing as long as you're keeping company with that slack coward.

Len   I think you'd best get home.

Joyce   What, and wait for you with my gob shut?

Len   You just shut it!

Joyce (*shouts*)   No, you just shut it! I don't care who's listening. Stan didn't even bother to write to her after the one letter. Six months alone with a kiddie and not a word, and your so-called mate here said he was going to be there for her till he found out he'd put her in the family way, then he couldn't scarper off quick enough. He's nowt but a coward. In fact, you're both the same, aren't you?

Len   If you know what's good for you you'll get out now.

Joyce   Or what? Leonard Kitson, you make me sick and I don't care who knows it. I mean look at you, you're not even a man, are you?

Len (*pushes back his chair and stands*)   You watch your mouth!

Joyce   What are you going to do? Hit me in front of all your mates? Go on, big man! I've made up a bed for you on the sofa so don't you even think of putting a finger on me or I swear to God I'll have you. It'll be the last thing you ever do!

Joyce *storms out of the pub and slams the door.*

Joyce (*voice-over*)   A few weeks later, I lay in bed and heard footsteps registering on the cobbles outside and then a hammering at the door. I listened as downstairs Len made his way from the sofa to the door.

Len *unbolts the front door.*

Len   Do you know what time it is?

Man #1   We're both here as representatives of the Price Regulation Committee of the North East Region based in Leeds.

Len   So what? What the hell do you think you're doing banging on my door at this hour?

Man #1   Don't play silly buggers with us, lad.

Man #2   We've got your farmer mate, and now you'll be coming with us.

Len   Like hell I will.

Man #1   For a start off, eggs can only be bought from a farmer for purposes of hatching. Really, what the hell have you two been up to?

Len (*shouts upstairs*)   Hey, what have you been saying? What have you told these blokes?

Man #1   Is there something your wife should have told us, Mr Kitson?

We hear **Joyce** *coming down the stairs.*

Man #1   Sorry to disturb you, Mrs Kitson.

Len (*to* **Joyce**)   Have you been telling lies on me?

Joyce (*to* **Len**)   I've never seen these men before in my life.

Man #1   You'll be coming with us now. Your wife can bring your things along later.

Len   Are you arresting me?

Man #2   Quick on the uptake this one.

Man #1   You've an appointment with a magistrate, my lad. I imagine you and your pal can look forward to a few years behind bars to ponder on why you think that while the rest of us have to tighten our belts and suffer it's alright for you pair of thieving clowns to profit.

Joyce (*voice-over*)   And that was it. They carted Len away and I was free of him, but it was clear that some people in the village believed that I'd grassed him out. However, I didn't much care what they thought for I had a shop to run and they needed me, and so we all performed the pantomime of being civil and then everything changed the night the Jerries bombed the town. That night we all stood high up on the hillside and looked down. (*We hear the sound of the bombing.*) First flares, then incendiaries, then the heavy bombs. The town soon looked like a thousand camp fires had been lit on it, beautiful little fairy lights blazing everywhere. The vicar started a chorus of 'Nearer my God to Thee' and others joined in.

We hear the **Villagers** *beginning to sing the hymn.*

Joyce (*voice-over*)   In the morning I took a bus down to the town to find my mother. All the familiar landmarks had gone, but eventually I found our street, and then I saw the ARPs and recognized old Mr Miles. He was cordoning off entrances. He handed his roll of string to another warden, then took off his tin helmet.

Mr Miles   I'm sorry, love. You know what your mother was like. She wouldn't go in the shelter.

Joyce   Where is she?

Mr Miles   They've taken her body off in a corporation bus with the rest of the unlucky ones. Really, **Joyce**, it were not good round here as a lot of folks took their chances. They weren't banking on a direct hit.

Joyce   I see.

Mr Miles   If you're a bit squeamish you'd best make yourself scarce. We've not finished yet and there's still more bodies trapped underneath that lot. (*Pause.*) Are you alright, love?

Joyce   I'm alright, Mr Miles. I'll be fine. You just take care of yourself.

Mr Miles   About time these Yanks pulled their fingers out and started to give us some proper help. I mean, how much more of this are we supposed to put up with by ourselves?

Mix through to the sound of birds. It's summer and a pleasant afternoon. We hear the distant rumbling of trucks approaching, and then a great roaring of engines as a convoy pulls into the village. **Joyce** *is serving a* **Customer** *in the shop.*

Woman #1   Can anybody actually eat this so-called National Loaf? It looks like bits of straw all baked together.

Joyce   Well, most people don't have any choice, I suppose. Will there be anything else?

Woman #2 (*shouts*)   They're here. I can see the Yanks getting out of their trucks now.

Woman #1   Hang on a minute, they didn't tell us that we'd be getting coloured ones. Why do we have to have them in our village?

We hear the raised voice of an **Officer** *barking orders to the disembarking Troops. 'Come on, hurry it along!' 'I said, move it!'*

Woman #2   Look at them staring at everything. I'm off out to take a look. Are you coming?

Woman #1   Hang on a minute. Let me reckon up with Joyce. (*To* **Joyce**.) How much have I got for you?

Woman #2   Look, there's more of them coming up the hill. We're being invaded by coloureds.

Rising sound of more trucks, and **Officers** *shouting, and* **Men** *disembarking as the Troops continue to arrive in the village. The crescendo of noise eventually starts to fade.*

Mix through to the barracks at night.

Travis (*voice-over*)   Dear Mavis, I appreciate your letter even if the contents were not what I was expecting.

Emile   Travis, turn out the lights, man. It's after hours.

Travis   Hey, relax, give me a couple more minutes.

Mavis (*voice-over*)   Travis, I've become friendly with a young man, Norville Washington. I believe you've met him, although you probably won't remember. He's a little younger than you and looks up to you as everybody does. However, he has some vision problems which mean he's not fit for service. Norville will be going off to attend theological college in Georgia and he's asked me to accompany him and . . . well, we leave tomorrow so I guess it's only proper that this should be my final letter to you.

Emile   Hey, Travis, what's the matter. Why you looking so blue?

Travis   Looks like Mavis has got herself a man.

Emile   Well, she ain't your girl so you should be pleased that she's happy.

Travis   I am, but Mavis was my link to back home. (*Pause.*) Damn, we've been in England for two weeks now in this stupid little village and we've not been allowed to do a thing for ourselves. All this 'Yes, sir, boss', 'No, sir, boss'. Man I'm twenty-three years old, and either I fight or I want to go home.

Emile   Easy now, Travis.

Travis   Easy now, nothing. I didn't come over here to be no labourer for the white troops. Give me a rifle and let me start shooting some Germans or turn me loose.

Emile   Put out the lights, Travis, and try and get some sleep, okay? I got an idea.

Travis   It's gonna take more than an idea to keep me from running crazy in this stupid little country.

Emile   Hit the lights, man. I told you, I got an idea, but let's talk about it in the morning.

Mix through to the sound of the shop doorbell. The door opens and closes.

Joyce   Can I help you?

Colonel   Morning, Duchess. I've come to talk with you about the servicemen we have stationed in your village. I'm Colonel Hungerford, the US commanding officer.

Joyce   You can take off the sunglasses, if you like. It's overcast today.

Colonel   Well, I guess you have a point.

Joyce   So it's taken you a fortnight to come and explain yourself. I reckon that whatever you have to say can't be all that important.

Colonel   Well, I just wanted to say that a lot of my boys are not used to citizens treating them as equals.

Joyce   What are they gonna do? Chuck themselves at our feet if we smile at them?

Colonel (*laughs*)   Do you mind if I smoke?

Joyce   I don't mind.

Colonel   Is your husband away?

Joyce   You might say.

Colonel   I see. (*Pause.*) Look, these are not very educated boys and they might need some time to adjust to your English ways and customs.

Joyce   So you've brought us a problem, is that what you're saying?

Colonel   No, ma'am. I'm just saying that a lot of Southern boys ain't ever seen life beyond the fields. We plucked some of them straight from the land and put 'em in uniform. If they start to get uppity we're gonna need your patience.

Joyce   And how have we been doing so far? Have we been patient enough for you?

Colonel   I guess so. You've all been exceedingly hospitable.

Joyce   Well, then, there's no problem is there?

Colonel   I guess not.

Mix through from the shop to the sound of **Travis** *and* **Emile** *walking up the street.*

Travis   Emile, you serious about this foolishness?

Emile   I told you I got an idea, now you in or you out?

Travis   I'm in, but I just don't see how you're gonna make this work.

Emile   Well, we just go into the shop and ask all nice and polite, simple as that.

A **Vicar** *approaches them.*

Vicar   Good afternoon, gentlemen.

Travis/Emile   Afternoon.

Vicar   Will I be seeing you on Sunday?

Travis   I'm sorry. I don't understand. Are we supposed to be some place on Sunday?

Vicar   Well, perhaps in church? I'm the local vicar and we like to welcome all guests to our house of worship.

Travis   To your church?

Vicar   Of course. And please spread the word. Bring your friends. In the meantime, have a good afternoon, and welcome to Cawthorne.

Vicar *walks off.*

Emile   Hey, is that guy for real?

Travis   What do you mean? He invited us to his church, didn't he?

Emile   Travis, you know we ain't allowed in no white church.

Travis   You heard the man invite us to his church so I'm going to the man's church.

Emile   You know this could mean trouble.

Travis   Seems to me like these English people ain't the ones trying to Jim Crow us.

Emile   So you're seriously going to go to the man's church?

Travis   You better believe me I'm going, and I'm taking along anybody who wants to come with me. These white English people ain't got no problem with us, so why should we have a problem with them? Now, you still want to go into the shop or what?

Mix through to the sound of shop doorbell.

Emile   Afternoon, ma'am.

Joyce   Good afternoon. Did the army teach you to take your hats off when you go inside somebody's house?

Travis   No, ma'am, the army didn't teach us that. I learned that from my daddy, and he learned it from *his* daddy.

Emile   Truth is, the army doesn't teach us much except how to say, 'Yes, sir' and 'No, sir' and then just sit around all day waiting for something to happen.

Joyce   Well, I hope you two haven't got it into your heads that you'll be coming in here to wait around all day. I've got customers who need serving.

Travis   I'm sorry, ma'am, but we didn't mean to be discourteous. I'm Private Travis Johnson and this here is Private Emile Sandford.

Joyce   Travis. Emile.

Emile   Pleased to meet you, ma'am.

Joyce   Likewise, I'm sure.

Emile   The thing is I'm organizing a dance on Saturday at the hall, and Travis and myself would like to invite you to come along.

Joyce   Really? What makes you think I can dance?

Travis   Well, Emile's planning on eventually inviting everyone in the village so we're not assuming that you can dance. It's more a general invitation.

Joyce   Flattered, I'm sure.

Emile   What Travis hasn't told you is that I've organized some of the boys into a band, and trust me you hear those boys start to cut up and you'll soon be on your feet and ready to dance. Some of the guys have played professionally.

Travis   Do you reckon we can count on seeing you, ma'am?

Joyce   The name's Joyce. And if I can find my dancing shoes, Travis, then maybe you'll see me on Saturday. Who knows.

Travis   Well, that's just great. (*Pause.*) Joyce.

Emile   Thanks, ma'am.

Joyce   Okay, Travis, Emile. Don't let the door hit you as you leave.

Travis   Say, what?

Joyce   Don't worry about it. Enjoy the afternoon sunshine while it lasts. Remember, you're in England. It could snow tomorrow.

We hear the door open and close.

Travis   That's one strange dame. What's she talking about snow for?

Emile   Wanna go back in and ask her? Forgotten all about Mavis, have we?

Travis   Man, you crazy? Emile, that's a white lady in there. I ain't ready to be strung up from no tree.

Emile   You said it yourself, they do things differently over here.

Travis   Emile, you better quit fooling. I'm just looking to take my Black backside home in one piece, brother. That's all. I just want to get back home in one piece, say hi to my folks, and then get on with my life. I reckon that ain't too much to ask, now is it?

We hear the sound of **Travis** *and* **Emile** *walking down the street. Mix through to* **Joyce** *in her bedroom.*

Joyce (*voice-over*)   I spent the whole week thinking about what to wear to the dance, but in the end I decided that a plain dress, some flat shoes and my blue cardigan would have to do just nicely, thank you very much, as I didn't have the money to go out and buy anything new. That Saturday night I walked through the village towards the hall, and then I saw a Yank soldier standing by the gate.

Soldier   Come for the dance, ma'am?

Joyce   Am I the only one?

Soldier   No, ma'am. Go straight down there, then cross over the grass and sidle up the stairs.

Joyce (*voice-over*)   I suppose nobody told them that you're not supposed to walk on the lawn in posh places, but the toffs had moved out for the duration so I suppose it didn't much matter. I walked up the stairs and into a big room where the first thing I saw was the food. They had stuff on the table that even I hadn't seen in years. Lemons and grapefruits. Tons of chocolate. Salami. Sliced tinned peaches.

Soldier   May I take your sweater, ma'am?

Joyce (*voice-over*)   So polite, I thought. I saw a few ATS girls from the next village, and some Land Army girls, and they were all sitting in a line and so I went and sat with them and listened to the gramophone records, but nobody was dancing. And then I noticed the band beginning to climb up onto the small stage, which was just some boxes pushed tightly together with a cloth drape tacked around the edges, but it looked proper. And then the band began to play 'Moonlight Serenade' and they were fantastic, but there was still a sitting line of us and a standing crowd of them and so I got to my feet. However, the Land Army girl next to me grabbed my arm.

We hear 'Moonlight Serenade' beginning to swell.

Girl   Where are you off to?

Joyce   Scarborough, where do you think?

Girl   But you can't just go up to them like that.

Joyce (*voice-over*)   I shook her off and walked straight up to Travis. I saw him smiling nervously at me and I could see the small gap in his teeth in the middle of the bottom row and I thought, that's different but I like it.

Joyce   Would you care to dance?

Travis   Dance? Are you sure?

Joyce   Do I look like I've made a mistake?

Travis   Dance with me?

Joyce   No, with Father Christmas.

Joyce (*voice-over*)   I put one hand ever so lightly on his shoulder and then held out the other one, and he stretched out his arm to meet it and steered me back and into the space that was the dance floor. Over his shoulder I could see it on everyone's faces that they were shocked, and maybe a little bit jealous, but I didn't care. And then one by one, the Yanks found the courage to go over to the girls and soon they were all dancing.

Travis   Well, it looks like you've started the party.

Joyce (*voice-over*)   I didn't say anything.

Travis   You don't seem shy and uneasy like the rest of them.

Joyce   You seem a bit different yourself. (*Pause.*) In an acceptable way, I suppose.

Travis   Acceptable?

Joyce   Well, so far. You Americans have got a reputation, you know.

Joyce (*voice-over*)   I listened to him and I listened to the music.

Travis   Are you from around here?

Joyce   Why?

Travis   Well, I guess you don't act like the others. I can't say how exactly, but they're nice people but kind of distant.

Joyce (*voice-over*)   And inside I was smiling because that was just what I wanted to hear. I wasn't from 'around here' and I never would be, but there was a war on so I had to muck in like everybody else. But at least on this particular Saturday night I was happy. I was dancing and I could forget the mess I'd made of everything by marrying Len. I looked at Travis and as we continued to dance I knew that neither of us cared about what anybody might be thinking for we kind of recognized each other. It was that straightforward. We recognized each other.

The music continues to play. Mix through to inside the church. We hear the sound of a hymn being sung by the American Troops which slowly becomes more rhythmic and then the Americans start to clap as the Anglican tones give way to gospel. Mix through to the shop.

Woman #1   I heard that when you were leaving the Yanks gave you all an orange, a pack of cigarettes and some chocolate.

Joyce   Well, I might still have a piece of chocolate if you're interested?

Woman #1   Really? (*Pause.*). I still don't like the idea of having them forced upon us, but do you happen to know if they're planning another do?

Joyce   I've no idea. I haven't seen much of them this week so I reckon they must be out on manoeuvres or something.

Shop bell rings as the door opens.

Woman #1   Well, it looks like one of them has managed to manoeuvre his way in here, no problem.

Travis   Good afternoon, ma'am.

Woman #1   Well, yes, it is that.

Travis   Joyce.

Joyce   Travis.

Woman #1   Well, I'll be on my way then. But don't forget about that chocolate that you promised me.

Joyce   I'll have a piece ready for you when you're next in.

Doorbell sounds as she exits.

Joyce   Well, you lot have gone and done it now, haven't you? Next time you have a dance she'll be bringing her begging bowl.

Travis   I don't know what these yellow flowers are called, but I picked some for you.

Joyce   You didn't have to do that. They're daffodils. Or daffs as we all call them. Mind the shop will you while I fetch a jam jar.

Travis (*shouts through*)   Is it okay if I smoke?

Joyce (*shouts*)   Of course it is.

Travis *lights a cigarette.*

Travis   I didn't want to come by in case you were busy.

Joyce *comes back through.*

Joyce   So that's your excuse for not showing your face for nearly a week.

Travis   I didn't want any awkwardness.

Joyce   At the dance you said you weren't wed, and you don't have a girlfriend.

Travis   I don't. I'm not lying.

Joyce (*laughs*)   So what's awkward? I won't bite. (*Pause.*) Look, it's a lovely day out. Do you fancy going for a walk?

Travis   A walk? With you?

Joyce   Or perhaps you're not allowed to do this? Go off limits, or whatever you call it.

Travis   Well, strictly speaking Sunday's our day for rest and recreation. Last Sunday I took some guys to church.

Joyce   Yes, I heard that you livened up the place a bit. Some of the villagers are still recovering.

Travis   I'd never been in a white church before.

Joyce   Well, you didn't catch anything did you?

Travis   What do you mean?

Joyce   I'm just joking. And what did you do after church?

Travis   Well, later on some of our guys went to your pub and drank that strange beer you've got.

Joyce   So you're free in the day? On Sunday, that is.

Travis   Sure. Sundays we're pretty much on our own.

Joyce   Right then, this Sunday we can go and see my mother. We can even take her these flowers.

Travis   See your mother?

Joyce   Don't worry yourself. It'll be alright. She's dead.

Travis   I don't understand.

Joyce   Look, I'll see you on Sunday. We'll go for our walk then, alright?

Travis   Listen, Joyce.

Joyce   What's up? You look confused. (*Pause.*) Well? What's the matter?

Travis   Nothing's the matter. Nothing. It's fine.

Joyce   Well, that's settled then. I'll see you on Sunday. Just come by after you've finished your church business.

Mix through to them standing in a cemetery looking down at a grave.

Joyce   Go on, just put the flowers on the slab. That'll get her attention.

Travis   Would you like me to say a prayer?

Joyce   Oh, Mother would go for you, she would. But no need, thanks. I think she'd find it strange if I started getting all religious at this stage.

Travis   Is your father still alive?

Joyce   You can find him on a bronze plaque by the town hall. He fell at the battle of the Somme in the last war. I was a baby, so I never got to know him and my mother never took up with another bloke. Well, there was Jesus, but I don't think he counts.

Travis   I'm sorry to hear about your father.

Joyce   Look, Travis, there's not really that much to see in the town since the Jerries had their go at it. (*Laughs.*) There wasn't much before either.

Travis   Well, let's just walk and talk.

Joyce   Alright then. (*They move off.*) Careful with the weeds and nettles around here. Maybe we could go to the Elektra and see a picture?

Travis   Sure, that way we can sit in the dark and people won't stare at us.

Joyce   Is it my imagination, or am I beginning to get the idea that you're not really comfortable being seen with me?

Travis   We have our customs back in the States.

Joyce   Well, you're not in America now. Are you really scared of what people are thinking?

Travis   I guess I'm still learning about your ways.

Joyce   Well, let me help you out. They think I'm just some tart and you're using me. I can see it on their faces. They nod at you but they won't look at me. But the truth is they're nodding at your uniform, not so much at you. As for me, they're disgusted with me.

Travis (*stops*)   Then why are you walking with me? Why bring me to your mother's grave?

Joyce   Haven't you ever been lonely, Travis?

Travis   Sure I have. I miss South Carolina and the folks back home.

Joyce   And right now you don't have anybody to talk to, do you?

Travis   Aside from Emile, I guess not.

Joyce   Well, then, what exactly don't you understand?

Travis   You're lonely?

Joyce   I like you, Travis.

Travis   And I like you too, Joyce. You're not scared of anything, are you?

Joyce   Can I slip my arm in yours? (*Pause.*) Good. Now we look the part. Right, you're still on for the Elektra are you?

Mix through to the sound of the cinema. A newsreel of the war. Then a feature film – Mrs Miniver. Then we mix through to footsteps scurrying and a bus pulling away.

Joyce   Oh dammit, we missed it. That's the last bus. I forgot that they've changed to a skeleton schedule because of the fuel shortages.

Travis   But can't we just get a cab?

Joyce   There aren't any taxis with the blackout and everything. You're going to be late back aren't you? And I know that's serious. I'm so sorry, Travis.

Travis   Listen, let's just start to walk.

Joyce   But it will take a couple of hours.

Travis   Once we get closer to the village we'll get picked up. The military police will be out on patrol.

Joyce   And they'll see you with me, won't they?

Travis   Nothing will happen to you, Joyce. I'll explain to them that we missed the last bus, and they'll take you back to the shop.

Joyce   For heaven's sake, I've made a right mess of everything, haven't I?

Travis   Hey, come on, we better get going. (*Laughs.*) You know, Miss Joyce, when you said we should go for a walk, I didn't realize that this was what you had in mind.

Sound of their footsteps as they walk off into the night. Mix through to an interior office. There is a knock on the door and then the door is pushed open.

Soldier   Colonel, there's a civilian from the village to see you.

Colonel   About what?

Soldier   She says it's about one of the men, sir.

Colonel   Okay, show her in.

Joyce *enters the office.*

Joyce   Hello again. You look more sensible without your dark glasses.

Colonel   Hello, Duchess. Take a seat. What can I do for you?

Joyce   You know why I'm here. It's my friend. He's being punished for something that's not his fault. I'm responsible for us missing the bus and his being late back.

Colonel   I take it we're talking about Private Travis Johnson?

Joyce   I took him down to town to introduce him to my mother.

Colonel   To your mother? Really?

Joyce   According to his mate, Emile, you've had him locked up for three weeks now. You're punishing him for my mistake? Or is he being punished for something else?

Colonel   Whoa! Calm down, Duchess. I'll look into it, okay? Had he been drinking?

Joyce   Drinking? Course not. We went to the pictures.

Colonel   I see. You're sure he hadn't been drinking?

Joyce   You must be hard of hearing or something? We saw my mother then went to the pictures.

Colonel   And if you don't mind my asking, how did he get along with your mother?

Joyce   Just grand. She didn't have a word to say against him and he was a credit to your country. He's a decent church-going fellar in case you haven't noticed.

Colonel   Yes, well, I'm sure he is, but Private Johnson seems to like to do things his own way.

Joyce   He's done nothing wrong apart from miss the last bus. How you do things in America is up to you, but you're in England now. We don't lock people up for missing the last bus, especially when there's a war on and fuel shortages.

Colonel   I'll look into this. I promise you, I will.

Joyce   Well, I hope you do. And sharpish.

Mix through to the pub in the evening. It is quiet with not many present. **Travis** *is returning from the bar.*

Travis   A whiskey for me and here's your half-pint. (*Pause.*) Do you think it's alright for us to drink together in this pub? People in here know your husband, don't they?

Joyce   Who gives a damn what *he* thinks, or what *they* think. You Yanks have doubled the landlord's profits so *he's* got no worries.

Travis   They released me from the hold as soon as you left the colonel's office. I don't know how to thank you.

Joyce   I mean it's mental. Who gets locked up for three weeks just for being late back to camp?

Travis   It's not that simple. After the MPs let you out at the shop they took me back down the hill and stopped by some woods and told me to step down from the jeep. That's when they beat me. In their report they said I was drunk and disorderly and that I took a swing at one of them. That's why I was being punished. I got word to Emile that he should let you know that I was being confined to camp. Seriously, I wasn't expecting you to speak up on my behalf.

Joyce   Well, in case you haven't noticed they don't make blokes like you around here. I care about you, Travis.

Travis   You care about me? (*Pause.*) No, Joyce, you can't do that.

Joyce   Why ever not?

Travis   Because we can't work back home in America. We don't do mixing. It's against the law. White and coloured got their own separate places. It's just the way it is.

Joyce   Then stay here. Why would you want to go back to such a stupid country?

Travis   It's home, Joyce.

Joyce   Don't you care about me?

Travis   How can you ask me that?

Joyce   Come back to the shop with me, Travis. I don't care how they look at us or what they think.

Travis   Joyce.

Joyce (*stands*)   I'm walking out of here with you, Travis. Take my arm, please. (*Pause.*) Travis, please stand and take my arm. (*He stands and takes her arm.*) Thank you. I'm walking out of here with you, Travis.

Mix through to **Joyce** *and* **Travis** *stumbling into the shop.* **Travis** *switches on a light.*

Joyce   Turn it off. (*He does so.*) There's a blackout, remember. Let me light the candle. (*We hear a match strike against a box.*) There, that's better. I can see you now. We *can* sit down on the sofa, you know.

Travis   Thanks.

Joyce   Who are you, Travis Johnson?

Travis My daddy's a schoolteacher at the coloured school in town. And my momma's a cook, for a lady who doesn't look much different from yourself.

Joyce But that's them. Who are *you*?

Travis A guy who's maybe in over his head.

Joyce Your head's telling you one thing, but your heart says something else, is that it?

Travis I guess so.

Joyce So how about no more listening to your head? (*She kisses him.*)

Travis Joyce, if things were different you know I'd never leave you here in this village with these people.

Joyce And how about no more talking? (*She kisses him again.*)

Mix through to dawn. Birds are singing.

Travis (*insistent whisper*) Joyce, I gotta go.

Joyce (*drowsy*) I understand. Just let yourself out. But take the spare key that's on the hallway table so you can come and go as you please.

Travis Joyce, I . . .

Joyce Sshh! Just go. I'll hear from you later or whenever you can.

She lies in bed and listens to him going downstairs and then the door opens and closes.

Mix through to the shop.

Joyce (*voice-over*) Four months later Travis got the news that his unit were finally being sent overseas and they had to begin to get ready to move out of Cawthorne. We didn't promise each other anything, and as the day of departure drew nearer we tried to be all grown up about things, but it was difficult. For both of us. Then Len came back and I had to close up the shop early so the two of us could have it out once and for all.

Joyce Len, I have no intention of living with you as man and wife and that's the end of it.

Len But I keep telling you we can sell up this shop and move away. We can begin again. You can't want rid of me just because I got put inside.

Joyce I want nothing to do with you, Len. I want a divorce.

Len So it's true, there *is* another bloke isn't there? I'd never have married you, and taken you out of that bloody dump with your mother, if I'd known you were going to behave like a common slut.

Joyce If you raise a single finger to me, Leonard Kitson, I promise you they'll find you with an American bullet in you.

Len You make me sick, Joyce. You're a traitor to your own kind and there's plenty around here who agree with me.

Joyce   You know, I wish you could see yourself, Len. Not even you would like what I'm looking at.

Len   Just shut it, you stupid cow. You can stop here in the shop till the end of the war then I'll be back and you're out. Do you hear me?

Joyce   Oh, I hear you, Len. I hear you loud and clear.

Len   Jesus, your kind sicken me, Joyce. You sicken all decent people.

He walks out and slams the door.

Mix through to trucks being loaded. Feet crunching on gravel. Shouting.

Emile   Travis, man, you're not even fixing on saying goodbye to her?

Travis   I said goodbye last night.

Emile   Yeah, I heard you sneaking back in at your regular time of six this morning.

Travis   Listen, Emile. I can't take her back to the States and so there's no point in making it any harder on the both of us.

Emile   But I *know* you got feelings for the woman.

Travis   Trust me, man, more feelings than I want to have. I love Joyce, but as messed up as it is, I love home too.

Emile   So, you've made your choice?

Travis   What choice? I'm a coloured man, no choice in that. And I'm also an American, no choice in that, either. Hell, Emile, I ain't got no choice. (*Pause.*) Man, let's go fight these Nazi jackasses then get home to South Carolina and start living again. Enough already with the cows and the sheep and this lousy English weather.

Emile   Travis, man, you sure about what you're doing?

Travis   Emile, truthfully I ain't sure about anything anymore but, please, let's just go. This place is breaking my heart.

Joyce (*voice-over*)   That afternoon all the Yanks, including Travis, left for Italy. Two months later I checked the rules to make sure. Pregnant women received extra concentrated orange juice. An extra pint of milk a day. An extra half-ration of meat a week. An extra egg – up to three a week. Free cod-liver oil. Free chocolate-covered vitamin tablets. And, of course, a baby. I wrote to Travis and told him that most of the village had sent me to Coventry, and the doctor said I was having a breakdown and a child. His commanding officer decided to give him seventy-two hours of compassionate leave to come and see me and get wed, because Travis told them that's what he wanted to do – and then he'd have to go back. I went down to town to meet him, but I nearly wept when I saw him getting off the train. He looked as thin as a door, and so tired, and he didn't have that same bounce in his step. There was no joy in his face and he was bent over under the weight of the bag on his back. As he walked towards me along the platform, with that long slow stride and those hunched shoulders, I could see that he hadn't shaved for days. He saw me, and the child pushing at my coat, and he just stopped and stared. I started to cry. The doctor was right, my nerves wanted building up. But so did his. This war was obviously taking a terrible toll on him. It had turned out the light inside of my Travis. I watched as he let his bag fall to the platform.

Travis   Joyce.

Joyce (*voice-over*)   . . . was all he said. And then he reached out and pulled me towards him. I couldn't believe it. He'd come back to me. It turned out he *really* wanted me. That day, crying on the platform safe in Travis's arms. He wouldn't let go of me and he promised me that once the war ended he was coming back to make a life in England. If he couldn't take his wife and child back to America then he promised me he would be stopping with us in England.

Mix through to living room in 1963 where **Joyce** *is sitting with her visitor.*

Joyce   When you were born they lifted you clear of my body and began to towel you down. You were beautiful. The nurse put you in my arms.

Nurse   He's like a cup of milky coffee isn't he, love?

Joyce   But she didn't mean anything by it. A few days later I left the hospital and I took you back to the shop. And then one morning there was a knock at the door and I hardly had time to set you down straight. The Red Cross man was about to knock again when I opened the door. He just handed me the telegram . . .

Red Cross Man   Here you go, love.

Joyce   Then he began to back away.

Red Cross Man   I'm sorry.

Joyce   The telegram didn't say much, so I had to try and imagine it. To die at dawn on the Italian coast. (*Sound effects of shooting.*) Fear. Mud. Shivering cold. Noise. Silence louder than any noise. Mortar fire. A young man, your dad, screaming in pain. My mother had once said to me, 'You should never marry a soldier for you'll just be left on your own.' But I wasn't on my own, I had you. A month or so later, at nine at night, the King made a speech on the wireless with his usual stammer and that was it, the war was over. People in the village poured out into the streets and lit fires and they started to dance the hokey-cokey. I'd done my bit, I'd supplied them with food. The bells started to ring again and some went off to church. I'd never had much time for the villagers but it was moving. Some of them even spoke to me, and they *all* smiled at you. You were a big hit. And then Len turned up and wanted his shop back, and I had no money or prospects, or anywhere to live even. And that's when the lady with the blue coat, and her silly dog called Monty, showed up.

Lady   You have to be sensible, Joyce, and give him a chance with a proper family. Just think about it, you'll soon be able to start a new life on your own.

Joyce   And so I was sensible and did as she said and put you into the care of the county council as an orphan. (*She starts to cry.*) I'm so sorry but I wasn't thinking straight. I was bloody stupid, and by the time I came to my senses it was too late. I'm sorry.

Joyce (*voice-over*)   For what seemed like the longest while he wouldn't meet my eyes. I thought, he's a handsome young man, and he looks just like his father. However, I was in pieces because I didn't know anything about him, not a single thing, and it was shameful to have to ask.

Joyce   I don't know how to say this, love, but my girls will be back from school any minute and I've no idea how to explain any of this to them.

Joyce (*voice-over*)   I watched as he slowly got to his feet without saying a word.

Joyce   After you went into care I left the village, the shop, Len, everything and went to live back in the town. For weeks afterwards I wandered around the park looking at women pushing their prams. I got work as a conductress on the buses, and eventually I met Alan, he's my husband, and while he knows about Len I've never said anything to him about you or your dad. But it's not because I'm not proud of you, it's just too painful, son. (*She begins to sob.*) It hurts too much.

Joyce (*voice-over*)   And it was that one word that finally broke the ice. 'Son'. As though it was his cue, my son stepped forward and took me in his arms the way his father did on that platform on that cold wintry morning.

Joyce (*sobbing*)   I don't even have a picture for you, or a letter, because once I married Alan, like a fool, I got rid of everything that Travis had sent to me for I was desperate to put it all behind me. I'm so sorry. Please forgive me, son. Forgive me.

She continues to sob. We hear 'Moonlight Serenade' rising.

Now that you've found me, I want to make everything right. And I promise you I will. (*Pause*) We were something, love, your mam and your dad. You'd have been proud of us the way we took the dance floor with everyone thinking, 'No way, they're not gonna dance together, are they?' But once we got up everyone followed us. That's what your mam and dad were like, love. (*Pause*). That's who we were. We recognized each other and in the end we didn't care what anybody thought.

Swell of 'Moonlight Serenade' by Glenn Miller.

Bibliography

Other Works by Caryl Phillips

Fiction

The Final Passage. London: Faber & Faber, 1985.
A State of Independence. London: Faber & Faber, 1986.
Higher Ground. London: Viking, 1989.
Cambridge. London: Bloomsbury, 1991.
Crossing the River. London: Bloomsbury, 1993.
The Nature of Blood. London: Faber & Faber, 1997.
A Distant Shore. London: Secker & Warburg, 2003.
Dancing in the Dark. London: Secker & Warburg, 2005.
In the Falling Snow. London: Harvill Secker, 2009.
The Lost Child. London: Oneworld, 2015.
A View of the Empire at Sunset. London: Vintage, 2018.

Non-Fiction

The European Tribe. London: Faber & Faber, 1987.
The Atlantic Sound. London: Faber & Faber, 2000.
A New World Order: Selected Essays. London: Secker & Warburg, 2001.
Foreigners: Three English Lives. London: Harvill Secker, 2007.
Colour Me English. London: Harvill Secker, 2011.

Stage Plays

Strange Fruit. Ambergate: Amber Lane Press, 1981; London: Oberon, 2019, with new preface by the author.
Where There Is Darkness. Ambergate: Amber Lane Press, 1982.
The Shelter. Oxford: Amber Lane Press, 1984.
Rough Crossings. London: Oberon, 2007.
Plays One. London: Oberon, 2019. Contains *Strange Fruit*, *Where There Is Darkness* and *The Shelter*.

Screenplays

Playing Away. London: Faber & Faber, 1987.
The Mystic Masseur: Essays and Excerpts from the Screenplay. Trinidad: Paria Publishing Company, 2001.

Further Readings on Caryl Phillips's Radio Plays

Ledent, Bénédicte. 'An Archival Exploration of Radio Dramatic Hinterlands: Caryl Phillips's *Hotel Cristobel*'. *Journal of West Indian Literature* 29, no. 1 (April 2021): 95–107.

Ledent, Bénédicte. 'Caryl Phillips's *Crossing the River* and the Chorus of Archival Memory'. *Commonwealth Essays and Studies* 40, no. 1 (Autumn 2017): 11–20.

Ledent, Bénédicte. 'Caryl Phillips's Drama: A Blueprint for a New Britishness?' In *Staging New Britain: Aspects of Black and South Asian Theatre Practice*, edited by Geoffrey V. Davis and Anne Fuchs, 189–201. Brussels: Peter Lang, 2006.

Ledent, Bénédicte. 'Radio Drama and Its Avatars in the Work of Caryl Phillips'. *Journal of Postcolonial Writing* 54, no. 1 (2018): 32–42.

Ranguin, Josiane. '"Happiness is not always fun": Caryl Phillips's *Crossing the River*, part IV (1993) and the BBC Radio Dramatization "Somewhere in England" (2016), Rainer Werner Fassbinder's *Ali: Fear Eats the Soul* (1975) and Robert Colescott's *My Shadow* (1977) and *Knowledge of the Past Is the Key to the Future* (St Sebastian) (1986)'. *Lectures du monde anglophone*, 4 (2018). http://publis-shs.univ-rouen.fr/eriac/index.php?id=438

Scafe, Suzanne. 'Home/lessness, Exile and Triangular Identities in the Drama of Caryl Phillips'. In *Modern and Contemporary Black British Drama*, edited by Mary Brewer, Lynette Goddard and Deirdre Osborne, 62–76. London: Palgrave, 2014.

Tempestoso, Carla. 'Silences that Ride the Air: Soundscaping Slavery in Caryl Phillips's *Crossing the River*', *Linguae* 1 (2020): 119–31.

A Caryl Phillips bibliography can be found at this address: http://www.cerep.ulg.ac.be/phillips/